THE
CLOSERS

BFG3 & ASSOCIATES

BEN GAY III
Salesman • Speaker
Sales Trainer • Consultant

Voice: (800) 248-3555
(530) 622-7777
Fax: (530) 295-9337
E-Mail: bfg3@directcon.net
WWW.BFG3.COM

P.O. Box 2481
Placerville, CA 95667-2481
USA

"**The Closers** is the most complete book on the art of selling I have ever seen... If I had to re-learn everything I know about this profession, I would start with **The Closers.**"
— Charles Rufkin, Pres. *Rufkin Dev. Co.*

"At last, a book that doesn't gloss over the hard facts of eye-to-eye selling, yet doesn't lose sight of the customer's humanity... I highly recommend **The Closers** to my salesmen, and anyone else who wants to get to the top of a very competitive profession."
— David Winston, Sr., Chrm. *Watteau Corp.*

"The author has written a book that is both lively and packed with good, solid information. He is one of the rare people who knows the ins and outs of selling and can communicate his knowledge in a readable, exciting way. I was delighted with **The Closers** from the first page to the last." — Winston Needleman, Sales Mgr. *Garden Estates*

"Some things are universal... **The Closers** embodies principles we want to teach our employees — respect for the customer and the drive to succeed."
— Tashumi Ichigeo, Personnel Training *Rhonnin Corp.*

"**The Closers** combines keen psychological insights with practical, how-to instructions... one of the most valuable books in the field."
— T.S. McTeague *McTeague & Blander Investments*

The Closers

ISBN 0-942645-00-6
Library of Congress #87-81170
Fifth Edition 2006

Published by:

The LJR Group/Hampton Books
P.O. Box 2481
Placerville, California 95667-2481
United States of America
Telephone: (530) 622-7777

PREFACE

The main purpose of this book is threefold. Firstly, it is a complete reference book on closing sales. Secondly, it's a professional closer's guide to new closes in today's market. Thirdly, and most importantly, it introduces a closing formula (Sam's secret) that has a proven success record which exceeds all other sales procedures and closes being used anywhere in the world. (FACT.)

This book is not a beginner's or self-help manual; it is a Closer's Bible. This book has not been written for the average, run-of-the-mill salesman or anyone who simply wants to read and "kind of" gain a little knowledge about sales closing.

This book has been designed to help Master Closers learn, brush up and study total closing procedures (performances).

There are no frills or superficial puffed-up chapters presented in this book (PERIOD). Just bottom-line closing facts to get the reader's closing average up at least thirty to forty percent above what he is currently producing. This book has been written for that one purpose and no other.

It is not the intention of the author to embarrass or upset anyone in the selling profession, although in places the book will take a close and very candid look at all salesmen. Any basic, hard-hitting, gut-penetrating, closing book — if it's worth anything at all — has to step on someone's toes, and this manual is no exception. This is a closing guide that actually tells you what all the other closing books *have not* and/or *will not*.

In the past writers have maintained a certain level of respect and circumspection toward customers, a respect level that salesmen generally acknowledge and accept. However, in this book no holds are barred. The customer is taken apart and completely dismantled, analyzed and thoroughly examined by the Master Closer. After this dissection, the closer can understand any customer's position. Then the closer, after developing a sound solution, can go in for the kill (the sale).

This book is a straightforward, honest discussion of proven tricks and traps that *do* produce sales. So, if you are really serious about your selling profession, no matter what field of sales you are in, then don't talk to another customer until you have read this book. This book covers virtually every objection from a customer that you will ever encounter. It gives you not only the answers but all the ammunition you will ever need to get the sale that day and keep it solid.

This book is in a league by itself, and you, the reader, can be guaranteed that you will not be disappointed in any way. The book is something for you personally and not to be shared indiscriminately. It's an aid to get the job done (the job of closing sales), and it does just that. *The Closers* will turn you into a Master Closer the minute you say "Hello" to your customer. You, the reader, will sell more than you ever have in your past sales experience. This is the only book you will ever need to close your customer one on one. The purpose of this book couldn't be put more simply. So, let's get started; you don't have to miss any more sales beginning right now...

FORWARD

Ben Gay, III

Welcome to an exciting experience! You are about to read *The Closers*. Authored by Jim Pickens, it is, in my opinion, the finest book on sales and closing skills ever written.

Whether you are an experienced Master Closer, one who aspires to be, or just entering the professional sales world, you will find *The Closers* to be easy-to-read, informative and an indispensible sales closing tool.

Now here's a suggestion: Contrary to what you were taught in school, make the book a working partner in your sales life. Underline or "Hi-Lite" important sentences, paragraphs — even entire chapters! Make notes in the margins and use the pages that have been set aside for note taking. I want you to literally wear the book out!

And don't read *The Closers* just one time and put it aside. Read the whole book several times. Then read the portions you've marked at least monthly. And note your calendar to read the entire book at least once a year — for as long as you are involved in professional selling.

As in any book, you won't agree with every single sentence, and you should tailor the book's lessons to your own personal style, but make no mistake about it, *The Closers* is written the way the sales world really is — at least for the TOP PRODUCERS!

Well, it's time for you to plunge in! As you use the lessons of *The Closers* in your day-to-day sales life, I wish you only the best.

Sincerely,

Ben Gay, III

NOTE:

Mr. Gay is one of the nation's top professional salesmen, sales-trainers and professional speakers. He served as president of one of the nation's largest direct sales organizations and, during the past twenty years, has spoken before over 200,000 men and women all over the free world.

Mr. Gay was dubbed "Attitude Coach" for the Astronauts and ground crews of Apollo 15, 16 and 17 and received national acclaim for his *People Builder's* success program, which he created and ran for the inmates and staff of California's infamous San Quentin State Prison.

CONTENTS

CHAPTER FOUR
THE CUSTOMER'S ATTITUDES

CHAPTER FIVE
PSYCHOLOGICAL MANIPULATION

CHAPTER SIX
CLOSER VS. CUSTOMER

CHAPTER SEVEN
THE SALES PRESENTATION

CHAPTER EIGHT
CLOSING THE CUSTOMER

PART I

PART II

PART III

CHAPTER NINE
THE TWENTY GREATEST "CLOSES"
ON EARTH

CHAPTER TEN

FIFTEEN CUSTOMER OBJECTIONS AND
FORTY-FIVE CLOSER RESPONSES

AUTHOR'S NOTE

All the information contained in this book is founded on closing facts and procedures that produce proven superior sales performances when utilized.

The story has been written to help illustrate a major closing point. All incidents, situations, and objects depicted in this book are fictional, and any similarity between characters presented herein and any living persons is coincidental.

All thoughts and situations contained in this book are based on the author's own experiences and writings.

This book was written to help the reader become a master closer — something any salesman should want and try to achieve.

It is the sincere hope of the author that the lessons learned from this book are beneficial, not only to the reader's future, but to his undying spirit.

Introduction

THE CLOSERS

I'm about to tell you of a remarkable experience that happened to me this past December. I've never written a book before, but facts and circumstances force me to try. On December 21st, something happened to me that was so fantastic and at the same time frightening that I felt it had to be shared, if for no other reason than that it made me believe in a phenomenon far beyond my own comprehension. The only way I could explain it to you was to take time off from my company and write it all down in my own words. This was a decision I accepted easily.

Before I start to tell you everything that happened that winter day, you should know something about me, so you will realize that I am quite serious about this book.

First of all, I'm a family man with a beautiful wife, four lovely children, and, with the help of many people, a very successful real estate developer, in the United States, and five foreign countries. The reason I'm telling you this is not to brag or to blow my own horn, but to let you know that an experience profound enough to make me drop nearly everything and take time off to write a book, something I've never done before, had to be of extraordinary importance. And believe me, I feel it was just that. I've been through a lot in my life, but nothing like you are about to read in this book.

The best place to start to understand the whole story is right from the beginning — a June morning seventeen years ago in my home town of Pittsburgh, Pennsylvania. That particular summer I was looking for a job, something to do so I could earn a little money to see me through the summer, and maybe have some saved for my sophomore year at Penn State University.

My freshman year had been very basic. I had ideas of studying law eventually. But now, the summer was the most important thing, and I just wanted to date and work outdoors, forgetting school and the Supreme Court Judgeship I envisioned. Oh yes, my dad — and this is just like him — had a great job lined up for me in a giant steel mill where he worked. Now it's true there was good money to be made there, but I wanted to do something different, something uncomplicated; you know, just something simple. I had to find a job that would meet my new university sophomore status, not just a freshman job.

As it happened, I was looking through the want ads one Sunday when I saw a job description that looked pretty interesting: "Outdoor recreational company looking for young, energetic people for summer employment in public relations work. Good salary and many company benefits."

Now to me, that hit the spot. The job was outdoors, with good pay, and some public relations; that was sophomore status enough. In addition, it was only fourteen miles away from my parents' home. This way, I could work and feel independent while still having my good old room at home. I decided that was the answer; that was the job I wanted.

So Monday morning I got all spruced up and, in my three-year-old Volkswagen, set out to conquer my objective — *get that public relations job.*

Driving out to the location given in the paper, I felt great. The weather was beautiful, and the foliage was in full bloom. It took me about forty minutes to get to my destination, and what a surprise! All of a sudden, I was looking at a huge building that must have been a magnificent old hotel at one time. All around this building bustled carpenters, plumbers, painters, people with filing cabinets, people moving desks — just about everyone was trying to bring this stately building up to par. To me, it looked as if it had been abandoned for about twenty years, but at the rate everyone was working, this old hotel would see better days very, very soon.

I parked my car and went inside with my newspaper clipping in hand, not knowing where to go or whom to see about a job. I noticed an important looking man sitting in the middle of this great hotel lobby; he was reading a newspaper. It looked strange because of all the movement and activity going on around him; he just sat there undisturbed. I went over and asked him where I should go to apply for summer employment. He looked up, then calmly stood. He was dressed in a golfing outfit and was very distinguished in appearance. He stared at me with a kind of puzzlement and finally asked what kind of job I wanted. Not knowing a good, solid answer I replied, "Oh, just anything." Then he asked me about my family, my studies, my ambitions, and said, "Can you start working right now?" Surprising myself, I said, "Yes!" So for the rest of that day and the next week I helped clean up around the old building, running errands, sweeping, moving, and being a good "go-fer," as they say.

It turned out the man I had asked about the job application was the vice president of the company. He was in charge of all the renovation and development being done. His name was Randell Billing, but it seemed like everyone called him "Big Bill." My new job under "Big Bill" was working for a company called the Duron Corporation. This company was a land and recreational development firm with headquarters located in New York City. The Duron Corporation had six developments in the Midwest and was starting a new one here in Pennsylvania. The name of this new project under development was "Green Vista Estates," and it had 15,000 acres of Pennsylvania hillside to its name.

I learned that the Duron Corporation was a solid and well respected real estate firm that was over twenty years old. So, all in all, I had lucked out. My new job amounted to doing anything and everything that would help out the total plan. That plan was simply this: The Duron Corporation was going to develop Green Vista Estates into a total recreational and retirement community. Facilities were to include private golf courses, tennis courts, lakes, swimming pools, town centers, and condominiums. The corporation was going to sell real estate (lots) and houses, along with building roads, country clubs, and every benefit one could think of to eventually develop what amounted to a private, well planned resort community. To accomplish this, not only were contractors and builders needed, but also sales personnel — in other words, the salesmen themselves.

This is where you will see the story start to take shape, and this is where I really begin to fit in. I wasn't a salesman yet, but as part of the Green Vista team, I began to join in and develop a positive attitude, cheering Green Vista Estates on toward its grand opening in July.

After a time, armed with my limited company knowledge, my positive attitude and aggressiveness, I felt I was ready to advance to a new and better job position. So I went to "Big Bill" and asked him for some of the public relations work the newspaper ad promised. After a long talk with "Big Bill" I got my new job assignment: parking cars for the duration of the summer. Oh well, at least it was outdoors, and there was some public relations work involved, I figured.

Time seemed to be most important now. All around and throughout the hotel everyone hustled to meet the July 1st deadline. That was the grand opening day, July 1st. Close enough to July 4th so it all sounded appropriate and patriotic. I wasn't too busy in my car parking job, since at first there weren't too many cars to park (no customers yet). So, I did a lot of other things to keep busy.

Things started looking up and getting more businesslike every day. The old hotel looked fantastic, after four hard weeks of solid restoration. Even the huge parking lot behind the hotel — my territory — was nearly finished. The only problem was that there were no trees in the parking lot, so consequently no shade; all I could think about was my original plan of wanting to be outside. Some plan.

At the far end of the parking area the company had constructed a guard gate and a guard house. It looked good because it was designed in the same mode as the old hotel. The purpose of the guard house and gate was obvious: it added to the atmosphere of privacy at Green Vista Estates. Green Vista Estates was going to be an exclusive resort, so the guard house would positively add to this overall concept. For a short time, I thought the company had an idea for me to be a security guard but no luck. They wanted an older person. Besides, I was only there for the summer, and I didn't need an air-conditioned guard house when I could be outside in the hot sun parking cars.

It was at this time, about one week before the grand opening, that I first met Sam Johnson, our new daytime security man. When we were introduced I was somewhat surprised because Sam Johnson was a fairly old man. In fact, he was old enough to be my grandfather. But he seemed like a very pleasant old gentleman. That first day we didn't talk much because he was busy learning his new job and duties down at the guard house; I was doing my usual running around, conquering all the errands no one else wanted to do.

At this point, I want you to keep in mind that Sam Johnson and I had a common bond between us from the beginning; you see, we were the only people working in or around the parking lot area. Everyone else was either inside the old hotel, (the new sales office) or scattered throughout the development working on construction projects.

On his second day of work Sam and I got to talking; he told me a little about himself, and in turn I told him some things about me. We really had nothing better to do than sit around in his guard house and get to know each other through small talk. (It seemed that everyone else was getting ready for sales, with all its promotion and excitement, or working with the builders and contractors who were scattered all over the place developing roads and other needed amenities.) So there I was, sitting and talking to my new acquaintance, old Sam Johnson, the security guard; just waiting for the day, our opening day, that grand day, when I could finally do my job — park cars. Well, it wasn't really so bad; parking cars could be a type of public relations work, sort of, and I was starting to get a pretty good tan. So things were looking up.

As I got to know Sam better, I realized that he was a peculiar and unique old man. Over the next few days, working and talking together, we became pretty close friends. For example, if I was ever late for work — and I usually was — Sam would cover for me. With this kind of relationship, we made the parking lot area a pretty good place to work. We'd tell jokes and talk about anything and everything that happened during our working hours. So time passed quickly for both of us.

About two days before the big opening, Sam told me something quite curious. He told me that he used to be a master sales closer and that he had worked all around the country selling real estate for many years. He told me about the company that we worked for now (its good points and its bad ones), and all about its history. He talked about his old selling days, the productive ones and not-so-productive ones. About getting in and out of all kinds of situations. The strange part was that it seemed the more I listened to Sam, the more intense, sincere, and serious he became about this special subject of his — the subject of selling.

We would talk for hours about selling when we weren't doing other things. I found myself becoming more interested in this old man and his tales. One day — and I'll never forget it — Sam told me that if he wanted to, he could out-sell any salesman Green Vista Estates would or could ever hire. Green Vista Estates was hiring the top closers in the country, and to hear Sam say something like that (sensing he really seemed to believe it) was kind of out in left field. I didn't say a word; but I just sat there and listened. The next thing I knew, Sam showed me a ring, a simple gold one that he was wearing. The ring was old and quite worn. It looked like an old crest ring but nothing more. It certainly wasn't expensive. Sam told me that the ring had a secret inscription on the inside that would make any man, no matter who he was, the greatest master sales closer in the world. The only thing a person had to do was read and understand the inscription and then practice what it said. Sam told me that this gold ring had made him a millionaire many times over, and when he practiced the ring's secret he never failed to get a sale.

Now I ask you, what would you do if some old man (and he certainly didn't look like a millionaire) just got through telling you a story like this? Well, what I did was human. I asked him if I could read the ring's inscription. But Sam replied, "I'll make a deal with you. We're going to be working together all summer long, just the two of us, and we're going to see a lot of customers and salesmen come and go. I'm tired and I don't want to sell anymore. But if you'll listen to me, I'll point out things about sales and closing that will make you the best sales closer anywhere. I'll make you a Master Closer. Not only that, but if you practice what I tell you, you will become a complete and total success in any kind of sales field that exists."

Sam said that I could learn all this in a very short time. All I would have to do is listen and understand what I would hear. Then at the end of the summer, if he thought that I had been a good student, he'd let me read the ring's inscription. He said, at this point, I'd know the secret that every salesman in the world would want. The secret that shows how to be the greatest closer alive.

That was Sam's answer to me. So what could I say? I thought for a moment and decided that since I was going to be here for the rest of the summer anyway — and since Sam just might know what he was talking about — why not? I might really learn something. I couldn't lose, and besides I wanted to know what that inscription said. I know myself, and curiosity gets me every time. I told Sam I would listen to him and try to learn what he would show and teach me. I knew that I would get to read the inscription eventually, and if it was a joke, a fake, or a real selling secret, at least I'd know what it said. If I could be a success in selling like Sam said he had been, then who really wanted to be a lawyer anyway? Certainly not me.

This is how it all started, seventeen years ago. Each day, Sam would talk to me and explain sales from top to bottom, and he didn't miss a thing. The extra benefit was that we were in the middle of one of the largest developments in the East, with all the top salesmen in the country around us. We had everything to study: the customers, the salesmen, plus plenty of excitement.

The Duron Corporation had hired only the best closers in the country. So to my way of thinking, if our company had the best closers around (and Sam told me that he was better than all of them), then I had to learn something about sales even if I didn't try.

Well, I learned, I mean I really learned! And just what did I learn? In the following chapters you will see and understand. You will also know Sam's ring's secret inscription which changed me so much. Because of what I was taught that summer, by one old man, I decided not to become a lawyer. Instead, I became president of the Duron Corporation, one of the top real estate developers in the United States. And a multi-millionaire at the age of 37.

This is the reason I have to share this experience with you; not what has been described so far, but what really took place last December 21st. This is just the beginning of a story that can make your sales performance and closing percentage far better than any salesman you know now or have ever known. This book is about what I learned from Sam. Not only what he knew concerning closing, but more importantly, just who Sam really was. It is all true, and all really works.

Chapter One

THE CLOSERS
(The Stone Cold Trapper)

A. Types of Salesmen
B. Types of Closers
C. Make-up of Closers
D. Characteristics of Closers
E. Why They Are Closers

NOTES

2

Chapter One

THE CLOSERS
(The Stone Cold Trapper)

Sam gave me my first lesson in sales — or rather, closing — the day our agreement began. In fact, I think I'll call our understanding the "gold ring agreement."

It didn't take me long to see old Sam didn't pull any punches when he spoke about sales and closers. He said exactly what he thought and always had closing a sale as the bottom line. Sam got so excited when he talked about closing and sales that I was beginning to believe there *was* a secret inscription on the inside of his ring.

The salesmen had already begun arriving at Green Vista Estates — about ninety-five in all. Sam said the salesmen, or better yet the closers, would be my first subject of study. He told me that by using closers as a starting point, I could learn the basics and go right on from there. With this in mind, we began.

The best way for me to tell you, is to simply put it all down as if Sam himself were doing the talking. In this chapter, you will see exactly what I learned about closers. But keep in mind that for Sam, closing was a very, very serious business. From here on out this book is strictly about closing and closers. It is "nuts and bolts" reading, not a novel.

The Types of Salesmen

Before we get into closers specifically, I want to explain the difference between salesmen and closers. You will see this in black and white before the chapter is over. But we have to understand salesmen before we can appreciate the skill of a Master Closer. All this really does is bring everything into proper perspective.

Order Takers or Tour Guides

This person knows all about the product; he knows all about the company. In fact, he has all the right answers, and he appears to be tailored for the job of selling. But there is one thing about him that's wrong: He cannot sell. Ever wonder why?

Well, there are a thousand reasons, but I'm not going to get into them now — you will understand once we get into closers. An order-taker shouldn't even call himself a salesman. The reason is he doesn't have that one little thing called "magic." But don't worry; you will soon see how to acquire that special ingredient, if you don't already have it.

An order taker is like a book with a lot of knowledge just sitting on a shelf, waiting for someone to open up the pages and read. In comparison, a Master Closer is like a smash broadway play; it jumps right out at you and hits you right between the eyes. It doesn't wait for anything; it's a full-scale production with all the trimmings.

The Salesman

He is better than the order taker; at least he can do some things on his own. He has some push, some drive, some determination. He makes a pretty good living, but that is where it ends. He requires help on too many deals. He doesn't study his profession to any great extent. He has his clients built up, is satisfied with that accomplishment, and that's it.

Everyone calls him a salesman, but I guarantee that when he is alone, looking in the mirror, he knows he could be better. But he just doesn't go that extra step; he doesn't want it badly enough. So, he settles for middle-of-the-road. He lacks that extra gut feeling of wanting to be the best. He does not want to upset his routine or self-styled pattern. He would rather be a good, so-so salesman than a Master Closer with professional class.

The Closer

Now here is a man who can do the whole nine yards. He can sell, charm, and hold the customer in a deal. He can do all the things that are necessary to be a top-notch man, and he is just that — always in front of the rest of the sales force. And do you know what? That is where he stops dead cold. He thinks he is so good he will not study or listen to anybody anymore. He thinks he can live on his past record and all the old war stories about sales will pull him through. He uses the same old pitches and closes and never changes except that he gets older.

Yes, he's a closer, and a good one, but not great, not a super-salesman, not a leader — just good. He thinks he is at the top, but in reality he isn't. He simply forgot to keep going and learning; that little oversight made him stop growing, and it shows.

The Master Closer (The King of Selling)

He's the person that everyone else calls for help on a deal. Why is he the one called and not you? Because he is the best, and everyone knows it. Something sets him apart from other salesmen. He not only acts like a Master Closer but thinks like one; he listens, he learns, understands, and uses a lot of charm to solve a problem simply and directly. He uses logic, and it is deadly.

Two things set a Master Closer apart from other salesmen; self-confidence and showmanship. A Master Closer knows he is good, and he shows it. He has manners, poise, and a super-positive attitude about himself. People want to be associated with him. He is good for everyone; he is a creative catalyst.

A Master Closer is special in many other ways. For example, he knows how to act when he enters a room, a football stadium, or just a phone booth. He is always in control, and it shows. If the truth were known, anyone can be that good if he knows how to act and direct himself — like a closer instead of a salesman. You can be a closer simply by understanding and learning.

A closer (I'm going to refer to Master Closers from now on) can chew up and spit out a salesman anytime he wants. I've seen it happen over and over again. The reason is that the salesman or a customer can't out-guess or out-maneuver the closer. The closer can out-mind-manipulate a customer every time. You will become aware of just how this is actually done in future chapters.

A closer can think faster and better on his feet than the customer and can change his approach to suit any environment he is in, any time. He simply blends into the surroundings as if he belonged there. He makes himself so comfortable that the customer feels comfortable.

If we want to talk about showmanship, a closer uses all the tools around him to sell his product the way an actor uses props. The closer doesn't miss a trick. He is entertaining to the customers and makes them feel appreciated. The customer feels confident about the closer and thus feels confident about the product.

The closer is forever selling, convincing, driving, and always winning — because he is sold not only on his product but on himself. This doesn't mean that a closer is egotistical but he likes himself and what he accomplishes. He likes people, and he wants them to like him. The closer is personal, personable, and in many ways, lovable. He is somewhat of a desperado and he can channel that quality as quickly as is necessary (desperado in the sense that he thinks for himself and is self-reliant). He can coordinate his own activities and is an independent self-motivator. He is hard to control to some degree, and that's good because what good sales manager would want the best to be totally controllable and mediocre?

So you see, the Master Closer is many things, but all the elements in his character are aggressive, charming, and positive. He is the one who can carry the ball anytime and make the touchdown. He'll always win. He knows it, the other salesmen know it, and the customer soon learns it. The Master Closer is the king of sales.

The Types of Closers

There are many different types of closers with their own styles and mannerisms, their own ways of doing things. But all closers have a common trait: they sell. Don't ever make the mistake of trying to be a certain kind of closer if it doesn't fit you. All you have to do is read and learn — your style will show itself sooner than you think.

The Jack Rabbit Closer

He's the one who talks a mile a minute; his enthusiasm is complete. His excitement is never-ending, and he is always happy. All this rubs off on the customers and gets them feeling happy too.

This kind of closer, like all closers, knows exactly what makes himself tick, and he uses it to his full advantage. This closer is a mover in every way; he is always on the go and always winding up in the same position: with a lot of sales under his belt.

The Turtle Closer

The "good old boy" attitude: slow and down-home. He presents an air of honesty, integrity, and kindness. He has a believable manner and acts like an old friend of the customer's. He moves in slow, deliberate motions and lulls the customer to sleep — and ultimately the sales.

The Positive Closer

He thinks and acts like everything is great. He is crisp and sharp, always seeing the good in people and any predicament that develops. He thinks any problem is no problem at all. He builds the customers up in such a positive way, they feel that they can't lose if they buy —

no matter what happens. This closer radiates good thoughts and attitudes; he can make everyone feel a lot better, no matter how they felt before meeting him.

The Negative Closer

He's the sleeper type. He has an "I don't care" manner as though he has other things on his mind, or is tired or lazy. He does a lot of listening to the customer and presents the customer with a take-it-or-leave-it thought plan. He gets the customer in such a position that the customer wants the product only because the closer seems to be holding back on some secret about the deal. The customer feels the deal is so good that if he does't get it, someone else will. The closer allows the customer to play mind games on himself. The closer is a country fox in every way. He is so good he can't lose.

The Jolly-Golly Closer

He is the clown of the closing bunch; he always has jokes handy and a happy-go-lucky air. He always gets laughs and is playing games on the other closers all the time. He clowns with the customers and gets them so relaxed and off-guard that they never know when he is going in for the close. All his customers love him. They don't realize that he is selling them all along. When the customer finally does realize what is happening, that old Mr. Jolly wasn't playing games all the time, it is too late — the sale has been made.

The Magic Man Closer

This is the closer who always keeps the customer off balance, always keeps him guessing and wondering what the closer is up to. With this closer, the customer never knows exactly what to expect next; he is always saying something interesting and amazing. He uses super-showmanship, keeping the customer entertained with his plays on words and antics. He doesn't create real mystery or doubts, but keeps the customer spellbound and fascinated with his personality. He's always pulling sayings or solutions out of his hat. He creates a magic, happy air about himself that keeps the sales coming all the time.

The Razzle-Dazzle Closer

He is not like the magic closer, so don't get the names confused. This closer is different; he is the one who always has the special deals, the secret ones no one else knows about. He can put together a package deal faster than anyone. He is always trying (and usually succeeding) to outwit the other salesmen; that is what he makes his own customers believe. He is always going and showing and telling and confusing and switching around ideas with everyone, until no one really knows where this closer stands on a subject. He's always jumbling up the issues, only to eventually come out the winner. The razzle-dazzle closer is a master of words, the whole double-talk vocabulary is his bag of tricks. He is good, intellectual, and he knows his stuff.

The Psychological/Methodical Closer

He is the thinker, the solver of problems. He uses logic as his selling tool. He knows the customer's make-up, backward and forward, and can dissect the customer's mind in ten minutes or less. He knows how to play mind games on the customer's objections, and knows how to overrule any thinking the customer may come up with. He analyzes the whole situation, then he makes his move. He is versatile, smart, and serious. He closes the professionals and he shows a lot of class when closing.

The High-Roller Closer

This closer shows the people all he has done with his life and how he has made it to the top. He says if he can do it — anyone can. He flashes his diamond rings and tells about his boats and cars. He is a master of intimidation and makes the customers feel out-of-place when they are with him because he has pitched himself so successfully. This closer knows his business, and he uses his props well. The high-roller closer has a purpose. He does his job, and people buy from him because he then turns around and makes them feel equal to him when they do buy. This is a closer who usually winds up burning someone if they don't see things his way and buy. But he sells; he does sell.

The College Joe Closer

Here comes the student, or a lost son or grandson; at least that is what he acts like. He dresses, looks, and talks the part, but don't you believe it. He can close. He uses honesty, innocence, and sincerity to sell. He does a super job. He looks like he wouldn't try to sell anything to anyone unless it was a great deal all the way around. He seems too clean shaven and inexperienced to be a mean old closer. He is well-mannered, polite, and he has all the ingredients needed to set the customer at ease — that's when he does his number and closes the deals, one by one, day after day, and always with a courteous smile.

*   *   *

Every closer I have just described can out-sell any salesman in any field. They are all different in their own ways, and they all use their own special characteristics to the best advantage possible. Whether you call them fronts, disguises, or just their natural style, all these closers have that ever-present common factor between them — they can all sell, anything, anywhere, anytime.

The Different Make-Ups of Closers

The Big Ticket Closer

He seems to want to sell only the high-priced items whether real estate, books, or cars. He won't sell something that is not top of the line with a big price tag attached to it. He feels that this is his specialty, and in many ways it is. He is a professional dealing with a class of customers that can afford his product.

The Small Ticket Closer

He's the bread-and-butter closer. He can sell more than anyone because his clients have a greater "affordability radius." He has a much larger field of customers than the big ticket closer. His sales volume might not be as large as the big ticket closer when the year is over, but his closing percentage will be up there with the winners. A closer who can sell the lower priced products can and will sell the higher priced items right in line with all the other closers. He realizes that you can always pull a customer up from a small ticket to a larger one if the client can handle the finances. But try to bring a customer down from a high priced ticket he cannot afford to something that would fit into his budget, and it's tough. The small ticket is a sure way to get more deals and keep from trapping yourself by over-pricing. So just be a small-item closer. If the customer wants more he will let you know. I call it a baby (lot, real estate) closer.

The Older Closer

This closer has some years on him; he is no spring chicken. He can come across in so many ways it's uncanny. This closer can be a father or grandfather figure. He can give advice, offer solid suggestions, and plenty of food for thought. He has an aura of truth and wisdom and uses it to his advantage. He is very good with younger customers who need guidance on this or that product. Remember, all closers (and I'll say it a hundred times over) are actors. They have to be versatile and durable while they are at it.

Closers Who Limp, Stutter, or Have Foreign Accents

Now we are getting to a tool that closers use all the time. If a closer has anything about himself that can be used to draw attention to himself, he should use it; it helps. In fact, a limp with a good story behind it gets sympathy from the customer. A closer who stutters gets interest and involvement from the customer. The closer who speaks with a Texas drawl, a Spanish accent, a French accent, a Brooklyn accent or anything else not only gets attention, but has a hypnotic fascination for the client. I knew one closer who took sugar pills and told the customers they were heart pills. He couldn't get too upset, or he would have a heart attack. Well, the customers were all afraid to say no to him; they did not want him to get upset. You see, use everything you have in order to gain the upper hand. You're the actor.

The Pressure Closers

What can I say? All closers are pressure salesmen, some more so than others. There is high pressure and low pressure — hard sell and soft sell. It is all in the approach to the customer: How you give it, and how the customer takes it. High-pressure or hard-sell closers are trappers and they do not give the customers any place to turn or save face. So in many, many instances the closer and the customer battle each other, and no sale is made. Sometimes, someone gets burned. High pressure is good if it is used right (as you will see later in this book), but you have to control high-pressure sales just as you control a pressure cooker. If you don't, it will explode. You must know exactly how to handle that safety valve.

Low pressure, or rather low key, soft sell closers are more tactful and subtle. They play mind games using traps that leave the client an out but keep him thinking sales. He can save face and still buy without feeling he was forced into anything. This is something we will also explore later in the book. Low pressure is good, solid, steady pressure, never letting up but ever so easily, minute by minute making the decision to buy for the customer plainer and plainer until, all at once, from nowhere a decision has to be made. This kind of pressure is very good for sneaking up on a customer and having that weight finally build so that a decision has to be made that day.

Characteristics of Closers

1. The closer knows how to give glamour to his product; he can make even the dullest product look great. He adds all the polish that is needed.

2. The closer is cunning and crafty; he knows the good and the bad points about his product, and he balances and arranges them to project the product in its most positive light.

3. He is an entrepreneur, a doer who wants to do things his own way, think of new ways to sell and then set a plan of action. He is his own man, made up of all he has learned in the past and will ever learn in the present or future.

4. He gives good service to his customers and stays with them, romancing them and taking care of their future needs.

5. A good closer is greedy; he has ambition and more motivation to obtain his goals than a customer has objections.

6. He has a great fascination with people; he learns from everyone and likes people because he wants to know what makes them tick. A closer really cares.

7. He's a self-starter. He can get himself pumped up for a sale all on his own initiative. He does not need a sales meeting to do it for him. He is aggressive, he is positive, and he is a winner.

8. The closer is, in many respects, a loner. He is a deep thinker who can console himself better than anyone else can. He knows himself best and would rather be alone at times — instead of out honking his own horn telling everyone how good he is when that fact is known already.

9. A closer is a helper. He will always assist a salesman or another closer when asked because he loves it. It is his life. Every time he is asked to help close a deal, that is just one more feather in his hat. As for religion, I have never known a closer who did not believe in God. Perhaps that is what makes him want to help others and like people so much.

10. He can make a stranger (customer) like him in ten minutes or less. But a closer knows no strangers.

The basic percentages of a closer's make-up are:

1. Enthusiasm...51%
2. Empathy and understanding...25%
3. Manners and charm...10%
4. Fun...7%
5. Product knowledge...7%

You will see that the least important ingredient is product knowledge and the most important is a positive, *enthusiastic* attitude. You can always learn facts about a product from closers, books, manuals, movies, etc., but you cannot manufacture enthusiasm unless you really want it in your heart.

The most important ingredient in a closer's make-up is something he gets from himself, not from anyone else. Every man is different, but if you want to become a closer, you can combine all the ingredients and add a huge batch of enthusiasm — then you've got it made.

Little Extras About Closers

Believe them or not, these facts are true, and they add up when talking about sales.

1. In closing a customer, a black man can sell better to whites than he can to blacks. A black man will buy much faster from a white man than he will from a black man. The reason is that most blacks feel a white closer has more knowledge about his product because he has had some advantages that a black closer hasn't. The reasoning on this might not be true, but the fact is correct.

2. There are two types of closers in the human feelings area:

(a) The Intellectual Type — He is the closer who is aiming at the mind, logic, and good common sense in customers.

(b) The Emotional Type — He is the one who aims at the heart of his customer; he works on all emotions, both good and bad. This type of closer is your winner, above all others.

3. The closers who carry too much sales material or too big a pitch book around with them always scare the customers. They look more like tax auditors than closers. When a closer is loaded down with sales paraphernalia he is weighted down physically and mentally as well. It's as though he were a racing boat dragging an anchor. So be light, calm and relaxed. All you need is your mind. If you have to give an in-home demonstration, you can always get your gear later, after you have said hello to your customers. I will explain later about this process and ways of presentation.

4. If you are a conservative closer, then forget the word "closer" because you are not one: you're a salesman. There is not a closer around who is conservative. A closer is a doer, a positive goer, an aggressor; there is nothing conservative about him. In sales there is no such thing as a conservative closer.

5. A closer is a compulsively driven person with a desire to win, to succeed, to sell, to become the best — and nothing less. That's why he

is a champion, and not just a winner. A champion knows there are going to be ups and downs in the game of sales so he keeps going. He is always striving for the sale. The winner is fine when he is ahead but when he's not, he is down and can't get back up by himself. The winner just cannot play the serious game like the champion can — and with his attitude, he never will.

Why They Are Closers

A closer is a man who can do more than any salesman ever thought about. Why? Because he knows how to get close to people, he knows how to get the customers feeling good about themselves. Customers like the closer because he shows interest in them; the closer builds the client up so high that he cannot possibly say no.

A closer is far more than a super-salesman; he gets the people on paper, on contracts, and he keeps them there by himself. He's the one who can step in on another salesman's troubled deal and solve the problem in minutes.

Don't think someone is a closer just because he says it. There are so many phonies running around it is hazardous to the selling industry. Some salesmen who call themselves closers are all talk and no show. A closer sells and that is enough to take the place of any self-enhancing talk.

A closer is a special kind of salesman that people like, people get excited with, people believe in, and people feel special around. A closer is true and convincing — he is sincere. He wins.

A closer looks like you, but acts and thinks like a closer — and so can you.

This is how I was introduced to closers by Sam. And this ended my first lesson.

Chapter Two

THE CLOSERS

CLOSER'S ATTITUDES
(Showing How a Closer Thinks)

A. The Do's and Don'ts Concerning Attitude

B. The Tidbit and Antidote Check List

C. The Closer's Personal Thoughts and Pressures

NOTES

Chapter 2

THE CLOSERS
(Showing How a Closer Thinks)

My first lesson was completed, and I could now see the difference in the sales closers' styles. I understood their make-up and their actions. Sam explained that from this point on we would now study the closers' attitudes, how the closers think, and exactly how they keep their minds on a high, positive note. Sam told me that a closer's attitude is his most precious or destructive weapon. Everything in sales closing depends on how the individual closer uses this very powerful force, attitude.

In this, my second lesson, I would also learn what really makes a sales closer go, what makes him tick, and how he is psychologically motivated towards himself and others. Sam stated that with this information in hand I could actually start to act and think like a Master Closer. So, listening closely, my lesson began.

The most important thing about a closer's attitude is his ever-present, positive enthusiasm. Sam put it this way: Enthusiasm is the one ingredient that makes us special; it is the base product that takes us away from being mediocre and commonplace, and develops a power in us that is indestructible. Sam said enthusiasm radiates and lights up our faces no matter what the surroundings may be. It is the catalyst that makes us sing and dance and makes people all around sing with us. He said enthusiasm is the maker of friends and the producer of smiles from all strangers. It is the builder of confidence and explains to the world, "I've got what it takes to win and accomplish." Enthusiasm tells and shows people everywhere that you like your job, the company you work for, and all the folks you work with. Enthusiasm is the inspiration that makes you want to wake

16

every morning and be alive. It's the thing that puts a spring in your step, a warmth and understanding in your heart, and a positive twinkle in your eyes. Sam said enthusiasm can turn a depressed salesman into a top closer, a pessimist into an optimist, and a loafer into a hustler — in just a heart-beat. Enthusiasm is all these things and more; without it, you will never be a closer or even close. You have to have a great emotional attitude to be a closer. To demonstrate exactly what I mean, I am including a do's and don'ts check list compiled by closers. These are the things a closer knows and is aware of all the time. These are the understandings that build and develop closers and keep them on top in the selling field. Without this check list of facts, a closer would be just another salesman in a world of thousands — and I do mean thousands.

Before studying the list, a note should be made at this point. Everyone is a salesman to some degree but most people don't realize it. Now, a salesman knows, but he has only gone so far in the pursuit of total awareness, and then he has fallen short. In truth, the closer is the one who actually knows the answers, the how's and the why's pertaining to attitudes and constructive outlooks — the ingredients that are needed to win. The closer utilizes them fully, all the time. This is where it all develops concerning attitude — using enthusiasm as the base power.

Do's and Don'ts for Closers

1. Don't sell if you're not sold.

Do not sell anything you are not already sold on personally. If you would not buy the product yourself, then get away from it. Find a product you can be sold on — something you can believe in. I've heard old timers say if you buy what you are selling, you are dead in that particular sales field. That statement is incorrect. The customers can sense through a closer's motions, reactions and intentions, if he is sincere about his product. So don't fool yourself and sell an item just because it is the going thing at the time — unless you're genuinely sold on it. If you do sell just to sell, you'll be the loser no matter how hot the item is. You'll be selling phony, and no closer alive can be the best if his heart isn't in it; selling phony doesn't do anything positive for the heart.

2. Don't sell just for commission.

I have seen many, many closers float from one product to another just for a larger commission — for example from land sales to steel siding just because the commission is bigger and there is more money to be made. All good, sound reasons to move around, right? Wrong. Now, if the transition can be made (knowing top quality closing is the same for all sales fields) from one product to another, it should be made because the closer is sold on that particular product with the same degree of enthusiasm he has for the commission being paid.

If a closer transfers or converts over for the commission only, he will not be as effective, as sharp, or as good as he thought he was. He will not be the same leading closer everyone had heard about because the commission-only attitude will show through to the customers, just like the product-only attitude. The closer will not be as productive, he will not be closing the same percentages as in the past, and he'll wind up thinking to himself, "With this great commission to be made and my past performance record, I could get rich selling this product no matter what it is. The commission is the only important thing. But I'm not selling. I wonder why?"

This question will answer itself in the long run because the closer is slowly killing himself trying to get rich through commission only and not through basic self and product belief. The same beliefs make you shine with style and polish rather than be dull and worrisome over commission.

A football coach once told his team, "Take pride in your work, prove yourself on every play, have dedication, and have a good time, and the score will take care of itself." I have found that applies in sales; the commission will be there if you do your job.

3. Small talk is out.

Don't listen to a lot of small talk around the office. Examples are old sales stories (unless you can learn something positive), negative talk: about the weather, salesmen, the developers, things that need to be done or undone by someone; whatever. All these nasty little statements build up to a big minus atmosphere. The best way to protect yourself is by being, in some respects, a loner.

Before you get with your customer, always get away from the other salesmen — go anywhere by yourself (the bathroom, closet, outside) and think to yourself only good, solid, positive thoughts. Believe you are going to go out there and sell that customer, and nothing in this world can stop you — except you. Then, when you have yourself in the right frame of mind, with a positive, sincere smile on your face, your clothes looking neat, it is time to meet your customer. He's yours alone; it's only the two of you involved, so be positive, alert and present yourself in the best manner possible.

Don't get close to any salesman who is feeling down or is feeling negative. Stay far away; he is poison. What can that kind of salesman do for you anyway? He can do nothing except try to make you feel as down as he feels. He will destroy you as you listen to him or remain in his presence. So become a loner before you get with your customer — and then go in and close.

4. Don't pre-qualify.

Of the negative attitudes that can destroy you, this is a giant. Pre-qualifying may occur when you meet your customer and find out he is from a state, town, or area where your product has not had much success. Or, your customer looks poorly dressed; or, he has a depressive air about himself; or, his house is about to fall in from old age.

Please, for the sake of all closers everywhere, don't say to yourself, "I'm beat," or "I'm going to lose; there are too many strikes against me already." That is the very best way to defeat yourself before you even start. Remember, it's one on one, and every customer is different. Customers will always have similar objections and questions concerning the product being sold. But the customers themselves are different and separate individuals.

So, don't pre-qualify or pre-guess them. When you come upon a situation that you think looks tough or depressing, get by yourself, regroup, and then turn around and go in — knowing that you will win and get the sale.

There is a secret to this regrouping action. It works like this: chances are that the customer was already pre-qualified by other salesmen and ignored because of his appearance. So, now here you are, treating the customer like a million dollars, showing him your best side, and putting him first; you are acting like he is going to buy and can afford it. Something happens at this point. The customer sees all this and feels the different approach he's receiving from you. He appreciates it, along with your showmanship — so he buys. He buys from you because you, the closer, made him feel special, made him feel wanted, and treated him like a millionaire no matter what he was driving or wearing or where he was living. You, the closer, have won again.

5. Don't get down on yourself.

If you miss a few sales or are in a slump due to personal problems, outside pressures or all the things happening around the sales office, don't let yourself get down. The first thing to do is to look at your sales slump and try to see a reason for it. Here you have to be honest with yourself.

Now, before we get into the subject of you and self-critique, let me tell you something about the sales that are missed. There is a good rule to know and remember: In sales there are two reasons why a customer will not buy. Number one is an objection, and number two is a condition.

An objection from a customer can and should be overcome by the closer. There should be no excuse for missing a legitimate, honest objection from the customer. This is the closer's job: to answer, get an agreement, and conquer (close).

But there is another reason people don't buy — the factor called condition. This is a different animal altogether. A condition from or about a customer cannot be overcome. There are exceptions, but basically a condition is beyond the closer's reach. The following is an example: Flatly, the customer cannot afford the product. Obviously, the closer involved cannot produce money for the customer. This is a genuine excuse not to buy. There are many different conditions that will develop and stand in the way of a sale everyday — conditions the closer has no control over cannot be avoided. If a closer misses a few customers, he should look back on his sales presentations and try to see what the reasons were for missing. If he feels that it was due to conditions involved, then forget those customers and go after the new ones.

But if a closer is missing because of customers' objections, then the people are selling the closer, and they are doing the winning. This is when the closer had better take a good, close look at his sales pitch — a hard corrective look. He should examine the total presentation to see if it needs any alteration or adjustment. If it does, then he should polish it up. The closer should start listening to other closers who are selling; he should see what they are doing that he is not, and then simply copy them until he is back on his selling feet.

Remember, you, as a closer, are in a numbers game, and you can make the numbers work for you if you hit every customer with a hundred percent effort — that total directed shot. But if you have missed some sales and are feeling sorry for yourself, if you are down and depressed, then you will probably stay that way; the numbers, the customers, and the whole closing business will beat you to death. And if you're that weak, you deserve to stay where you are.

A closer knows the score of the game and always keeps on trying, hitting harder with more enthusiasm, and winning. So, analyze the problem; see if it is you or the customer or both, and do something about it. Then, when you get to your next customer you can give him your revised best. Be a professional closer, and don't get down on yourself. It's not worth it.

6. You can get angry.

I just told you not to get down on yourself. That statement is correct. But you can and should get angry or annoyed with yourself if you miss a sale and know that it was your fault. That's good for you; take some pressure off — get out in a field and yell at the top of your voice — anything you want. I've seen top-notch closers throw chairs hit walls and doors, yell at the trees, and be so mad at themselves for their stupid mistakes that the secretaries all run for a corner. I guess these men can control their fits of anger if they want to, but that's not my point. The point is this: a closer who knows he has lost a sale through his mistake and consequently gets mad at himself is better than a salesman who misses a deal and says, "It's the customer's fault; you can't win 'em all." If you're going to be a closer, act like one.

If you lose a sale through your own fault, then admit it to yourself; don't allow it to happen again. Don't put up excuses or alibis or push your loss off on the customer. Remember, the sales percentages tell all in the long run. The company you're working for didn't hire the customer to win the selling game, they hired you. If you mess up and get angry at yourself, that is your right.

Don't dwell on the customers that you miss, just learn from them. Remember your mistakes so you don't make the same ones again. Go from there. The rule is: Don't look backward for very long; that is not the way to progress.

7. You can't learn enough.

We're talking here about learning for closing reasons and that wanting-sales attitude. You will always have things to learn about closing and yourself; that relationship is one and equal. You learn new ways about how to work, how to improve your closing habits, distinguish your style, and polish your manners. You discover improvements you need to make. You learn every day, and you learn from everybody, no matter who they are or where you are. Every single customer you have, whether you win or lose, makes you that much stronger. You learn with every objection, problem, situation, or maneuver you encounter; these make you a much better Master Closer. Always keep your eyes and ears open. You cannot learn a thing with them closed and your mouth open. Acknowledge all that goes on around you. Be aware and alert. Watch and observe what the top closers are doing, and follow their pattern.

To improve your closing percentages you must become an awake closer. You have to study and learn everything so that you will know something about any subject — jobs, or geographic areas, or anything your customer might bring up. The knowledge that you pick up will open new horizons for you with your customers. With that knowledge you will make them feel at home and relaxed with you. Both of you have something in common to talk about. This common ground is your springboard for selling that customer — the common bond you have established because you learned and studied about something you both could talk about. It's easy. The more you know, the taller you grow; and, a Master Closer grows pretty tall, mentally.

8. You're the giant.

We are not talking about physical size in people. Different heights, weights, looks, long hair or short, thin or fat, old or young — in closers it does not matter. All you need to be a master closer is your mind. You do not have to be a 6'7" football star to be a good closer; you don't have to look like a movie star to sell. You don't even have to be a university graduate to be a top closer. All you need is your mind — and that wonderful thing called heart.

I'll put it this way: You need love for people and a fighting spirit. With these two assets, plus wanting to be the best, you've got it made. That's all it takes, really, and a little know-how.

For example, I've seen closers sell who couldn't even talk because of laryngitis. I've seen men sell who couldn't walk, write or understand English, and sell more than ten so-called salesmen put together. They believed in themselves, and they wanted that sale badly enough to go get it. If you want to be a Master Closer, if you give it your best shot and know that you will win, then you will win. No matter what size you are or what you look like, it's all that is inside you that counts. Basic desire and spirit is your key.

9. Feel comfortable.

Keep your mind and thoughts geared and cleared so you never feel uncomfortable around your people or in their environment. You are in charge and in control. At least you should be. If you feel awkward or out of place around your people, they will feel this. Before you know it, the situation will be out of hand, creating an atmosphere that is not conducive to any kind of sales, much less closing. By feeling out of place, you create another obstacle that does not have to be there. If you make your job easy and you feel at home around your customers, they, in turn, feel comfortable around you.

I'm not only talking environments, but customers themselves. They might be completely opposite from you racially, financially, and geographically. You may be in their home, and it might be a shack or a mansion. Just analyze the situation and comprehend it; relax, be courteous, and become chameleon-like — blend in. Belong. This way, you will actually be the calming factor that the situation demands. Use charm, manners, and class as your key.

10. You're hot; stay that way.

How many times have you heard it said, "You are what you think you are"? It is true. The saying, "When you're hot, you're hot, and when you're not, you're not," is wrong. So don't believe it. If you are a closer, the saying goes like this: "When you're hot, you're hot, and when you're not, you get hot."

As a closer you have to know deep down that you are top drawer material. A power inside you drives you to be the best. If you know you're hot, then who in this world is going to say you are not? Do you think any other salesman or manager is going to try to stop you from believing in yourself? When you really do, and you're out there talking to customers and trying, you always know that you have what it takes. You never give up.

There is not a closer in the world who wouldn't respect and appreciate that kind of effort. That kind of working and tenacity creates sales. One cannot help it. See for yourself who is out-selling everyone around. It will be you — all because you believed in something pretty special; you believed in you. You made yourself hot and you are keeping it that way. There is no earthly way you can lose.

11. Be confident.

This is a super-must. You have to show confidence in yourself. It's like believing in yourself, but to a different degree. This is how it will work to your benefit.

If you show confidence in yourself when you walk into a room, your customer begins to feel confidence in you. This makes the customer feel secure in believing the things you say and secure in the feeling he can give his money to you. Through confidence, you build up trust in yourself — something the client has to have before you can sell him anything. Confidence is positive; it is power. Confidence is the leadership quality that a closer needs and has to have. To acquire confidence dress well, smile, stand tall, be polite, be courteous to everyone, and show your best manners. If you do these things confidence will radiate from you. You will not be able to hold it back.

Another thing about confidence and how to keep it: Don't get frustrated or up tight when things start happening too quickly or unevenly. Stay calm and tackle one problem at a time. All this time your customer is watching you and saying nothing; he is thinking and forming his opinion about you. So show that confidence in yourself, and the customer will be on your side. He really wants a strong leader selling him, not a salesman who is unsure of himself or shows weakness. This is showmanship at its best. Confidence can make or break a sale, so be aware of it at all times. The confidence in you will show if you let it.

12. You can be replaced.

No matter how good you are, or think you are, there is someone else out there in this world who is standing by to take your place on the sales line. That person probably has more energy, enthusiasm and go than you do. You had better remember this, because if you let up, slide, or coast on your past sales history, it is back on the interstate for you. If you keep this fact in front of you, you'll be ahead of the game.

A good lesson for closers who think they're indispensable is this: Go put your finger in a bowl of water, then pull it out. Watch how long the hole lasts. Get the point? You have to keep on top of everything to be the best and to stay there.

13. Burn your bridges.

I like this way of thinking — go for it; don't forgo it. In other words, to get a sale, go all out and give it everything you've got. Burn your bridges behind you, so even if you feel like backing out of something or retreating, you can't do it. You have to go forward and win.

The customer is your challenge. Your job is to sell. How can you sell going into a presentation if you know you can back out of a corner if you have to? I'll tell you how. If your pitch is half-hearted, just fifty percent — then so is your closing average. Burn your bridges and charge toward the sale. Don't worry; you'll get it. Again, a positive, aggressive attitude wins.

14. Leave your work.

A good rule to remember: Don't take your work home with you.

When the day is over and all has been done, relax, hang it up until the next day; take a break. Get your mind off the hook for awhile. This will do a very important thing for you and that is to keep your mind and your entire self sharper. That's why all sports have halftimes and breaks.

The same holds true in the closing field. You have to learn to relax, regroup, and calm down so you can be at maximum strength the following day. You're recharging. It's normal and makes closing a lot more fun. When closing and sales become work for you, and you are starting to fight it, then your sales will go right down the drain — faster than the blink of an eye. So keep things in perspective; you work hard at closing, so play hard with your free time.

To go along with this, plan your days off. When you're working, concentrate and devote total energy to closing; when you have a day off, enjoy it. Forget closing, customers and the office. Get them all out of your system. By planning your days off and knowing when they are, you give full attention to your closings and to your selling time. You should have nothing else on your mind while closing. Work is work, and days off are just that. You've got to understand the difference; and make the difference work for you. You are a professional, so treat yourself like one.

* * *

We have been talking about the do's and don'ts of attitudes for closers. Now we are going to get into some tactful things to know — all the little notes and phrases that keep the closer alive. Everything you see and learn concerning attitudes are a culmination of tidbits that fit together; they congeal to form a sound working pattern for the closer. To have an attitude that is positive, you have to be aware of everything that makes you think better and clearer. So, the following is a closer's tidbit chart showing the little things you have to know.

1. Treat them with respect.

Every man, no matter what his character or behavioral pattern, wants to be a winner, and he wants to be accepted and appreciated by others. Use this approach with your customers to build them up for sales decisions. This build-up comes through your attitude toward your customer, how you treat him and think of him. You've got to show the customer you are interested in him — and make him believe it.

2. Compete with yourself first.

The less you concern yourself about out-selling the other salesmen the better your closing percentage will be. You should be competitive but you will not sell anything by watching the other closers sell and standing there in awe. Remember, it is you and your customer that make the sale, not the other salesmen who are looking on. If you want to compete in sales, be competitive with yourself first. Then, at the end of your selling season, you won't have to worry about the other salesmen because you'll be the winner. They will be the ones worried about you.

3. The closer, then the product.

The main thing in sales is not really the product but the closer himself. He represents the item being sold, and he is the company's personal representative. The closer is the one who shows the product's positive points and plays down the negative ones, and everything else that goes with the final sale. It all has to be filtered and shown through the closer, no one else. He is the front door for the whole company, and the closer is the first impression presented to the customer.

4. Your impression.

The customer will develop and form an impression of you when you first meet; whether that impression is good or bad depends only on you. Your attitude and appearance are the initial keys. It is easier to sell when that very first impression, even without a word being said, is positive.

So, act like you want a sale, and give that image. It will show in your manners and actions. You have to act positive and be in control when you meet your customer.

5. Customers are people.

If you forget that the customer is a warm human being, with feelings and a family, with emotions and needs just like yours, if you look at him as a dollar sign, a way to get your commission, then you better hang it up. You're not a closer but a wimp. You will show about as much class and professionalism as a genuine loser or a salesman who thinks he is a winner and is really only as close to being a closer as a hobo is to becoming president of a large oil company. Keep your customers first; treat them with love and understanding, then the sale will develop — producing your commission.

6. Build up the customer.

Get the customer sold on himself; set him on a shining pedestal. Always let the customer see himself in the best light possible; make him want to be with you for the respect and admiration you show him. Make your customer feel special, a cut above other prospective buyers. When you have him feeling high on himself, he has gained the self-confidence you have instilled in him. Then, when you ask for the sale, you'll get it because the customer has built himself up so much that he would be intimidated and embarrassed to say no.

7. Be organized.

Keep yourself and your business organized. Keep records of all your sales; keep names, addresses, phone numbers — everything — not only for tax purposes but also for referrals and future business. Know your own good and bad points; and your own habits. Work on the poorer ones so you can get control of every situation in which you are involved.

By keeping yourself and your business records organized, your mind will be free to concentrate on sales and closing. This eliminates all the nit-picking items that a good closer should not be bothered with in the first place. Organization is the foundation of total professionalism.

8. Contribute to team work.

To work in a sales office with others, you must have teamwork — if you want a total sales effort going on around you. Be constructive. Help other closers when asked, and be happy for them when they sell; you'll have your turn many, many times over.

If things get petty around the sales office, such as little differences of opinion, tacky gossip, and jealousy, put yourself above and beyond it. Just go out and sell your customers; they are not involved in your office politics. Remember, your customers are the ones you make your living from — not the office range wars. In a sales office, whether it has teamwork or the aforementioned problems, always keep things in the right perspective — sales first.

9. Don't procrastinate.

Don't delay a customer who calls you after the sale has been made. Call him right back. It could be good news, a product pay-off or a new referral. Or the customer might want his hand held; he might need reassurance from the closer that everything is fine. If your customer has bad news, at least you can deal with the problem immediately — nip it in the bud. Whatever you do, don't procrastinate; the problem involved only gets bigger.

If you have a new customer when an old customer calls, wait until you've sold the one you're with before you call back. If you don't, and the old customer gives you bad news — for example, a cancellation — your negative thoughts could ruin the deal with your present customer. You'll lose two customers instead of one. Use your head. Keep things in order.

Another thing concerning calls and old customers: when you do call back, and you solve the situation, don't just solve it temporarily. Get it over with so the same problem doesn't keep coming back to mess up your mind.

10. How to kick the slump habit.

There are three good ways to get yourself out of a sales slump. First, instead of giving your presentation in your regular or usual way, reverse it and give your pitch backward, from last to front. This gives you back the enthusiasm and momentum you didn't realize you had lost. When you pitch backwards, that is explain your product in reverse, you don't really know what you are going to say next to the customer. You are extra alert and on your toes to keep the presentation organized. This automatically creates a spark in you, the missing enthusiasm, and you will sell. After selling the customer, go back to your original sales presentation format; if you keep using the reverse pitch it will lose its unique quality and purpose. Remember, the purpose is to get you out of your slump.

The second way to re-group and start selling again is simple. Instead of trying harder to sell, go completely negative. When you get with your customer, act like you don't care if you sell or not. Tell him you've already sold today, and you're tired. Tell him the product is better than you can even try to explain right now, and if the customer really wants a good deal, then he should buy the product. Assume a take-it-or-leave-it attitude, and watch the customer turn around. The customer builds up his own presentation for the product, thinking it's too good to pass up. Because of your attitude he then buys. Try it — it works.

The third rule is a fun way to get out of a sales slump. Just go out and buy something — a sports coat, a shirt, a new pen, a car, anything. But, you have to spend some money on yourself and no one else. Then go back to the office or project and get your next customer. You'll sell him. This gets the excitement back in you that you had lost from being in your sales slump.

In studying attitudes keep in mind that enthusiasm is always your base power. To think like a closer you must be aware of all the factors that affect the closer's total outlook. You have to understand how a closer views each new situation and solves it. All the pointers in this chapter are designed to produce a positive attitude. Every statement contributes, and you can't cut one short or underestimate any of them.

*   *   *

We are now going to look at some "closer's anecdotes" or "short shot ideas" that add to the development of a closer's attitude.

1. There is only one you, and you are unique. No one else can do what you can in the same way you do it. Always show your personal style, and don't try to be anyone else. Exhibit your own brave, generous spirit.

2. "If you got money, you're a honey; if you're broke, you're a joke." Sound silly? Think about it.

3. In selling a customer, some rules of thumb:
   Your heart equals his heart.
   Your mind equals his mind.
   Your understanding equals his understanding.
   Your reasons equal his reasons.
   Your sales presentation equals his acceptance.

4. Some salesmen say, "Good morning, Lord." Some say, "Good Lord, it's morning!" Guess which ones are the producers.

5. When you have used all the mental tricks you know to get psyched up for a sales presentation and you're *still* not ready to face the customer, tell him your problem, and start a polite conversation. Your customer will help you out, believe it or not — and buy.

6. Every person you talk to is a potential customer — a person who makes your living for you. Always treat people in that manner.

7. With the combined ingredients of enthusiasm, control and product knowledge, you can sell to anybody.

8. To be a top quality closer you have to have self-confidence, self-control, and self-respect; these produce self-satisfaction.

9. A good point to remember: "A man is stagnant if his dreams equal his present existence."

10. Talk about having a good attitude, a closer went broke one time on his own business venture, and another salesman asked him, "How are you doing, 'Has Been'?" The closer was calm. He smiled and answered, "Pretty good, 'Never Was'." Closers do have a strong attitude.

11. There is not a customer anywhere who wants to do business with a semi-pro when they could be doing business with a professional. Act like what you're supposed to be — a professional closer.

12. If you don't sell the customer then somebody else down the line will. Ask yourself: are the other salesmen better than you?

13. Some salesmen think it is a big joke when they sell a customer something that he doesn't need or if they sell the customer more of the same product. Well, it is a joke all right, but only on the salesman. It all comes back to haunt him and disrupt future sales. That's the way a salesman creates problems for himself.

14. A salesman who is forever telling old sales stories (war tales) about himself and elaborating on all he's sold is bragging only to build up his own ego. Chances are he has an inferiority complex and has never done very much in the world of closing; he probably never will.

15. Know how to expound on a particular subject; know how to use the correct words and phrases to express yourself.

16. A good thing to keep in mind: when most of a closer's bad dreams disappear it is a sign his subconscious mind is clearing.

17. Be a closer to your customer, not just a good conversationalist; anyone can talk.

18. If you take the letter "C" out of the word closer, you have the word "loser." The "C" stands for confidence, control, compassion, and courage.

In studying the closer's attitudes, we must look for a moment at the closer's personal thoughts and pressures to understand that dimension of his world.

To a closer it is a great feeling to know that he is the best in his selling field because not only he knows it, but all the other salesmen know it as well. The main goal is staying a winner, to be the master closer you want to be. But every closer, no matter what he may say, has a hidden fear of being known as a loser; it's a feeling any kind of competitor has. It's built-in, and it is normal. It is all part of being a closer. The fears stem from the pressures. Being a closer involves coping with many personal pressures, as the graph on page illustrates. This is why the closer's attitude is so important. A closer cannot do his job, he cannot function, if he is not prepared mentally.

A closer also has to think about his goals in life. (See illustration, page 32.) A closer knows about the ups and downs of life and he also knows you have to stay on a base game-plan — something you can home-in on. If you don't have a long-range goal, you could be in real trouble. You'll drift and never gain anything in life. One day you will look back and say, "What happened? Where did it all go?" Then it will be too late.

To have a closer's attitude, you have to be bold enough, gutsy enough, humble enough, classy enough, and most of all, human enough. You have to want to be number one and be willing to go out and work for it. It all happens with an understanding and love for people and that ever-present enthusiasm that will make you become, anytime you decide, a Master Closer.

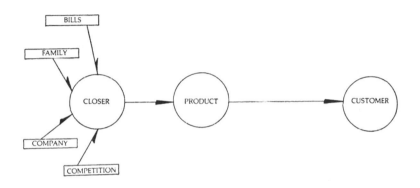

The Closer's Personal Pressure Exposure

Closers have the same problems everyone else has except for one thing: A closer can't afford to get down. If he does, his closing percentage is shot. This is why a positive attitude is so important. Being a closer is the only profession in which you must be mentally up all the time.

The customer can get down, feel bad, but it's the closer who has to be up mentally so he can get the customer feeling good, and make the sale. On top of being up mentally for the customer the closer has to be a big brother, a father, a minister, a friend, an advisor, a baby sitter, and a good listener just to get a word in.

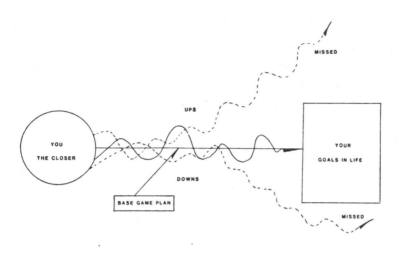

Closer's Goals

Every closer has to look into the future at one point or the other and see what direction he is going. If he doesn't, any goal he had hoped for will vanish. It's like driving a car: If you take your eyes off the road, you'll run into a ditch. You'll have the same ups and downs but you'll be off the track and miss your original objective. Just think for a second how many closers you have seen that have all the talent in the world but are down and broke. The above illustration is one of the reasons for that happening. It didn't have to be that way. Keep your eyes on your goal, and go for it.

A good note for yourself:

Write down on a piece of paper your ultimate goal in life. Then look at it. Review it every day — this is a simple way to constantly check yourself. See if you are maintaining your original course toward your objective. Above all, be honest with yourself because you are the person who is either going to make it or fail.

Chapter Three

THE CLOSERS

THE CUSTOMER
(The Opponent)

This chapter describes the characteristics of customers and shows how the Master Closer handles each one in preparation for the close.

NOTES

Chapter 3

THE CLOSERS
(The Opponent)

July the first had finally arrived at Green Vista Estates, and our grand opening was in full swing. The customers were arriving from all across the country thanks to our company's outstanding marketing department. Everywhere there was activity and excitement. As for me, I was parking cars like there was no tomorrow — and enjoying every minute of it.

Sam wasn't just sitting around, either; he was at the guard gate giving directions and information to everyone. In fact, Sam was so busy he looked like a swamped-under travel agent. Whenever we got, or took, a work break, we'd sit down together and continue our discussions about sales and closers. Sam had explained sales closers to me over the past weeks in a way I could understand and I came to appreciate the job they actually do.

But the time had come to start studying, observing, and learning about the closer's number one opponent: the customer himself. Sam told me that no matter what label you put on a customer — an up, an out, a unit, a bimbo, a peep — the customer is the fascinating element of sales work. Before we start, two facts have to be stated. First, the customer is the name of the selling game, and the closer has to know everything he can about his customer. If the closer wants to make a sale, he must know his customer as well as a surgeon knows his patient. If you think people involved in a sales situation are different in Boston than they are in Kansas City or Los Angeles, you're kidding yourself. People are customers, and customers are just that — customers. Period.

People will have different accents and mannerisms, and they act and react differently because of their environments. But when it comes down to bottom-line sales — the close — all customers are basically the same. They will have the same basic thought patterns, the same objections and questions, and the same hesitations. It's as though they all read the same cue cards and scripts.

It is important not to confuse sales presentations with closing. True, customers are individuals. They have to be treated and approached in many different ways in a progressive sales presentation, but we are not talking about that now. We are talking about closing a sale on a product, whatever it may be. The customers are the same in that they are the opponents — with all the aforementioned common basics. They are either going to tell the closer yes or no. As stated previously, the customer is the name of the selling game. With this understanding we can start to study the many fascinating types of customers.

A closer knows that the first thing to learn about a customer is the kind of customer he is dealing with. Then the closer uses that information to develop a sales presentation suited for that particular customer.

Categories and Types of Customers

(Using a one-to-ten scale for measuring the customer's degree of closing difficulty, ten is the most troublesome customer.)

The Yes Man

(Description) This is the customer who will agree with you on everything; he will nod his head in the affirmative and say "yes" to every statement that is made. The closer could give any kind of ridiculous sales presentation, and this customer would still agree.

(In Reality) The customer has already made up his mind that no matter what the closer says he isn't going to buy today (if ever). This customer keeps agreeing just to get the sales presentation over. He thinks the affirmative nod of the head, or an occasional "yes," will pacify the closer into letting up on the sales pitch. This customer is basically scared that if he does let his guard down, the closer will indeed sell him. This customer is pretty easy to close, and on a scale of one to ten (with ten being the most difficult) the yes man is rated a solid four.

(Solution) To snap this customer out of the "yes" habit, the closer should turn around and ask the customer directly, "Why aren't you going to buy today?" This kind of shock question will catch the customer off guard, and he will most likely give you a legitimate answer, not knowing anything else to say. With this, the closer can then work toward the final close.

The Know-it-all

(Description) The title speaks for itself. This customer already has all the answers and thinks he knows more about the product than you do. He will tell you that he personally knows the president of your company or that at one time or the other he was in your particular business. This customer will say just about anything to make you feel off balance or uncomfortable. He continually acts as a smart-aleck, to some degree, and tries to take control of the sales presentation. His favorite statements are, "I know," or "I understand."

(In Reality) This customer does not want to be out-classed, out-shown or intimidated by the closer. He knows that he is weak around a good closer, so he puts up that strong "I know" guard to protect himself. He feels he has to show-out in front of everyone around when he is with a closer so the sales closer will not make him look like an uneducated idiot about the product. This customer is fun to work with because you can program him easily. On a scale of one to ten, this customer rates a four.

(Solution) Let the customer trap himself; go along with him and allow him to explain the product to himself. All you, the closer, have to do is be polite and agree with him, acting like you are learning something yourself. This customer will keep talking and eventually talk himself into a corner. This is when you ask him, "Well, since you know all the advantages of this product, how many do you want?" Then you take his answer and run with it. The customer will feel all the pressure because he explained the product himself and now has to answer the closer in front of other people. He won't know what to say and will most likely start backing down. That is when the closer moves in for the sale.

The High Roller

(Description) This customer has to tell you all about how much he is worth, how much he owns, and all the things he has been into and accomplished. He will tell you about all the important people he associates with, and he'll explain that if he likes your product enough he will even buy a dozen or so — money is no problem. He'll flash the diamonds, the gold watches, and make sure you know he is a man of means. And, if you're lucky, you can visit his country club sometime as his guest.

(In Reality) This high-rolling customer is most likely up to his eyeballs in debt. He lives a pretty good life, or so it would seem, but nothing is really paid for. He probably spends more nights awake worrying about bills to be paid than about where he will invest his money. The customer sees himself as something he is not and tries to get that facade across to the closer. This client is polite and shows manners, but he is hurting for cash and he will not admit it to the closer. He just plays his own game in his own world. On a scale of one to ten, he rates about a four.

(Solution)Go along with the customer, be impressed with him and all he has acquired. Show admiration, and ask him for his secrets of success. Become his friend by idolizing him to a degree. Then, when it comes time to close, ask him how much time he would need to transfer some of his investment monies so he can purchase your product. This gives him time to accumulate some money and save face and embarrassment by not being asked if he has money now. Do not confront him by telling him you know that he does not have the ready cash; just act as if he does and don't let on that you know differently. This customer will trap himself every time, so the closer should just give him some room. The client will high roll himself into his own sale.

The Thinker; The Quiet One

(Description) This is the customer who just sits back and doesn't say a word. He could be smoking his pipe or looking out of the window, but he simply will not talk. He'll look at you with skepticism in his eyes and act bored. He will have a firm handshake and be quite courteous when he meets you, but that's when it all stops. He makes you feel like an actor on a stage, and he's the audience just waiting for the performance to begin. This customer instills the feeling of pressure on the closer because of his silence.

(In Reality) The silent customer is really a thinker; he wants to listen to what you have to say, and he wants to see if you're honest and sincere. He is analyzing you and sizing you up. This customer is most likely pretty intelligent and probably somewhat knowledgable about your product and your company. He is more like a country fox than a city tiger. He is cautious, slow moving and protective of his statements and answers directed to you. On a scale of one to ten, this customer is about an eight.

(Solution) First of all, be on your toes and keep alert to everything this customer has to say. Pick up on any little hint or slip he might make so that you can figure out this client's thinking. Be courteous, sincere, and give a somewhat negative pitch; go soft sell and low key. Don't get over-excited. Instead, present basic logic about your product and company. Also, explain something about yourself, your family, and your job. You just do the talking and relax. This will let the customer get to know you better first; he, in turn, then relaxes his own guard and lets you know something about himself. This opens up a conversation so the closer can accumulate some ammunition to use for the sale. Treat this customer as an equal; you are the professional and know your product completely and with confidence. ★Note: This customer will send you more business than anyone else!

The Scared-to-Death Customer

(Description) If you should sneak up behind this customer and yell, he would have a heart attack. This customer is so nervous it sometimes even scares the closer. This person is always looking around and never staying in one place; it seems he is fidgeting with a pencil or something on the sales desk continuously. This customer is afraid of the closer, and it shows. He is wound up tight and talks sharply to his family and friends, even in the presence of the closer.

(In Reality) He is scared because he thinks he will be put in an embarrassing position and have to answer personal questions. For example: the closer may ask something about which the customer is ashamed. The customer doesn't want an outsider, the closer, to find out something that he would rather not have known. He feels out of place and totally uncomfortable around sales closers because he also knows he can be persuaded to buy anything. He knows his weaknesses and doesn't want them to show, but he knows they do. On a scale of one to ten, this customer is a three.

(Solution) Treat this customer with kid gloves. Be slow, low-keyed, and compliment the customer on something good that you observe about him; this way you can build up his confidence. Make him relax by talking about yourself and not about him. Hit on his job lightly in conversation, and don't dig deeply into his personal life. Make a friend out of him. Find a similarity in your life and his own. This will help ease the tension. Put this customer up on a pedestal, and show him that you think he's special. This will be an experience that this customer has never had before. He will be easy to control and close. All he needs is confidence in himself and the leadership and friendship of a Master Closer.

The I-Don't-Care Customer

(Description) He fits the name. He acts like it is no big deal if he buys or not. This customer has a take-it-or-leave-it attitude with the closer. He seems to care less if the product is great or if it will just barely do the job. This client is nonchalant and acts like the closer is boring him. He could be rude and discourteous in his manners and hard to get to know.

(In Reality) This client does not want to be pressured or sold by a closer. He wants to examine the product for himself and not be bothered with a sales presentation. This customer could be the silent type or the boisterous kind. He wants to do things on his own and in his own time. But don't let him trick you. This customer acts as though he doesn't care, but he is wide awake and alert. He is taking in all the information he can find, and he is thinking about all that is being said. On a scale of one to ten, this customer is a seven.

(Solution) Don't try to sell him with the usual presentation or you will be fighting a losing battle. This customer has to be turned around and injected with excitement about the product. The closer has to create a sudden interest in the product for the customer and spark his curiosity. This curiosity will cause the customer to show more interest and get more involved in the closer's presentation. This will then develop into a more normal closer-customer relationship and the closer can progress toward the final close.

The "We Don't Buy Today" Customer or "The Looker"

(Description) This customer says to the closer the minute he meets him, "I'm not going to buy anything today, it's my policy." Or, "I'm just looking; I wouldn't buy today for any reason." This customer will not let the closer even say one word until that fact is out in the open. This is the customer who sounds like he memorized his questions and answers before he entered the sales office. He is ready for the closer. He thinks he is prepared.

(In Reality) This customer is easy to sell — probably one of the easiest. He puts up a negative front because he knows when that is destroyed, he is finished. He will buy anything. This client is likeable once you get to know him, and his sales resistance is very weak. All this customer can do is give the closer that one big "no" on the front end of the sales presentation, and from then on it's easy sailing for the closer. On a scale of one to ten, this client is a three.

(Solution) Don't listen to his first statement; let it go in one ear and out the other, because he doesn't mean it anyway. Give him your regular sales pitch with a lot of enthusiasm and kindness. Show a special sales price for this particular customer only — and you have a sale. This customer cannot resist a good deal. In essence, that's what he is saying to you when you first meet. He is telling you that he is a pushover and to please not present a good deal on a product or he will buy. These customers are fun.

The Curious Customer

(Description) He really doesn't have any buying questions, he just wants to know what is going on. This customer wants information to take home so he can read about the product. He is willing to listen to a complete sales presentation if time allows, and he is nearly always polite and courteous. This customer can get involved in your sales pitch easily and start to participate by asking questions — and some good, positive questions at that. This customer is a bright spot on a slow day.

(In Reality) This customer is a buyer all the way. He first has to like what he sees and then develop a desire for the product. This person is a shopper but also an impulse buyer who can make a decision at any time if he is motivated. He has a good personality to go along with his curiosity and is a good person to get to know. This customer wants to buy — and will, if he feels good about the closer, the sales office, the environment, and the product itself. On a scale of one to ten, this customer is a solid three.

(Solution) Give a dynamic sales presentation with a lot of showmanship; get the customer excited and involved. Get him thinking about how he would feel owning this product. Work on his ego and his pride. Tell the customer that there is an inventory situation involved and the customer can really take advantage of the price. This customer just needs to feel that he has stumbled onto something great and special. With that planted in his mind, he will buy anything.

The Good Natured Customer

(Description) This customer is polite, courteous, and shows class. He is open-minded and respectful to the closer. He will sometimes even tell you (in a light manner) that he is hard to sell. This client is a winner, and thank heavens for him.

(In Reality) To be short and sweet, this customer is genuine and for real. He does have an open mind and is willing to listen to what the closer has to say. He usually has the money to buy but will turn away from a high-pressure salesman. He wants to be treated the same way he treats other people. This customer is a breath of fresh air to any closer. He makes the sales business that much more enjoyable. On a scale of one to ten, he is rated four.

(Solution) Treat him very courteously, with a lot of charm. Show your professionalism with gentlemanly manners. Give this customer a solid, logical sales presentation without going overboard in any one area. Assume he is going to buy from you from the beginning; then treat the close as something quite normal. This kind of customer is especially good for your referral business. Do *not* high pressure or push this customer.

The Rude, Skeptical Customer

(Description) This customer comes into the sales office with a chip on his shoulder. He is far from being the nicest customer that you ever had. He acts as if you are the cause of all his problems, and it would be easy for a bad situation to develop between you and this customer. He doesn't believe anything you say and has great doubts about the product. In all, this customer is a problem, not only to the closer but to anyone in the general area.

(In Reality) This customer has personal problems; it could be in his home life, job, finances, or anything. He will try to take it out on someone else — and it could very well be the closer. Remember, this customer is not in his usual frame of mind. But if he is always like that, he could very well have a serious problem. He is just looking for any excuse to start an argument. On a scale of one to ten, he rates about a seven.

(Solution) Destroy him with kindness. Do not get into an argument. Stay away from any pressure subjects — they might irritate him. Play your sales presentation down, low-key. Be polite, and show concern for his predicament. Ask him if there is anything you can do for him. Become his friend, and he will calm down because he doesn't have anyone to spar with. He will start to talk to you, and then you can present your product in a calm and orderly manner. It would be easy to forget this customer and let him go without making a sales pitch. To stay with him — to turn him around — is the difference between a professional closer and a salesman. Be nice to this customer; he needs that friendship first — the sale will follow right in line.

* * *

We are now going to take a look at the circumstance customers. This area of study has more to do with couples and families. It shows the different kinds of situations the closer is regularly confronted with. We will also see the procedure you should use to channel each circumstance customer toward the sale.

The Elderly Customer

(How They Think) The label "elderly customer" also pertains to couples, widows and widowers. Older people have a common characteristic: loneliness. They might have a large family and friends or a small family and not know many people, but they still have a great deal of time on their hands. The older customer wants to contribute and do something with his life; he wants to be involved in activities and surrounded with creative projects. This customer does not want to feel left-out or useless, which is a problem he is facing in many ways everyday. The elderly customer wants to be able to do things without the help of relatives so he doesn't feel a depressing dependency on them. This customer has an understanding personality and simply wants to fit in somewhere — to belong. Having the peace of mind that comes with knowing he is sincerely wanted, the elderly customer is slow to act and react. To him, decision-making is not urgent. When this customer is unsure about any sales or buying situation, he will most likely want to seek advice from a friend or family member. This customer wants to believe in the closer, but he knows elderly people are always being taken advantage of and is therefore cautious.

(How To Treat Him) The closer has to do one thing right off the bat which is imperative for this kind of customer: he must slow down his sales presentation. The closer has to be deliberate with his words and demonstrate understanding with a sincere attitude toward the customer. The closer cannot push or pressure the customer at the end of the presentation. Instead, he has to builld up to a decision-making point. This process is accomplished by a slow, steady, positive and gentlemanly sales presentation. The closer has to show warmth and charm toward the elderly customer and must always take the time to listen to his stories. This customer needs patience from the closer, combined with ever-present empathy. The closer has to make this customer feel wanted, appreciated, and needed. The closer has to show the customer not only the benefits of buying the product, but how the product will help meet the needs of the elderly person. This can be illustrated in many ways. The key is to get the customer involved so he can trust the closer. When this is done, the closer not only has made himself a good friend but has gotten himself a sale.

The Young Couple and Single Person Customers

(How They Think) These two types of customers can be approached and treated in the same manner. They both have a common factor when it comes to any sales dealings — excitement. Both of these types also want a financial program that will help them become secure and advance in today's world. These couples may have just gotten married, or they may have just gotten a divorce; they may have children or only be dating; in sales it doesn't matter. Younger couples want something that will put them ahead of people in their own age bracket. They are aggressive when it comes to self-advancement.

The younger customers will probably have financial problems and won't be willing to admit it to the closer. But they have something that will, in most cases, counterbalance that negative problem. That is their optimistic outlook and their willingness to do something to change things. The closer simply has to show friendship, authority, and leadership, and the sale will be made.

(How To Treat Them) The closer has to demonstrate a lot of enthusiasm and showmanship. The sales presentation can be made a little faster than with the average customer, and the presentation should have a great deal of excitement. The closer can turn the younger customer into an impulse-buyer by using emotions involving family, future, and self-pride.

The closer will have to work out finances with this customer in most cases, but he should always act as though it were the normal sales procedure. This keeps the younger customer in a more comfortable frame of mind.

The closer can use this customer's children as leverage. The younger customer will take the pressure better than the older customer. This customer can easily be intimidated into a sale, but in most cases that will not be necessary.

The closer should draw a parallel between his life and the young customer's, showing how making the right decision about the product will pay off in the long run. The closer has to be confident in himself and the product, and sympathetic about any problem the customer may bring up. The younger customer will buy if he is excited and believes in the product. These elements can be produced for the sale, if the closer keeps the younger customer fascinated and involved with the product.

The Middle-aged Customer

(How They Think) This is the customer who has a family and a good job. He might own his own company or be working his way up in one. This customer has a good education and is at that special age where he is not a youngster anymore but neither is he ready to retire. This customer wants more from life than he has and is concerned about his future. This customer is aggressive and tries to think and stay younger than he is.

The middle-aged customer is a person who thinks, deep-down, that everything is going to change for the better, either through a sudden lucky break, or through a run of good fortune.

The middle-aged customer wants only good things for his family and he is willing to fight for them. This customer can make his own decisions and can take care of any problem or situation he encounters. If this customer is sold on a product, he will buy it. He is a closer's bread and butter.

(How To Treat Him) The closer has to become a friend to this customer. The closer should show respect and admiration for the customer and his family. Treat this customer as though he is younger than he really is, and be sure to tell him that his future looks great, according to what he has told you. Build the customer up, work on his ego, and create a positive world for him. Show this client how your product will contribute to his future success. Put this customer first in everything you do and make him feel very special. Use emotions involving his family's future and compliment him on the progress he has made so far. This customer will buy if you put a spark of spirit in him — something he needs. Then proceed on to the close. This customer can get excited and motivated about your product if you speak to him as an equal and show him he has what it takes to make it big in the world. The closer can compliment this customer into a sale every time.

A word of caution: The technique of complimenting can back-fire on the closer if it is not handled properly. When the closer compliments a client on anything, he had better be honest and sincere. If the closer thinks that he can fake compliments, he is in for a big surprise; the customer will know exactly what is happening and simply walk out — and I don't blame him one bit. The closer has to use his head before he can use his knowledge.

*   *   *

The Ethnic Posture of Customers

This is an area of sales study that has to be touched upon if any sales closer wants an honest guideline to follow relating to the ethnic mannerisms of customers. The statements that will be given are based on general transactions and sales presentations. They are not intended to imply that every customer has these characteristics. These statements are all sales-oriented and have been compiled over many years of closer's observations. The examples of customers are based on people who can afford a particular product.

The Black Customer

This customer is unique in many respects because of his background. Black people have not always enjoyed total freedom of buying. With that past history, black people have evolved into two distinct types of customers.

The first type is the older customer who remembers the years of limited sales freedom. This customer is still, to some degree, reluctant to purchase and cautious when buying. This customer has total trust in most people and has to be treated with empathy and leadership by the closer. This customer wants to buy if finances can be handled in an uncomplicated manner. The older black customer is a wonderful referral generator, and he is a good, solid customer if he believes in the closer's sincerity. This customer is a buyer all the way if treated with respect and friendship.

The second type of black customer is the younger and middle-aged client. We can treat both of these customers as one; their thinking is closely related. This customer is aggressive in a positive, creative way; he takes every opportunity to advance and carry his own responsibilities. This customer is a willing buyer and eager to listen to a good sales presentation. The younger black customer has to see how the product will contribute to his future plans. This customer can and will get excited about a product if the closer uses good showmanship with enthusiasm. With this customer, because he is an impulse-buyer, the closer should use an emotional sales presentation relating to the customer's family; he should explain the buying opportunity the customer now enjoys. With this, the closer can go in easily for the sale.

This client is the type who buys from the closer personally, not from the large company the closer represents. This customer buys because of the trust inspired by the closer and will continue to be a good customer if the closer does not misuse that trust.

The Hispanic Customer

This customer is totally family-oriented. The closer must involve the entire household when giving a sales presentation. The Hispanic customer is a delight to work with, and he will buy easily if he feels the closer is being honest and understanding toward his personal situation. This customer will make payments on time, even if the whole family or distant relatives have to help out. This customer has a very religious background, and friendship means a great deal; he is also good with referrals, and is an asset to any closer's customer list.

Always treat this customer with respect for his family history, and create a desire to buy the product through total family participation and enjoyment. The Hispanic customer will go out of his way to buy if he feels the closer is working with him to get the best deal possible. The closer has to become part of the customer's family, and the customer will invite this relationship if the closer shows personal concern and sincerity.

The Jewish Customer

Any statement on this customer has to be brief. The Jewish customer wants one thing — a good bottom-line deal on the product. This customer is easy to deal with if the closer shows the best price possible and refrains from a long sales presentation. This customer probably knows about the product beforehand and wants only the pertinent information. This customer is not the easiest to sell and should not be confronted with any kind of argument pertaining to the product or he will walk out and do business elsewhere. This customer is business, and when he buys it is a good solid sale. The closer should show professionalism and low-key pressure, keeping the customer as the center of interest and importance.

The Oriental Customer

This customer should receive a slow and deliberate sales presentation. The closer should use logic and documented facts. This customer is intelligent and a thinker. He is not the easiest person to enthuse over a product. This customer is business and consumer-oriented in most respects. The extroverted closer will find it hard to establish an immediate close relationship with this client. The Oriental customer is thinking in basic realities. The closer must show sincerity, honesty, and good common sense to relate to this customer. The Oriental customer will buy — and buy hard — if and when he has convinced himself of the product.

The Professions, Businesses and Trades of Customers

This arrangement of customers will show the general thinking and financial outlines that exist with each client's business life. This chart will allow the closer to give a proper sales presentation when confronting a specific customer.

☆ ☆ ☆

Accountants

They are skeptical and conservative in their thinking. They have to study all the financial statements about the product before buying. They have to display their accounting education even if they do not understand the subject being discussed.

They can be closed using a negative presentation, with steady intimidating pressure applied. The closer should let the accountant think he is in control. The customer will trap himself.

☆ ☆ ☆

Airline Pilots

They are between conservative and aggressive. They are decision makers and individualists with a high degree of professional pride. They are good-natured, personable and open-minded. They are logical and optimistic.

They are happy-go-lucky in outlook. They are buyers all the way. They can be closed by building up their ego and showing respect for their profession. An enthusiastic sales presentation is a must.

☆ ☆ ☆

Commercial Artists

They are thinkers and have to be brought down to reality. They tend to see products in a different light. They are both optimistic and pessimistic in their outlooks, and they tend to drift in their trains of thought, looking at the world with an air of lightness.

They can be closed by demonstrating the advantages of owning the product. Steady, hard-hitting pressure is needed to show reality. The closer could even use a mild shock presentation.

☆ ☆ ☆

Bankers

They are conservative and skeptical to a degree. They are thinkers, not excited doers. They will analyze and pick a product apart with an air of supremacy. They don't like pressure and want everything organized.

They can be closed by a negative sales presentation with a confident air of professionalism. Low-key pressure can be used with an assumptive close.

Barbers-Stylists

They are individualists who can make a decision; they see things with some optimism and a creative mind. They are artists to a degree and will have about the same characteristics as the artist, except that they are more logical in their thinking.

They can be closed with a solid, logical, positive sales presentation. The keys are enthusiasm and ownership advantage. The closer needs to work on the stylists' egos.

Bartenders and Club Owners

Individualists who can make a decision, they are doers and will act like it. They will make a buying decision. They are independent thinkers who know what they want and go after it. They are personable, understanding, and self-motivated. They are good for referrals.

They can be closed by using a positive, enthusiastic sales presentation with friendship and excitement. The closer should make them feel as if they are a part of the sales team — on the inside.

Residential and Commercial Builders

They are money-oriented and will buy anything if shown the advantages of the product. They are a positive and decision-making group. They will not go into great detail over a product, but want to be fairly sure the product is sound. They are personable and will take a chance. They are buyers all the way.

They can be closed by showing logical financial advantage and excitement concerning the product. A positive aggressive sales presentation should be used. The closer should allow the customer to have some control.

☆ ☆ ☆

Professional Bus Drivers

These customers are personable and understanding. They have an open mind and are somewhat security conscious. They are buyers and self-motivators. They can make a decision, and will when asked.

These customers can be closed by showing ownership advantage and basic logic. A good negative sales presentation can be used. The closer should work on ego and listen to bus stories. The customers should be made to feel special.

Coaches

They can make a buying decision, but they have to be led. They tend to be out of place when not around the team, where they are leaders. They are not as self-motivated as you might expect. They want a good deal and don't worry much about details. Their base is a school teacher's attitude.

They can be closed by working on their ego and pride. A positive pressure presentation should be used. The closer should get involved with the coaches' sports field. Everyone should be made to feel comfortable.

☆ ☆ ☆

Construction Worker — Light

They are open-minded, and want a good deal. They are hard workers who play hard. They will buy on impulse, and will get excited easily if motivated by the closer. They are aggressive and individualistic in thinking.

They can be closed by pressure, aimed at the future security of their families. They can also be closed by a positive presentation. The closer can work on emotion and ownership advantage.

☆ ☆ ☆

Construction Worker — Heavy

These customers are about the same as the light construction workers except these customers usually have more financial power. They will buy if sold, and will buy hard. They are good for referral business, and they are open-minded.

They can be closed with a negative or positive pressure presentation. The closer has to make friends and show ownership advantage.

☆ ☆ ☆

Data Processing Technicians

They are not excitable and must be guided into a buying decision. They are numbers closing customers and tend to look into too much detail. They are not self-motivators nor the greatest conversationalists.

They can be closed with a pressure close using intimidation. They have to be pushed into the sale. To accomplish this, the closer should build them up and make them feel special.

Dentists

They do not have the same self-centered air that physicians do, but they are still thinkers and not impulse buyers. They want logic and facts concerning a product. They are individualists and will make a decision if sold in a professional manner.

They can be closed with facts and a very personable sales presentation. Enthusiasm and manners are most beneficial with a professional client.

Electricians

They are buyers, and they will react on impulse if excited about a product. They are very open-minded and will ask only basic buying questions. They are not detail people; they just want the satisfaction of knowing they got a good deal. They are good referral customers.

They can be closed with a positive, enthusiastic sales presentation. Use friendship and some leadership when closing.

Engineers

They are numbers people. They want to examine and analyze everything. They are thinkers and to some degree procrastinators. They are not impulse buyers and are difficult to motivate. They think logically and reason with little emotion.

They can be closed by a negative presentation using logic and facts. They have to think they are in control and conducting the conversation. They will trap themselves if given enough time by the closer.

Entertainers

They can be sold if taken away from their ego-personalities. They are optimistic and aggressive. They can be very individualistic and stubborn in their decision-making, but are easily persuaded if motivated. They are moody and need some leadership. Work on their egos.

They can be closed with a sales presentation that is full of excitement and enthusiasm. The closer should go out of his way to make this customer feel important, something the customer is not used to.

☆　☆　☆

Farmers

They are conservative in their thinking and are strong individualists. They can make a decision when they want to, but they are independent and open-minded. They are personable and understanding, and they will give anyone the benefit of the doubt.

They can be closed by using logic, friendship and a positive, enthusiastic sales presentation. They will use common sense more than emotion. They will buy hard if they believe in the closer.

☆　☆　☆

Firemen

They are personable and understanding. They have open minds and are security-oriented. They are individual in their thinking and can make a buying decision. They want only a good deal and are excellent on referrals. They are buyers all the way.

They can be closed by showing respect for their job. The closer should show enthusiasm and advantages of ownership. The closer should listen to hero stories that build up these customers' egos.

☆　☆　☆

Entrepreneurs

They can lead themselves; they are self-motivated and optimistic. They are open-minded and very aggressive in their thinking. They can and will make a buying decision on the spot. These people can handle themselves and know the score.

They can be closed by showing admiration for their successes. The closer should give a positive, enthusiastic sales presentation while all the time working on their egos.

Executives

Believe it or not, these people need leadership. They are self-motivated and optimistic but need a pushing guidance. They want a good deal and like to think they made the decision themselves concerning a product. They can be sold all the way if their egos are built up.

The closer should show professionalism and logic, treating the executive as the owner of his company instead of an executive. Work on this customer's ego and ability to make a decision.

Factory Workers

They want security for themselves and their families. They are money-conscious and skeptical. They think everyone is out to get their hard-earned money. They are basic thinkers. They need to see proof of the product's claims.

Government Workers

They need leadership and are not self-motivated. They can get excited and enthused if shown the advantages of the product that would advance them personally. They are security-minded, but can be turned into impulse buyers. They are bureaucratic in thinking and have to be pushed into buying.

They can be closed by using pressure in a low-key presentation. They can be intimidated into buying. The closer can use enthusiasm to a great extent, but should always be pushing toward a final close.

Jewlers

They are individualists who can think on their own. They can make a decision once they are convinced it is a good deal. They are personable, logical and understanding. They are optimistic in their thinking and have an air of confidence about themselves.

They can be closed by using a good, solid, positive sales presentation. They can be brought to a decision-making point by building up their egos and showing admiration for their artistic tastes.

Judges

They are conservative and slow in their decision-making. They have an optimistic attitude and a gentlemanly air about themselves. They work with logic and reason and cannot be pressured. They are individual in their ways and open-minded.

They can be closed by showing a great deal of respect for their profession and their achievement in the judicial system. They should be given a positive, enthusiastic sales presentation. The closer should show professionalism.

Lawyers

They tend to have a know-it-all attitude about every subject under discussion. They are aggressive and open-minded. They are individuals who think with optimism. They will make a decision when necessary but have to be enthused, motivated and led.

They can be closed by working on their egos and building them up. The closer can use pressure in a positive form and should show professionalism to equal the customer's thoughts about himself.

Managers, Administrators

They have to be led into a decision. They are personable but feel out-of-place when not in their own environment. They are not very open-minded and can be pressured into a sale. They are not overly optimistic, but can be motivated by working on their egos.

They can be closed by showing appreciation for their job and the responsibility they hold. Work on their egos and show parallels between your job and theirs. Use pressure and make them feel decision-making is their second nature.

Mechanics

They are hard workers who play hard. They want advancement for themselves and security for their families. They are open-minded when it comes to a good deal. They will buy if convinced of the product's quality. They are personable and trusting to some degree.

They can be closed by giving an enthusiastic and exciting sales presentation. They need to be shown emotion more than logic in most cases. They will buy all the way if they are motivated and believe in the product's ownership advantage. They can be pressured in a positive, low-key manner.

☆   ☆   ☆

Military Personnel, Officers

They have to think they are in control and making the decision. They are open-minded when they think they are the center of attention. They can make a decision, and will. They can be motivated easily when the ego is played upon because they are sold on themselves.

They can be closed by making them a part of the team. Let them think they are on the inside concerning the sale. Let them trap themselves with their own knowledge.

Military Personnel, Enlisted

They are buyers all the way. They can be enthused and excited with little effort. They are completely optimistic and desire a good future for themselves. They want a good deal and show a lot of trust. They can be pressured, and do require leadership.

They can be closed by giving an enthusiastic sales presentation. Use a great deal of positive excitement. Show the customer an optimistic outlook with plenty of charm and respect. The closer has to build this customer up in front of his family.

☆ ☆ ☆

Ministers

They all seem to want a super-discount or to be treated special in some way. They can be pressured into buying, but have a tendency to cancel. They can be led and motivated easily. They think optimistically and are personable because of their vocation. They are not as self-motivated as presumed.

They can be closed with pressure and intimidation. They can be trapped easily with a positive sales presentation. With this customer the closer can be aggressive.

☆ ☆ ☆

Nurses

These people are proud of their profession and will make a decision if motivated just a little. They think they make enough money to gamble for something better. They are aggressive and will think about any product with optimism. They are open-minded and personable.

They can be closed by using a positive, optimistic sales presentation. The closer has to use enthusiasm and show respect for this profession. The closer can use logic, but emotions work far better.

Physicians

They imagine themselves to be prima-donnas, standing on a golden pedestal. They have a conservative air and are highly intelligent, though they demonstrate it quietly. They are thinkers, and will buy eventually — if shown logic and the financial advantages of the product.

The closer can sell every one if he shows professionalism and class. The closer should work on ego, saying "Doctor" and not "Doc." He also must show control and not let titles scare him.

Plumbers

These are individualists who make money and will spend it. They have open minds and are good-natured. They are not overly skeptical but want the best and want to believe the closer is showing them just that. They will buy if shown basic logic.

They can be closed by giving an enthusiastic and exciting sales presentation. The closer should work on a friendship, good ol' deal approach. Showmanship will do the job.

Policemen

They think in a skeptical manner and try to find fault in the sales presentation and the product. They are personable if there is a common factor to talk about. They are proud of their profession and will show it. Policemen can be good customers if friendship is established. They like themselves.

They can be closed by working on their egos. The closer should listen to police stories and show great respect. The closer can use an enthusiastic, exciting sales presentation with friendship as the base factor.

☆ ☆ ☆

Postmen

Conservative bureaucrats, but they do their share of the work. They are security minded and they hesitate to do anything that will interefere with well-laid plans for the future. They are very low-keyed, and not self-motivators. They think they are deliberate in their actions, but in many ways they are unsure of themselves.

They can be closed with a low-key, logical sales presentation. The closer should show how the product will benefit them and not disrupt their very well laid-out future plans. The closer can use pressure in a soft sell manner and should always have control of these customers.

Professors

Very conservative, will converse on a lecture basis; professors are most definitely thinkers. They are "mull-it-over" customers. They are not excitable, and are very low-keyed. They will ask questions about the product that no one else would ever think about.

They can be closed by showing respect, and by building up their egos to a degree. They can be complimented on their knowledge. The closer should try to learn something from these customers (or at least make the customers think that). These customers should be shown a positive, enthusiastic sales presentation.

Retired

They are worried and concerned about their futures. They are on a limited income, and will be ultra-conservative. They are slow in their actions and in their decision making policies. They will not jump into anything. They will be fairly passive to most enthusiastic, aggressive sales presentations.

Surprisingly, they can be closed by giving an exciting and enthusiastic sales presentation at first, just to wake them up. Then by showing logic and soft sell, lower pressure, the closer can develop emotion and spirit in this customer. The closer should show a trust, sincere and understanding friendship.

Salesmen

They can be sold just about anything. They are aggressive and individualistic people. They are positive thinkers and will make an impulse decision when buying. They are motivated and optimistic — always looking for a good deal.

They can be closed by making them feel they know the inside story concerning the product. The closer needs to build up their egos and show enthusiasm for their sales knowledge. The closer should put the salesmen first and then let them trap themselves. Intimidation and pressure will close them if necessary.

School Teachers

They are used to talking and will show that in conversation. They think in a conservative manner and will not jump into something until they really understand it. They are low-keyed and not highly self-motivated. They are not overly optimistic in their thinking.

They can be closed by showing respect for their profession, and listening to their favorite student stories. They can be pressured into a decision-making situation. The closer should work on ego and give a positive, low-key presentation.

Small Business Men

They will make a decision and stand by it. They are aggressive, self-motivated, optimistic, personable thinkers. They are so-so with referrals but will help your sales with good comments. This customer understands your problem.

To close these customers all you need is a very positive, progressive sales presentation. The closer should show plenty of enthusiasm and excitement. Be professional, work on ego and show respect for accomplishments. Use showmanship.

Social Worker

They are conservative and hesitate to make decisions without leadership guidance. They are bureaucratic individualists and will have to be guided toward a product with pressure. They are very proud of their work, but tend to get their job thinking involved in all sales situations.

They can be closed by building up their egos and showing respect for the job they do. They can be pressured into a sale, but not with intimidation. The closer should show ownership and opportunity advantage.

☆ ☆ ☆

Technicians

They are followers and need leadership. They will buy when given direction. They are instructed workers and consumer-oriented to some degree. They are not self-motivators, and view things on a less than optimistic scale. They are security-minded.

They can be closed by using pressure, and showing the advantages of ownership. An aggressive, positive sales presentation should be used. The closer needs to get this customer excited.

☆ ☆ ☆

Train Engineers

They are thinkers and personable; they are loners to some degree and will study any situation before buying. They are mostly conservative in their thinking.

They can be closed with logic. Do not use pressure; if anything, use friendship and a positive, enthusiastic sales presentation. The closer should be more low-keyed.

Truck Driver

Aggressive, individualistic, truck drivers can make a decision when asked. They are common sense thinkers who use logic in nearly all situations. They are personable and good humored.

They can be closed through logic, reason and showmanship. The closer needs to show excitement coupled with a plain ol' good deal. The closer should ask for and listen to truck stories; build up egos by expressing respect for these customers' jobs.

Welders

Hard, individualistic workers who can and will make a buying decision. They are in the same field as electricians and plumbers. These customers make money and spend it just as fast.

They can be closed if given a strong enthusiastic sales presentation. The closer should extend plenty of friendship and show a super deal, being genuinely sincere. They are aggressive and open-minded.

There are many professions and businesses not mentioned here, but the idea is basic. Customers are individuals and must be approached as such. The closer has to take each customer one by one and solve each individual problem. This can only be done by listening and observing; there are no short cuts, so don't expect any if you want to be the best.

Knick-knack Facts To Know About Customers

This list contains insights and observations concerning customers. Without these facts, the closer could never understand the customer, if that is possible in the first place.

1. If a closer asks a customer directly if he can afford the product, the customer will automatically say yes. Even if the client is

completely broke, he will lie to the closer because no man will admit his finances are in that kind of condition. When you hear this kind of statement, remember: Buyers are liars.

2. When working with couples, no matter how strong a family leader the man appears to be, the wife is the most important in general terms.

a) The wife, in many families, handles the finances.

b) The wife will have an extra job, along with being the homemaker and domestic engineer.

c) The wife will be the one who worries most about the sale.

d) The wife can get enthused about the product and help the closer make the sale.

e) The wife can suggest shopping around first and thus lose the sale for the closer.

f) The wife can handle the children.

g) The wife can, and does, handle the husband.

3. People are followers, in most cases. Customers are like sheep: they want to be led and have someone else do the thinking for them. Try this experiment: get in front of a group of people and say, "Come here." Then walk off. Most of the group will follow you and not even ask why. If you find someone in the group still standing there, you have found another leader. Simple but true.

4. The customer wants something for nothing. He is, in most cases, a good, healthy mooch. He is looking for the best price on the product, and has a grain of free-loader in him. This is a fact that every closer uses in order to sell.

5. People like to spend money. They really want to buy something for themselves or their families. This is true of all customers because buying something new makes them feel good.

6. Most people like to feel that they made the buying decision themselves, without being pressured by the salesman. This is why a closer has the highest percentage of sales: he can lead a customer into a sale without the customer ever knowing it was the closer's idea in the first place.

7. Don't dare underestimate the customer for one second. He has a brain, and he can use it. The old saying, "Simple men believe everything they hear; and smart men want proof," is not the rule of thumb anymore. Customers are thinkers; they know more than you think they do.

8. If the closer goes out of his way to make the customer feel important and appreciated, that customer will buy anything. The customer wants someone to show genuine interest in him.

9. Customers want a good deal on a product, they don't want to be taken for a ride. Take a look at all the people who bought land that was under water. These customers lost money, true, but then they turned right around and invested more of their money somewhere else, hoping this time to win. Customers will buy with optimism, but don't try to hoodwink them.

10. The customers that are thinkers and can sometimes be spotted in a minute. This list highlights give-aways to customer attitudes.
   a) A pipe-smoker equals thinker.
   b) White socks, not worn as sportswear, equals thinker.
   c) Crew-cut hair equals thinker.
   d) Jump-suit wearer equals thinker.
   e) Camera carrier equals buyer.
   f) Loud or flashy clothes equals buyer.
   g) Cigar smokers equal buyers
   h) Cowboy boots equal buyers.

11. The closer has to know in his own heart that people are really great. There is some super good in everyone and it is the closer's job to find it. He must bring it out, and use it toward the sale. Everybody — no matter who they are — loves something. With that knowledge, the closer should find the love in the customer and develop it into a positive selling tool.

In summing up customers, this one thought will suffice: People are distinctly themselves; They have their individual likes and dislikes, good points and bad, they are unique beings unto themselves. To really get to know a person, the closer has to get him away from others, away from all outside influences. When the closer is alone with a customer, that person's real self appears. This is when the closer can get to know and relate to that individual. When someone is alone with the closer, there is no pretense or faking, as long as the person is not trying to put on airs. He won't be doing that if the closer has been honest with him. When a closer has a person alone, all sales defenses go down and both parties converse as equals. With this level of respect and understanding, the only reason the closer wouldn't sell would be due to a condition on the part of the customer — something beyond the closer's control. If the closer has done his job correctly, both he and the client are satisfied.

A sales presentation is only as good as the closer's attitude about himself, his product, and most important — his customer. This all relates to knowing and understanding people.

Sam enjoyed telling me about customers, and one thing I knew for sure: He did know people and how to describe them. This lesson was complete, and I was certainly impressed and eager to learn more. Sam was in a good mood and knew I was totally involved.

Chapter Four

THE CLOSERS

THE CUSTOMERS' ATTITUDES
(Both Serious and Foolish)

A. Customers' basic thoughts, both personal
and secret. What they really think about
themselves and the closers.

B. How the customers scheme against the
closer.

C. Recognizing customer attitude give-aways.

D. "Hot Notes" to remember concerning
customers' attitudes.

NOTES

Chapter 4

THE CLOSERS
(The Customers' Attitudes, Both Serious and Foolish)

After describing the customers' characteristics Sam said it was time to learn exactly how customers think and reason. He said no one can really know what a customer is thinking every moment, but a master closer would know about 93.7 percent of the time and the other 6.3 percent of the time he could guess correctly.

With this statement as my guide, Sam began to explain customers' attitudes. The key fact is that a customer is human, with normal human needs — food, shelter and clothing. Security, love, understanding and recognition are also needs of every human being. Everyone knows that about everyone else.

In addition, most customers are scared, awkward, skeptical individuals. They know very little about the product being presented and are afraid of being intimidated, embarrassed, pressured and pounded into buying.

They are equally afraid of missing a chance or overlooking an opportunity. This creates a customer who feels out of place with a master closer. A master closer has to understand the customer's thoughts and motives and develop them into a progressive, positive action — an action that produces a sale.

All the information about the customer's attitudes is vitally important, because without understanding the customer's reasoning and actions the closer cannot understand the problems and objections that arise during a sales presentation. The customer's attitudes make up the customer's personality and if those attitudes are understood, so are the people who produce them.

To understand customer attitudes we are going to take a look at how the customer sees himself and the closer.

A. Customers' Personal and Secret Thoughts About Themselves and Closers.

1. Two true words: scared and uncomfortable. The customer is basically nervous and feels out of place when he enters a buying and selling situation, especially when he is in the closer's sales office. This applies not only to the customer who is financially well off but to the customer who has a limited budget. The reason is simple: the customer doesn't know the closer as an old acquaintance, in most instances, so an air of friendship is missing.

Also the customer is in the closer's territory — his sales office — and this makes the customer feel even more out of place and awkward. This puts the customer in a guest position, with limited privileges and many doubts, ranging from where the bathroom is located, to whether or not he can smoke. The customer isn't totally himself because he isn't at home or in familiar surroundings where he feels relaxed and more in control.

Just think back for a minute and remember all the customers who said they had to go home first before making a buying decision. This does not include the customer who just plain wasn't sold, but the customer who sincerely feels he can make a better buying decision in his own home surrounded by familiar environment. The Master Closer must acknowledge this basic fact and do everything in his power to make the customer feel totally comfortable.

This can be accomplished through charm, personality, understanding and a sincere interest on the closer's part in the customer's needs. If the closer can relax the customer and make him feel comfortable this objection about going home first will never materialize.

2. The unknown presentation (pitch). The customer is always unprepared for the closer's sales presentation. Although the customer knows he's going to hear a sales pitch he doesn't know how the closer is going to present it. This unknown element makes the customer more suspicious and guarded about what he does and says. It's a great advantage for the closer to know and recognize this uneasiness. If the closer does not understand this fact he will think the customer is stand-offish, or make some other misjudgement. The closer can accomplish a great deal if he will only look through the customer's eyes and see his viewpoint during the sales presentation.

3. The lead shield. The closer *must* keep in mind that the customer does not want to feel pressured or tricked into buying a product.

The customer wants to have the last word himself, keeping his self-respect and integrity intact. The closer has to remember that the customer has been telling himself and his family he will not make a buying decision the same day the product is presented to him. This attitude makes the customer feel he has control and won't be trapped into buying. To maintain this attitude the customer has built up a lead shield around himself and his family to resist any and all sales temptations presented by the closer. The customer has been telling his family and himself all the way to the sales office the many reasons a decision should not be made that day. And I assure you the customer has every intention of keeping that self-proclaimed commitment. The customer and his family can come up with some fantastic stories and excuses for not buying, and I mean some real academy award material.

The Master Closer who understands that lead shield can destroy any excuse with logic and charm, sprinkled with enthusiasm.

4. The white hat. The customer sees himself as the good guy *all the way*. *He* is the one who is going to make a decision to buy or not to buy, and *he* has the money to execute that decision. *He* is the one who can make the closer his commission — or deny it to him. The customer thinks he is in complete control, wearing his white hat and pulling all the strings. (He's still scared and uncomfortable, but we are not talking about that attitude at this point.) The customer thinks he knows where he stands against the bad guy (closer) and expects the closer to pull some sneaky sales trick or hide the truth.

He is in his good guy role, determined, ready and waiting. The customer feels if he himself stretches the truth or misleads the closer in some way it's all fine and fair. The customer's reasoning is "Let the buyer beware." The customer wears the white hat and the closer wears the black hat, as far as the customer is concerned.

This is something every closer in the world should know and accept. If a closer doesn't realize the customer sees himself in that light he will never have a chance of getting close to the customer and then simply switching hats (by letting the customer see him in the white hat) through personality, understanding and charm.

5. His creed is greed — the customer is greedy. By "greedy" I don't mean the customer is rude or dishonest, but that he wants to use his money to its fullest advantage in any sales situation. He wants the best deal possible and will use every trick he knows to reach that objective.

The customer will try to outmaneuver a closer through some hard luck story, a "I can get a better deal some other place" story.

That is wonderful for the Master Closer — the more greed in a customer the harder he will bite. A customer will trap himself every time if greed is his creed. A Master Closer can always come up with a bottom line close when faced with this attitude.

Now we're going to examine how customers scheme and connive against their opponents the closers. This is a truism if there ever was one. Customers have that basic feeling of "I'm going to be taken," so they prepare for it and set a game plan. There are even classes that teach customers how not to be intimidated or trapped by a closer.

B. How the Customers Scheme Against the Closer

1. The customer game plan - The customers — husband and wife with family — will all have their speeches and parts down pat before meeting a closer. They will have all their excuses outlined and perfected well before any objection is needed in the sales presentation. (The closer must realize this and relax that defensive feeling so the customers will be attentive and open-minded or the customer will never hear a word of the sales presentation.) This will be studied later in the book but a note at this point is important.

The customers will say, "We don't have that much money" or "Our kids have to look at it before we decide," batting it back and forth between each other, like the good guy, bad guy approach many closers use in selling. The husband and wife will play off each other until the closer hears one customer say, "We might buy if you would do this or that," making the customers feel that they got the best deal by working on the closer together and wearing him down.

The closer should go along with this game plan, because any sale is better than no sale at all, and the Master Closer is the one who can recognize this plot in no time.

2. Customers won't tell - The customer will never tell the closer how much money he has or doesn't have. He will not volunteer any information to the closer that makes the sale easy, and the customer will lie to the closer in a second if he feels the closer is about to bait a trap or intimidate him. Remember, the customer has a game plan and is suspicious of his enemy, the closer.

3. Customer and friends (customers feel safer with friends) - The customer will arrive at the sales office with a friend or another couple and try to use this third party as the "bad guy" who won't let him make a buying decision that day. The customer will rely on this third party to speak negatively and give the customer his way out. The customer may also use the telephone to call his brother or lawyer, or whoever, as an invisible third party excuse.

But don't worry, it's all been planned and as we will see later it's really no big problem. The customer, with all due respect, is at least trying, and the closer knows this.

4. Comparison customers - The customer will be simply shopping around, but won't tell the closer he just wants to see what the closer's product is and compare it with a similar product he has pretty much made his mind up to buy. This type of customer always wants the full sales presentation from the closer and nothing else will do.

5. Discount Customer - The customer will tell you he wants a discount for paying cash or no deal. The customer knows you have spent valuable time with him and to get a sale you will go for a take-it-or-leave-it cash deal. So what; let the customer play his game, the closer is the one who gets the sale.

In looking at some of the schemes customers use it's basically a bottom line fact that they have a set story arranged to protect themselves and their money. The closer has to be aware of this fact and keep it in mind, because every customer has an individual approach and character; he is truly a fascinating opponent for the Master Closer.

At this point we are going to examine the customer's attitudes about himself, which he communicates without being aware of it. We will see how a Master Closer can detect attitude give-aways by simply observing the customer and his environment. This is not to be misunderstood as pre-qualifying the customer, but a study of the customer strictly through "telltale" signs the customer himself lets slip.

C. Recognizing Attitude Give-aways By Observing the Customer

The Master Closer knows there are two basic ways to observe the customer: The first is for the closer to be selling a product in the customer's home or office (in home sales); the second way of observing is for the customer to be in the closer's territory (on-site sales). From these two vantage points, we will look at the customer and study his give-away attitudes.

1. In-home observation — If a closer is selling books, vacuum cleaners, home improvements or any such product, he will be in the home of the customer. In that situation the closer will have an open book on the customer's life. Simply by looking around the closer can know the life style of the customer, his attitudes about himself and his family, and nearly anything one would like to know about a customer. So how in the world can a closer miss a sale?

In a home the closer can observe if the customer is religious or if he is poor or rich. The closer can see the customer's neighborhood, if the drapes in his home are clean or dirty, his furniture, the floors, wall pictures, cars — everything. The closer can tell if the customer has pride in his home or not. The closer can write a book about the customer without having said a word! With that kind of information in hand the closer will know how to present his product and what sales avenue to use.

I've seen many sales missed because the salesman didn't even look around and make a mental note of the customer's environment. Such information gives the closer a complete picture of the customer's attitudes. There is no excuse for a lost sale with such a wealth of information at hand. (Later in the book, Chapter 7, Part II, we will look at a list of rules and notes that will be helpful in never making an in-home mistake.)

2. On-site observation — This is where the closer has to use every little bit of information the customer brings with him (not like the in-home attitude observation, where everything is spelled out for the closer). The best way to describe on-site observation and connect it with a customer's attitude is to look at some fact-notes that are give-aways from the customer.

(a) Car observation — Always try to see what kind of car the customer drove up in. This is the fastest and the best way to get a quick idea of the customer's attitude. If it's an old car that looks run down don't pre-qualify; look at the tires and see if they are new or safe. If they are there is a good chance the customer simply likes that old car or uses it on errands and his other car is at home. But if you look at an old car whose tires are bald and about to fall apart, there is a good possibility the customer is hurting financially. Think, what kind of customer would risk his his family's lives on unsafe tires if he had the money to replace them. With that information the closer knows what approach to use with the customer and how to give his sales presentation without even talking to the customer first. (Note: if you didn't see the customer's car, be polite and ask the customer where he parked; he'll tell you. Then you can examine it for yourself.)

(b) Financial appearance — If the customer drives up in a new car, notice the model, the size of his family, the age of the customer and how he is dressed. Then the closer can evaluate the car payments and get a pretty good picture of the customer's financial situation before knowing what kind of business the customer is in. (Now everything will fall into place when the closer talks to the customer and finds out more information, but at least the closer has a fairly sound idea of the customer's attitude through this quick and easy observation.)

(c) Clothes and things — When the customer meets with you, notice the customer's fingernails, his hair, his appearance and his wife's and children's clothes as well. Every little thing that the closer sees tells him something important about the customer, and I mean everything. Shoes, rings, watches and jewelry are always a good give-away. The closer shouldn't miss a thing because without all this information how in the world can he know how to begin a sales presentation geared to this particular customer? If a closer has the wrong presentation for the customer, the sale is lost.

(d) Wise guy laugh — If a customer laughs a lot and does silly things, or acts like a smart aleck, the closer shouldn't think that he has a problem customer. It simply means the customer is scared to death. He is nervous, and nothing more. I've seen many sales lost because the closer sees his customer laughing and acting like everything was a big joke, when in reality the customer just needs a friend in the closer, so he can relax a little and settle down. (The customer needs to know that the closer is a friend and not someone who is going to try to intimidate him.) No closer should misjudge this and believe the customer is a wise guy; the customer, in nearly all cases, is not.

(e) Customer poise — Always notice the customer's manners, his etiquette, how he controls his children and how his wife behaves. By observing, the closer can see who runs the family, who gives the orders, and who controls the money. The closer can tell a great many things by how a man controls himself and his family. The closer should observe the customer's vocabulary, which will indicate his educational background. All this is noticed without really getting into detail with the customer himself. At this point the closer can tell the customer what he wants to about himself, but the customer (if observed properly) is an open book. And yet sales are still lost. Unbelievable.

(f) Home location — Be observant about where the customer comes from, where he lives, whether it is a big city, farm country, north, south, the west coast. Everything will tell the closer something about the customer's attitude. Always keep in mind that the closer shouldn't think every customer from one area thinks the same way, but there are common attitudes that go with different geographic areas. The closer should prepare and direct his sales presentation toward those attitudes.

(g) Wait, watch and learn — If a closer watches the customer for a little while, the customer will tell all. The closer can see if the customer has a limp or has something physically wrong with him. He can tell whether the customer is nervous, by noticing if he goes to the restroom too often. He can see if the customer has an outgoing personality, and makes friends easily, or if the customer is introverted. The closer should be patient and just observe, use logic, and be alert. By observing details the closer can know his customer before a word is spoken.

The information just given is true in virtually every instance. The closer should never pre-judge or pre-qualify any customer, and I mean never. But a closer can make a logical and basic assumption about the customer before ever being introduced by waiting, watching and learning. This is a professional process the Master Closer must use, because the attitude of the customer *is* the customer. Observation is the only way the closer will understand the customer.

D. "Hot Notes" To Remember Concerning the Customer's Attitudes

1. The customer will not buy a product if he has legs crossed or is sitting lumped in a chair or has a more-than-relaxed posture. The customer has to have both feet on the floor when sitting at the closer's desk, and has to have an alert posture to make a buying decision. Body language tells a lot about attitude, and a closer must be aware of this kind of communication.

2. A closer can tell if a customer is lying from some of the following signs:
  (a) Dryness of the mouth, so-called cotton mouth.
  (b) Sudden perspiration on the brow, sweating hands.
  (c) Nervous movements, shuffling of the feet, twitching of an eye.

(d) The customer won't look the closer straight in the eye for very long. He looks down when talking, and has an ashamed look or attitude.

(e) The customer will stumble on his words and use to many "uhs" or whatever, because he's not sure of himself.

(f) The customer will start licking his lips more often.

(g) The customer's voice will change to a more deliberate and soft tone.

3. A customer wants to be proud of his purchase, he wants to feel good about it so he can brag on it and feel comfortable with it.

4. All customers have been burnt on a product before and they expect to be burnt again so their guard is always up at first meeting.

5. Customers want to be treated special and because they are around new faces in a sales office they want to hold on to their individuality. It's up to the closer to make them feel important so they relax to some degree.

6. The customer has a weakness, somewhere, and he knows it, so in this area the customer will be over-protective. The closer has got to find this weak point. (This will be illustrated later.)

7. The closer can just sit and observe a customer and all his actions and, believe it or not, the closer will wind up liking the customer.

8. To a closer this is most important and it can't be stated enough — take mental notes, and listen to everything the customer says. *Don't pre-qualify.*

9. If a customer can develop a positive attitude for the closer, it really doesn't matter what product is being sold; the customer will buy with enthusiasm.

10. The customer's actions can be shaped by the closer's actions, but the customer's attitude can only be shaped by the closer's heart.

This completed my study of customer attitudes. Smiling, Sam told me to always keep in mind that when a closer goes to buy something, *he* becomes the customer. (Something to think about.)

One thing a closer should always remember: Customers are people with their families' interests at heart; and any attitude derived from this fact can only be based on concern and love. The closer should accept this and treat that attitude with respect. The customer is the closer's opponent, with an adversary's attitude; but the customer is also the closer's way of life.

Sam was starting to see my sincere respect for all the things he said. As far as I was concerned I was more than ready for my next lesson.

Chapter Five

THE CLOSERS

PSYCHOLOGICAL MANIPULATION
(Head Game Warfare)

The Basic Foundation For All Sales Closing

A. How the closer manipulates the customer to think as he wants

B. Customers' different listening levels

C. Why a customer won't buy

D. The Master Closer and His Rules

E. The Weapon Called Reverse Psychology

F. Customers and Money

G. Thirty-five Tactic Notes on Psychological Manipulation (The Master Closer's Head Game List)

NOTES

Chapter 5

THE CLOSERS

By the later part of July sales at Green Vista Estates were going out of this world. Every single goal the Duron Corporation had set for the start of the selling season was being surpassed by the Master Closers.

Green Vista Estates was developing into one of the most exclusive private resorts in the country, and I was more than proud to be a small part of it.

Every once in a while "Big Bill" would come out to the parking area and ask me what I thought about the development and selling industry. I would always tell him that I thought it was unbelievable and liked everything about it. That seemed to make "Big Bill" happy, because he would tell me that I wouldn't be parking cars forever and that I could go a long way in the company. This made me feel pretty good, especially coming from "Big Bill." (He never was known for his compliments in the first place.)

Anyway, all I really wanted to do was get back with Sam Johnson and learn more about sales closing and Master Closers. Sam was still at the guard house, directing traffic and giving out customer information.

By this time Sam and I had become very good friends, and he knew that now, more than ever, I wanted to see what the inscription on the inside of his ring said. Sam had asked me many times in our conversations if I could guess what was written inside the gold ring, but despite all the information I had learned so far about closing I really didn't have any idea. He said I would just have to wait a little while longer, until my sales closing lessons were over before he would let me read the ring's secret--the secret that would make anyone who practiced it the best Master Closer in the world.

Sam said my next lesson would be on the psychological warfare used in actual closing procedures to get a sale.

So far we had studied the closer and the customer separately. Now it was time to get the two opponents together and develop a sales situation. Sam said "closing psychology" was the bottom supporting line in any sales area. He said that to understand "head game phenomena" the closer has to know certain closing rules and also must know how to manipulate the customer. Sam stressed that from this point on, we would be getting into the subject of sales closing itself.

Closing By Psychological Manipulation
(The Basic Foundation for All Sales Closings)

Now we are getting down to the subject of "head game warfare," or "psychological manipulation," and how it is used by the Master Closer. This is the foundation for all sales closings, the way the closer sells to his customer one on one, eyeball to eyeball.

First this important note — The Master Closer has to know everything that goes on around him and his customer that might interfere with or help a sale. The closer should be aware of any distracting factors that might catch the attention of the customer: another sales presentation going on in the same area, loud noises such as traffic, music, or other customers talking. The closer has to keep an eye on everything and anything. *The closer and his customer should be the only important relationship that exists!* The customer has to concentrate on the closer's voice and actions, and the closer must pay strict attention to every word the customer says. One missed word or sentence could lose a sale. (The closer has to have full control of the customer in every situation.)

Psychological manipulation is simply a head game the closer plays with his customer. But the closer has to have control before this process is effective. By using psychological manipulation the closer can examine and analyze a customer and determine exactly what tactics are necessary to get a sale. The closer can also guide the customer's thinking so he will be open-minded and receptive to any sales presentation.

In other words the Master Closer can actually gear the customer to think as he wants. This can be accomplished by the following list of procedures. This list will tell how to set the customer up in a manner that will let the closer give his sales presentation with control, and have the customer stay attentive.

Before we start there is one rule a closer should keep in mind: A customer can't be conditioned totally unless he wants to be, and the only way he will want to is to believe in the master closer first.

A. How the Closer Manipulates the Customer Thinking

1. Tell about you — Tell the customer about yourself. Tell the customer you are a family man, where you are from originally, and about your life to some degree. This makes the customer more relaxed, and he will feel some obligation to tell you about himself.

The customer won't listen to you if he thinks you're a mystery man or just another salesman with a commission in mind. A customer wants to be appreciated and liked. He wants to feel like he is part of an inner circle of your friends. The customer has to trust you from the start, and that can be accomplished by sharing a little of your life story with him. The customer will feel this sharing is something special, and that you think enough of the customer to relate that personal inside glance of yourself.

2. Ask the customer about himself — The closer should ask the customer about himself, what type of business he's in, about his family, about his home — if he has any pets, everything. (Note: The closer can do this sincerely, without looking nosey.) The closer will get all the answers he wants if he shows genuine concern, understanding, and appreciation for the customer. But if the closer shows the slightest hint of an "I don't really care" attitude, everything will be lost. The customer can spot this insincerity in less than one ten-thousandth of a second, and this is something the closer should never forget.

When the closer is asking the customer questions, he had better involve the whole family. Don't leave anyone in the customer's party out, because the person who was left out of the conversation will be the one to kill the sale, every time.

3. Common bond subject — When the closer first meets a customer, he should find some kind of common bond, such as kids, business news, sports, an illness in the family, etc. Just about any subject will do. But the closer has to set this common bond early in the sales presentation. It not only relaxes the customer, but puts the product being sold in a second subject state. This makes the customer lower his guard somewhat, because he won't be defensive talking about a subject that doesn't relate to the sale. This common bond will be a springboard for the closer later in the sales presentation, and a good equalizing tool between the customer and the closer since both parties can relate to the common subject. The closer should always use it to the fullest extent.

4. Five thousand and one words to the wife — In talking to a customer team (husband and wife) if you say five thousand words to the husband, you'd better say five thousand and one words to the wife. The wife is the most important part of a husband and wife team. What man wouldn't buy something if his wife seriously really wanted it?

The closer can even go as far as talking *only* to the wife, and never saying a word to the husband. This sounds ridiculous, but it's true. No man would let a stranger talk to his wife and not hear every word being said. Even if the husband looks uninterested, believe me, he's listening to the closer — closely. So when the closer talks to a husband and wife team, let the conversation go 49 percent to the husband and 51 percent to the wife.

5. The secret rule — Here are four fundamental rules which, if used properly, will never fail to get a sale.

(Rule A.) For the customer to like the closer, the closer must first like the customer.

(Rule B.) If the customer likes the closer, he will listen to what the closer has to say.

(Rule C.) If the customer listens to the closer, he will believe the closer.

(Rule D.) If the customer believes the closer, he will buy. PERIOD.

To illustrate this, let me take each rule and explain how it works.

Rule A. The closer has to look hard and deep into the customer and find something he really likes about the him. It could be his children or something the customer has accomplished — whatever. But it has to be sincere on the closer's part. If it is faked the customer will feel it and all is lost. The closer can and will find something to like about the customer; it might take a few seconds or it might take thirty minutes. But the customer *does* possess some likeable quality and the closer must find it. When this is accomplished the closer should comment to the customer on that quality. This makes the customer feel great, because he knows the closer sincerely means the compliment. (Note: The customer knows what his likeable quality is and he was proud of it before he ever met the Master Closer, so the customer can tell if the closer is sincere or not.) This does one basic thing: It makes the customer immediately like the closer. There is no way it can fail.

Let's say you know someone who robs old ladies and steals bicycles from kids, a real louse. All right, let's say this bad guy comes up to you and tells you he really likes you, and means it — then he just walks off down the road. No matter what everyone else says about how bad he was, there is no way you, personally, could dislike him. Think back, and see if you've ever disliked anyone who genuinely liked you. You just can't do it. The customer will automatically like the closer if the closer likes the customer first.

Rule B. This step is easy because the customer now likes the closer, so he will listen more attentively to the closer and be open-minded about what he hears.

Rule C. This is where the customer starts to believe the closer, simply because the customer is listening and because of the closer's enthusiastic presentation.

Rule D. This is the final phase, when the customer buys because he believes in the closer and what he is saying.

The whole secret is encompassed in these four words, LIKE, LISTEN, BELIEVE, and BUY. This rule is so true it can't be stated enough. If it is followed correctly it won't fail.

6. Kill the "I have to think about it," line before it is said — This is a sure way of never having a customer say at the end of a sales presentation, "I have to think about it." The following statement will put the customer at ease and pull down nearly all the defenses the customer has developed before the opening sales conversation. This opening statement will work every time, if it is executed properly. The best way to illustrate this opening remark is to show it as if it were being given by a closer:

"Mr. and Mrs. Smith, my name is Sam Johnson. May I call you Bob and Mary? Just call me Sam, the mister scares me. You know I'm a salesman and I'm going to to try to sell you something, right? Well, I'll tell you what I'm going to do. I'm going to make an agreement with you, and I think you're going to like it. I'm not going to try to sell you a thing. I promise. All I'm going to do is tell you why other people bought. If it makes sense to you and you like it, or you think it's advantageous to yourselves and your family, and it fits into your budget, then try it, buy it, get your foot in the door. But if you don't like it, or you don't think it's a good product for your family, or it doesn't fit into your budget at this time, then don't buy it. Now is that fair enough?"

The customer will answer this question with a "Yes, that's fair enough," every time. But the customer is really saying that he will give you either a yes or a no at the end of your sales presentation. This opening statement also relaxes the customer, because then he isn't being sold something, he is merely listening to the reasons other people have bought. To the customer's way of thinking this lets him off the hook, so he relaxes his defenses.

When you say, "Then try it, buy it, get your foot in the door. But if you don't like it etc. . ." you should emphasize the word *but*, and keep on talking. Don't pause at this critical point or the customer will put a word in and that ruins the whole statement. Don't allow the train of thought to be broken.

This kind of front-end pitch is a great way to channel the customer and get him off guard. The customer never expects a statement like, "I'm going to try to sell you something, right?" This knocks the customer off balance every time.

7. **Friendship degrees** — There are different degrees of friendship, and a closer has to establish a friendly relationship with the customer within a certain time period.

To understand this time element better, we'll look at three different degrees of friendship, and see how each one can help the closer get a sale. The first degree of friendship is a light one, but it works. The higher we go in degrees the more solidarity the relationship has.

First degree friendship: This friendship can be developed early. People love themselves, so talk about them and the many accomplishments they've made; flatter their egos, but always with genuine sincerity. (This is a shallow way to get someone to like you, but it works.)

Second degree friendship: This type of friendship can be cultivated if the customer has known the closer for a period of time, and both parties have been through hard and good times together. This kind of friendship is based on mutual trust and respect, but it has to be built on happenings and it has to have time to develop.

Third degree friendship: This degree of friendship will exist when two parties have known each other for a very long time or all their lives. This relationship shares a common ground, in that both parties know each other completely, all the good and bad habits. And still the parties remain close friends. This friendship will endure many, many hardships because it is based on a past history of friendship. This degree of friendship is of the highest quality and the most lasting.

The closer needs time to establish a friendship with the customer, and time is not usually on the closer's side.

To get as close as possible to the customer in a limited time period, the closer can do something rather simple: He can identify with the customer, share a common experience and relate to a common belief, such as religion or politics. This will develop into a friendship that is deeper than the "First Degree Friendship Level" and will expand into the "Second Degree Friendship Level" in a short period of time.

8. **The mirror technique** — This is a way to control the customer in any manner the closer wants. It's a difficult process, because it takes total concentration on the closer's part. If the closer uses this method with every customer he talks to (let's say he sees three or four customers a day), the closer will be completely exhausted by the end of the day. This mirror technique works every time, but it isn't easy.

This is how it is used: When a closer looks into a mirror he sees himself in a perfect reflection; if the closer smiles so does the mirror reflection. This kind of reflection works with the customer. The closer should imagine the customer's face as a mirror, reflecting the closer's face. If the customer is smiling, it's because the closer is smiling; if the customer is sad or unhappy, it's because the closer is reflecting that same image. The closer can look the customer straight in the eye and produce any expression he wants on the customer's face. This is true, but it takes total concentration on the closer's part. This method is a complete mind game and it works. The closer can also control the customer's mental impressions, because the customer is listening to the closer with great intensity and is totally involved. This makes it easy for the customer to reflect the same expressions and impressions the closer produces. (Remember the customer is doing this subconsciously, and isn't even aware of what's taking place.) Of course, this method has to be practiced many times, but when the closer feels comfortable with the technique, it becomes a powerful closing weapon.

9. **Gear your sales presentation** — When a closer talks to a customer, he has to gear his pitch at a sharp, clear, crisp pace. If a closer talks slowly and draws his words and sentences out, the customer has to keep pace with the closer to pay attention. So if the sales presentation is slow and relaxed, the customer is going to be listening in a slow and relaxed way. Then, when the closer asks the customer for a buying decision, the customer will automatically say, "I have to think about it." This happens because the closer geared the customer for a slow and relaxed decision. It is all the closer's fault and he winds up saying "What happened? Where did I go wrong?" (Note: with older customers, a slow, deliberate presentation is needed. But we're not talking about that now, we're talking about the average middle-aged customer.)

The customer has to be attentive, or he won't understand what's being said. So, just like the "mirror technique," the closer can control the customer through his voice and speech patterns. If the closer uses a sharp, crisp, snappy presentation, the customer has to be attentive so he won't get lost or left behind in the conversation. Don't use a fast and furious sales presentation either; use a pace that moves right along in an understandable fashion, with enthusiasm and freshness. The closer can keep a customer alert, awake and excited with this type of speech control.

A closer can lull a customer into indifference or just plain boredom if he uses a slow, low-geared, drawn-out pitch. The closer has to be aware of the fact that he is gearing the customer's mind through his own speech and voice patterns. If a closer wants an attentive, alert and listening customer, then he'd better have that same attentive and alert attitude himself. This way the customer will make a buying decision when the closer asks for one, because he was geared that way from the beginning of the sales presentation.

10. Build on emotion — To keep control of a customer from the start of a sales pitch until it is closed, the closer can depend on one powerful word, *emotion*. If a closer uses this correctly and builds on it, he will always have a captive audience in the customer. Emotion will produce some type of action in a customer every time. Emotion will make a buying decision, emotion will react to what is being said; emotion can produce friendly or hostile forces. I don't care how often the closer uses this closing tool, he must always use it with respect.

The closer can relate to a customer's problems and develop a rapport with the customer by using emotion. To illustrate the effect of emotion: The closer can show emotion by thinking of something sad or disheartening from his own past. Then, working up some tears, the closer can tell the customer his story and instantly the closer has a captive audience. Customers love to think they know the real closer, and such a sad emotional story will do the trick. When a customer hears such a story he will relate to the closer a lot better, and will let his guard down a little more.

The closer can also use the customer's children, his love for his family, and concern for their future as emotional leverage. Every customer wants the best for his family and a good closer should use that great emotion to get action out of the customer. Believe me it will.

Many sales books stay away from the use of emotions as leverage. Because emotions are the most powerful movers of man the closer must be careful when using this tool on a customer. But the closer can and should use emotions with intelligence. The closer should always keep in mind that a customer won't buy if he is hurt or upset by emotions, but he will buy if he sees a sound reason, shown through emotion. (Note: emotion can be shown by the closer through his voice control: soft and deliberate, or excited; his eye contact: with tears for sadness or happiness; and his facial expressions that reflect the emotional feelings needed at a particular time, whether happiness, sadness or concern.)

One more thing the closer should remember about emotions: Love, fear and self pity are the most powerful factors that make up a customer's emotional force field.

Sam said that since we have seen different ways to control customers in sales situations through mind manipulation, we were ready to study how the customers listen to sales presentations.

B. Customers' Different Listening Levels

First of all the closer has to understand the three different levels of customer listening. This understanding is basic and it can't be stressed enough.

The three distinct levels of understanding and thinking the customer will exhibit during a sales presentation are:

1. First Level — The customer hears only sounds from the closer. Not words but noises. The reason is that the customer is not concentrating on the conversation — he simply lets the sounds go in one ear and out of the other.

2. Second Level — The customer hears the closer's words and sentences and will understand what is being said, but that's it. The conversation with the closer just does not register with the customer.

3. Third Level — The customer hears what the closer is saying, understands what is being said and then — the most important thing of all — *thinks* about what is being said. This is the level of listening a closer must inspire in his customer. Because if the customer is on any other level, there won't be any sale. If a sale is made with the customer on the first or second level, it will most likely be cancelled when the customer gets home, because he bought the product without full understanding.

C. Why a Customer Won't Buy

(A) He doesn't like the product.
(B) He doesn't believe the closer.
(C) He has some unseen personal reason or problem.
(D) He can't afford the product.

Objection A — A closer should solve this problem with showmanship, persuasion, ownership advantage and reverse psychology. (We will study reverse psychology in closing later in this chapter.) The closer can overcome Objection A. If a sale is not made because of Objection A, it's the closer's fault.

Objection B — The closer can overcome this problem by using printed material, customer testimonials, consumer reports and actual test results for product. The closer has to be sincere, have an interest in the customer's needs, and genuinely believe in his product. If the sale is not made because of Objection B, it's also the closer's fault.

Objection C — The closer can conquer this objection by uncovering the customer's problem through friendship, interest, understanding and empathy. The closer should help with the problem and find a solution for the customer. The closer should read between the lines to understand what the customer is really saying. When the problem is out in the open and a solution is found, the sale can be made, and not before. If a sale is not made because of Objection C, again the closer is at fault.

Objection D — The closer should do one thing when he feels he has exhausted all avenues to close a customer. The closer should just acknowledge that the customer cannot afford the product. The closer must accept this as a fact and believe he has done his very best. The closer should never get mad at the customer for this condition or burn him. Instead, the closer should wish the customer well and tell him that when he is in better financial shape to please come back and see him. This will make the customer feel more comfortable and will let the closer demonstrate a little class. The closer can't make the customer's money for him, so if a sale is lost because of Objection D it is not the closer's fault.

It might sound like I'm preaching, and I'm not one to preach, but a point has to be made at this time. I just mentioned burning the customer — making the customer mad through emotions or intimidation. The point to be remembered by the closer is this: If you have a glass bottle of sulphuric acid and you want to destroy something, pour the acid on it and it will be ruined. But the inside of the bottle that was holding the sulphuric acid has been more damaged than the object you wanted to destroy. The same holds true for a closer who intentionally burns a customer. The closer might upset the customer, but the closer will be the one who really suffers because the closer will be upset and he still has new customers to contend with, while the customer he just burned gets up and goes on his way.

Concerning the four customer objections, only one — Objection D —is beyond a closer's power to overcome. The other three objections could have been overcome by the closer. So a Master Closer should be able to resolve 75 percent of the objections raised.

Now, that is how black and white is. The Master Closer can out-sell anyone, anywhere, anytime through head games, psychological manipulation, and knowledge. He just has to think.

D. The Master Closer and His Rules

Sam taught me an ironclad rule associated with psychological warfare and customer control. Few closers think about it or acknowledge it, but it is of vital importance: *The Master Closer should know beforehand all the questions the customer is going to ask about the product and have all the answers.* The Master Closer should also know more about the product's good and bad points than the customer.

The customer is on unfamiliar ground with the closer, because he does not know the closer's methods of presentation. The closer knows the rules and runs the whole affair; the customer is at a great disadvantage.

At this point the contest begins between the closer and the customer. If the customer wins and there is no sale, it means the closer lost control.

With all the advantages the closer has over the customer, shouldn't the closer win? Of course he should. The closer has the upper hand from the beginning; it only stands to reason that the closer should win.

E. The Weapon Called Reverse Psychology

When we talk about psychological manipulation, warfare tactics and head games, there is a very powerful approach the closer can and should use. This method of selling is a phenomenon in itself — one of the strongest closing weapons the Master Closer possesses; reverse psychology.

The closer can sell as much as he wants, as long as he wants, by using reverse psychology. But the closer has to know how it works and how to prepare for using it. To use reverse psychology the closer has to know every other method of closing backwards and forwards. The closer cannot use the reverse psychology method correctly if he doesn't have a good closing knowledge background. (Note: A closer could use reverse psychology once in awhile and get away with it, without having a complete sales closing background. But that same closer couldn't use this method day in and day out, because he would start missing too many sales and wouldn't understand the reason why.)

Reverse psychology works in this manner:

Customers are aware that in any sales situation, the closer will give a positive, aggressive sales presentation. The customer is alert and geared for this. By doing the exact opposite, the closer can completely disarm and destroy the customer's resistance.

For example: The closer should meet the customer with a positive greeting and assume a nonchalant attitude from that point on. The closer shouldn't be rude or take an "I don't care" attitude, but should act as if it's no big deal if the customer buys or not. The closer should let the customer know that sales are going great, and should act as if he has had a very good day in sales. The closer should explain his product in a simple, relaxed fashion, with an air of satisfaction and contentment. This impression has to be conveyed to the customer, or the reverse psychology method won't work. (The customer has to believe the closer and think he is not worried about getting a sale.)

The closer should answer the customer's questions calmly, and not seem too eager. The closer should simply be polite, cool and reserved.

What this does for the customer is unbelievable. The customer can't understand this approach and will let his guard down every time, because he is not prepared for such an indifferent attitude from the closer. The customer can't spar with an opponent because the closer is not acting like an opponent.

So the customer is completely off balance. This makes the customer even more alert and attentive because he is trying to find out what is really going on in the closer's mind. Far more attentive than if the closer had used any other kind of sales approach.

The customer will start to think that the product is far more special than the closer is letting on, and he will start selling *himself* on the product. The customer will let his imagination go to work and that's one of the best selling tools ever.

All this goes back to the customer's greed and ego. Customers don't want to miss something good, or something secret that will benefit them. So when the closer acts like it's not the end of the world if the customer doesn't buy, the customer will then become more inquisitive, attentive and aggressive in his attitude.

The reason a closer who does not have a complete sales closing background can't use reverse psychology every day is this: A closer will see many different types of customers, and if he acts negatively toward everyone, trying to use reverse psychology all the time, he will become negative himself, and genuinely lackadaisical. He will short-cut the customer (not giving the complete sales presentation) or act so reversed in his pitch that the customer thinks the closer really doesn't care, and will leave.

To use reverse psychology the Master Closer has to know when to be positive and aggressive with the customer to get a sale. If a closer doesn't have a well-rounded closing background he won't know when to stop going in reverse or when to accelerate into a close. Reverse psychology is a great weapon, but the closer has to know the basics before he can use this special sales closing method.

F. Customers and Money

Sam made an observation about money and customers to me, which explained a way of thinking that made sense. Sam said the only reason for a customer not to buy a product from a closer, if he is completely sold on it, would be the objection of money. In other words, if the customer wants to spend his money or not.

To illustrate this let's say we are giving away old used Volkswagens on a street corner, and the only thing people have to do is tow the cars away. No strings attached, no money needed, just take the car and receive the title free. I don't care how many Volkswagens we had on that street corner, in one hour there wouldn't be a single car left. Every one would be gone, even if people had to push them away. If something is given away, it will be taken.

That is true of sales too, with only one difference — money. If a closer gave his product away, he wouldn't have a product left at the end of the day. Since money is the only obstacle, the closer must simply justify the cost of the product to make his sale. Sales closing is that simple when it comes down to the nitty-gritty. But to get it on that level and to close the sale, the Master Closer must use his knowledge and techniques of psychological manipulation.

In this section of the chapter, we're going to look at some notes and reminders you must use when you are with a customer. These notes are closing tactics that keep you in control. The following information should be viewed as a closer's head game list:

G. Tactical Notes on Psychological Manipulation

1. Touch people. Use your hands to touch their hands and arms, making personal touch contact. This makes people more attentive and draws them closer to you. Use your hands and fingers for explaining and pointing; this has a hypnotic effect on the customer. (Use this

approach with discretion and courtesy.) Touching is the most basic form of communication — talking is the second degree of communication.

2. Don't ever use a red pen or pencil to sell a customer. This makes the customer subconsciously think, *stop!* (Red is usually associated with danger.) Don't wear any red clothing or have red markings on your sales material. Always, when possible, use blues and greens — they are more relaxing for both you and the customer.

3. Remember: "If you confuse them, you lose them." The closer should always keep his sales presentation simple.

4. Don't ever complain about your customer — you'll be defeated before you start. Always think positively about him and go in knowing you will get a sale.

5. You might have a million problems, but nothing makes you feel better than a sale. A closer can cure himself of all his ailments by getting one little sale; that one sale creates others and it goes on from there.

6. When you are giving a sales presentation, always nod your head in the affirmative. Give a positive "yes attitude" to your customer. The customer will react subconsciously by nodding yes also. This is like the mirror technique. It works to the closer's advantage every time. Note: Be subtle when you use this positive nodding movement with the customer; don't over-act. If the customer is aware of what you are doing (or even if he's not), he will think you are a nut.

7. If it's raining, snowing or if it's just a dreary day, you will usually sell. Most people think you have to have beautiful weather, blue skies, birds singing, and all of that to get a customer in a good frame of mind. But on a bad day the customer will most likely have nothing else to do, so he will spend more time with the closer. The customer will not have as many distractions on a cold, rainy day as he would on a sunny day, so he'll be more attentive. This gives you more control and time with the customer, making the sale a little easier.

8. If you create or make the customer feel some nervous tension during or after the sales presentation, a sale will be lost every time.

9. You have to get on the same level the customer is on. You should do or say something the customer can relate to. For example, if the customer drives a truck so does your father; if the customer is a welder, so is your father, etc. The customer needs some common ground to feel comfortable with you.

10. You should always tell the customer a secret, some information no one else knows. Customers love to think they know something special, so you ought to let the customer in on something, no matter what it is. Tell the customer the secret is not to be made public. Believe me, the customer won't tell.

11. No customer, no matter how much money he has or does not have, is poor. Every customer you talk to is rich in some way. It could be the customer's children, his health, his past or his dreams, but every customer has something worth more than money, and you should appreciate and be aware of this fact.

12. You should be alert to the moods of the customer. You should be able to read between the lines and know if the customer is under-reacting or over-reacting to a normal situation. (The customer may have had a fight with his wife or cross words with his kids just prior to his meeting with you.) You must decipher the customer's moods and make an appropriate adjustment in your sales presentation. This adjustment will enable both you and the customer to become more comfortable and receptive.

13. You should never let the customer team (husband and wife) get mad at each other. You must make them feel the buying decision is a fifty-fifty agreement, between both of them. You should always be a referee and keep both parties involved in the sale. If you lose control of one of the parties the sale will be lost, in most cases. (This will be studied in more detail later in this book.)

14. You are selling to a customer team (husband and wife); it's you against both of them, one against two. But during the sales presentation, when you start to win over one of the customers, it becomes two (closer and customer) against one (customer). This creates more pressure on the one remaining customer, and the sale is that much closer to being consummated. (Note: If you have more than one couple to deal with, it is obviously going to make it more difficult for you to control the situation. You should use the very same procedure as you do with the husband and wife. All you have to do is win over one customer at a time, until the odds are in your favor.)

15. Customers are very suspicious people. If they don't understand something, there is a good chance they won't mention it to you. The customer will only think about it to himself in some negative way. This negative idea will stay locked in his mind and become an unseen obstacle for you. Many sales are lost because of this unasked and unanswered question. The solution is to answer

everything you feel might be a question in the customer's mind, up front and voluntarily. For example: explain why you have out of state license plates, if you're selling away from home; or why you are giving such a discount on a product. You should explain your position in your company, and anything else that might become a hidden objection in the customer's suspicious mind.

16. This is a good thought for every closer to remember: The customer who is hard to close — I mean *really* difficult, has to have been sold by someone, sometime. The customer has clothes, a house and a car. So there *is* someone out there who can close him. Is that someone better than you?

17. You should never wear dark sunglasses, either inside a building or outside, when talking to a customer. The customer has to see your eyes to gauge your sincerity.If the customer can't see your true facial expressions, he will think you are hiding something or there is something shady about the product. The same is true for the customer. You must see the customer's eyes also. If the customer is wearing sunglasses, you can get them off by simply saying, "I have a pair of glasses just like yours, may I see them?" or "I really like your glasses, may I see them?" Then, when you get hold of the glasses, look at them and give some kind of a compliment, and set them down. Don't give them back to the customer. (This can be done courteously and subtly without anyone becoming offended.)

18. You should never say, "I'm sorry" about anything. Instead say, "I apologize" or "Excuse me." When you say, "I'm sorry," your subconscious mind will soak up that expression and it will affect your thinking. It's a negative thought. You should remember you are a closer and not a sorry person.

19. It's a good idea to tell your customer he is the most important part of your company, and that your company would be nothing without him. You should state that the customer comes first and will always be first in the eyes of the company. The statement, "We are only as good as our people" will work wonders on the customer. You should always work on the customer's ego.

20. You have to build a dream for the customer, a dream that fits into his own personal goals. When you have established this vision for him, you can proceed to close, using emotion to relate to the customer's future and his family's welfare.

21. When you are giving a sales presentation, and the customer answers questions with "Ummmmmm" (meaning yes) or a silent nod of the head, stop right there and take action. The customer is not really listening to you. You have to make the customer say the word "Yes" or "No" aloud. The customer can then actually hear himself respond and his subconscious mind will be more aware and alert to what is going on in the sales pitch. This can be accomplished by politely saying, "I didn't hear you," or, "Pardon me, what did you say?"

22.   It's all right to tell the customer you are the best Master Closer around. You must have a positive air and use charm when you make this statement. Don't say it with a snobby attitude. If it is handled correctly, the customer won't mind. The customer would much rather be with the best closer around than someone who is a loser.

23. Don't ever argue with the customer. You might be right, but it won't help get a sale. Instead, use a tactful approach and let the customer correct himself. You might win an argument but you'll lose the sale in the long run. Besides, if you lose an argument and get the sale with its commission, who really is the winner?

24. You should realize that through the whole sales presentation, from the front end until closing, the customer will open up more and more, telling you everything about himself. In other words, you will get more ammunition to use against the customer all the time. All you have to do is be polite, understanding, and — most importantly — listen. Sooner or later the customer will let his weakness be known.

25. You should allow the customer to think he is in control to some degree. Let the customer believe he is in the driver's seat some of the time. If the customer sees you have had complete control, he will feel resentful, and cancel as soon as you leave, if for no other reason than to get back some of his self-esteem.

26. Should something bad happen while you are with a customer (example: someone says something rude to someone else and you and your customer overhear it) do *not* ignore it. Comment to the customer about it, and apologize for that rudeness. This action will bring the customer closer to you, making you and the customer a more tightly knit unit.

27. If anyone asks you, "How are things going?" or, "How's business?" tell him everything is great. Be positive. This attitude will rub off on others and will produce a better atmosphere for sales. I don't care if you are sick as a dog, you should project that winning attitude. Believe it or not, the good feelings you spark in others will rub off on you and then you will start feeling better too. Note: You have to work harder at being positive than being negative. To illustrate this point: a negative sign only takes one mark to make (−), but a positive sign takes two marks (+). The positive sign will always take more effort than the negative sign, but the effort will be well worth it. Something to remember.

28. You should be aware of the weapon of intimidation, in every sales presentation. For example: A customer goes into a clothing store looking for a dress shirt. The customer finds one and asks how much it will cost. The closer tell the customer it's a very expensive shirt, and the less expensive ones are on the other counter. Well, the customer gets mad because he thinks the closer believes he can't afford the nicer shirt. Just to show up the closer, the customer buys ten expensive shirts, instead of one. This is a good example of selling the customer by intimidation. There are many, many ways to use intimidation in sales closing, and they will be studied later in this book.

29. You should use third party stories with a customer. This is an excellent way to put real pressure on the customer indirectly.

To get your customer to relate to the third party story, use a fictional or factual customer who is on the same level as your customer. Also, the third party customer has to have a similar problem or objection. Then show how the third party's problem was solved, through a story illustration. This approach is a wonderful closing tool, if done properly. But you must show sincerity and true emotion when telling the story. The third party story can have either a good or bad ending, depending on how it is needed. (This method of closing does work, but the story had better sound convincing or it will look like a joke.)

30. You should use a small degree of hypnotism when talking to a customer, especially when closing. One way is for you to be above the customer. This can be arranged by using chairs of different heights, or by sitting on the edge of your desk. The main factor is for your eyes to be higher than the customer's eyes. This makes the customer look up at you. Subconsciously the customer will feel less defensive, and more attentive to your words. In movie theatres, the screen is elevated

above the audience and the patrons sit in quiet concentration, watching the movie. You can use the same approach and have the same effect on the customer.

31. You should realize that you can over-sell. You can be too enthusiastic, too excited, too pushy, and too talkative. You can actually scare the customer off. You should use reason and control, not only with the customer, but with yourself.

You can also lose a sale by over-selling the product. You can show too many facts, relate too many testimonials and demonstrate the product too many times. All this makes the customer think you may be trying to cover something up or over-compensate for a flaw in the product. An unseen objection develops and the sale is lost. You should know the product and yourself well enough to deliver a sales presentation that is well-balanced, comfortable, controlled, and understandable.

32. If you are shorter, taller, thinner, or fatter than your customer, mention it with humor. For example: If you are short and the customer is tall, say, "Where did you play pro-ball?" or anything that will flatter the customer's ego.

You should build the customer up a degree or two above himself, making him feel special and proud. You should make fun of yourself a little to get the customer on the level you want. When this is accomplished, you can go ahead and give your sales pitch. Now the customer will be open-minded and attentive, because he will feel that he is really somewhat superior to you. He will feel the least he can do is show you some courtesy and listen. (The customer won't even realize it was your intention to make him feel that way in the first place.) This is where it all falls into place and the fun begins. When you ask the customer to buy, he can't say "No" without getting down off that pedestal you put him on. He won't want to step down because he's been acting big in front of you and if he steps down a degree or two he'll be on your level where he knows you could tear him apart. So the customer will stay on that level and buy the product. The customer let himself get trapped by his own ego. It works every time.

33. This is a little reminder for closers. If you don't understand the product, how can your customer? If you don't believe in your product, how can your customer? If you are not happy or excited about your product, then how in the world is your customer going to be?

34. You can't sell anyone anything, if you don't understand the customer. You have to take the time to think about what makes this customer tick. You have to examine the customer and develop a sound approach for that customer. What this all breaks down to is this: "You can't close if you can't open." You have to open up the mind of the customer and know his thinking, before you can get a sale closed.

35. The customer does not depend on you; *you* depend on the customer.

Sam said that this ended my lesson on psychological manipulation. He said the head game war was actually much more complex, but I had enough information about it to be able to continue my studies of Master Closers.

Sam summed up all the material I had learned in this lesson, with one statement that stuck out in my mind: "A Master Closer is the person who finds a positive solution for a customer's problems through mind manipulation."

NOTES

Chapter Six

THE CLOSERS

CLOSER VS. CUSTOMER
(The First Meeting)

A. The master closer's strategy (The attack plan)

B. The closer's initial approach to the customer (Five essential steps)

C. Twenty tips and tactics that work (Candid information to use and remember)

August the second started out poorly. On my way to work at "Green Vista Estates" my car broke down, and when I got the thing going again, the tire went flat. The delays made me late, and "Big Bill" did not like to have any of his people running behind schedule.

When I finally got to my job, Sam was waiting for me. He seemed particularly happy and excited — quite the opposite of how I felt. "Big Bill" had just given me his late-to-work lecture and it didn't do much for my morale.

Sam called me over and told me that today was going to be special. Not only would we be starting an important sales lesson, but for the first time we were going to study the master closers' initial approach to customers and the procedures that are used. Sam said it was finally time to put the two opponents together, closer and customer. Now I could see how the closer literally channels, programs and controls his customer, from the first eye contact until the beginning of the basic sales presentation. This was the point where all the sales lessons started to fit together and go into action.

This was the subject I had been waiting for: the first meeting of the closer and customer, one-on-one. My day had started out somewhat off-center, but now I was eager and alert to hear what Sam had to say.

Chapter 6

THE CLOSER'S STRATEGY
(Attack Plan)

Sam told me the first thing a closer must do — even before he meets his customer — is establish a game plan. The closer must have some kind of strategy outlined in his mind if he wants to get a sale. If a closer does not have a game plan, he might as well give his customer to some rookie salesman and hope for the best.

Game plan strategy simply means that the closer has pre-developed an attack plan for his customer. The closer not only knows how he will approach his customer, but he knows his inventory, his product and himself, backwards and forwards, one thousand percent. The closer also knows where he is going with his customer, and how to get there with confidence. In fact, the closer has already envisioned a closed sale.

The following notes will provide a basic foundation on which to build a game plan and outline the techniques a closer uses to prepare himself for a customer, both physically and mentally.

Note: There is *no* certain time or set place in the sales presentation to actually close the customer. The Master Closer is continually (from the first second he says "Hello" to his customer, until the sale is made) going after the sale with every question and statement he can think of. The Master Closer knows that every single "Yes" or positive response he gets from his customer is a step that much closer to getting the sale consummated.

---

1. Fifty percent positive

When the closer is with his customer, it's one on one. No one else is involved. The closer is fifty percent of the sales situation, and the customer is the other fifty percent. With this in mind the closer should go somewhere to be alone, before he meets his customer.

The reason for this is simple: By being alone and thinking nothing but aggressive thoughts, the closer will build up a positive magnetic field that will completely surround him. When the closer feels positive, strong, and comfortable enough, he can meet the customer for the first time. This positive force field around the closer will always rub off on the customer to some degree. When the closer and the customer meet, the positive half (the closer) will always be more powerful and dynamic than the neutral or negative half (the customer) because positive forces are always greater than negative forces. This is a mental attitude the closer must use if he wants to win.

2. Product Knowledge

The closer must know his inventory, his price list, his product, the monthly payments, the pay schedules and company facts before he ever meets a customer. When a closer has all this information down pat, he will feel more confident and relaxed. This self-confidence will show when he encounters his customer for the first time. A closer cannot be completely confident in himself and feel well balanced and poised if he does not know what he is talking about. The customer can spot this weakness in a closer in no time, and the sale will be lost.

Without detailed knowledge of his product, the closer will be vulnerable to any kind of detail question or trick question the customer might come up with, and this too can easily kill a sale. The closer should never be in the position where he can be caught off guard.

3. Look in the Mirror

The closer should take time to stand alone in front of a mirror before he meets his customer. The closer should check his clothes, shoes, fingernails, hair and overall appearance; he should make sure he doesn't have bad breath, dandruff or body odor. The closer has to look neat, well groomed and sharp if he wants to make a sale. (Remember the customer will not see the closer as he sees himself.)

Something else that is important about looking in the mirror: The closer should look at himself and tell himself he's the best closer around and that he *is* going to get a sale, no matter what. Sound silly? It isn't. A closer can actually psyche himself up and build his confidence by looking in the mirror for a few minutes and telling himself these things. (It's a form of self-hypnosis and it works.) There is only one you, so you'd better make it the best you possible. No one else is going to help you succeed.

The closer should remember he is an actor getting ready to go on stage for his customer, so if he has butterflies, it is normal.

The closer should loosen up before meeting his customer by shaking his arms at his sides and over his head. This will make the closer more relaxed and get his blood flowing.

The closer should present the customer with a good appearance, and an air of confidence. The mirror can do just that for the closer, if it is used properly.

4. Self-Made Enthusiasm

The closer has to have enthusiasm before he meets any customer. Here are two ways to build enthusiasm and excitement: The closer can simply start tapping a pencil or pen on a table, slowly, then faster and faster until he feels himself come alive. The same results can be achieved if the closer claps his hands together, slowly at first, but building the tempo. All this movement and noise builds excitement in the closer and excitement is enthusiasm's first cousin.

The closer has to be alert and standing on "Go" before he meets his customer for the first time. To achieve that frame of mind, he has to use enthusiasm, excitement and positive thinking. These qualities are always available to the closer and are always on his side. But it's up to him to put them there and use them.

5. Pre-Game Strategy

To establish any type of pre-game strategy, the closer must know his product first. When he feels confident of that knowledge, he can develop his attack plan.

Pre-game strategy is illustrated in this example: The closer already knows where he wants his customer to sit, or what room he wants to use for his sales presentation. The closer will already know what product, model or piece of real estate he is going to show the customer. He also knows what price range he wants to work in or around. The closer has all this information prepared and pre-planned so he will know exactly what he is going to do and how to do it. He has total control and confidence in himself, and it shows. With a solidly prepared game plan the closer will have a basic foundation to work from and build on. The closer can then give the customer an organized and understandable sales presentation, leading the customer in any direction he wants. He can show a more expensive product, or a smaller product, a different model or other real estate locations. It doesn't matter because the closer's basic game plan foundation will always act as his focal point.

Another benefit to having a game plan is that the customer too will have a basic starting point to compare with other models and prices the closer shows him. This way the customer can listen to the entire sales presentation in proper perspective. A game plan keeps the customer from getting confused, and gives him a basic knowledge of the product.

The closer's game plan or pre-game strategy is just the closer's ability to develop a controlled sales situation before he meets the customer. The closer knows what steps he is going to take with his customer and he has enough product knowledge to have back-up plans ready, if needed. He understands the need for a solid sales presentation with a pre-developed foundation that can be built on and expanded in any direction necessary to get the sale.

Game Plan Notes and Ideas

1. The closer should remember that he is the leader. He is the person who will take control and lead his customer toward the sale. The closer has to get himself in that frame of mind and show that quality when he meets the customer. The closer should not confuse this attitude with arrogance.

2. The closer should think of nothing but victory when he meets his customer. He should go into the first meeting knowing he will like the customer, and will get a sale.

3. The closer has to know what direction he is going with his customer, and how to maintain control. The closer can't be distracted with side conversations and petty questions, or let the customer knock him off balance.

4. The closer should never have a canned sales pitch. It sounds phony and stupid. His basic sales presentation should have a good foundation, and be flexible.

5. When psyching up for a customer the closer should tell himself, "You are going to use everything you've got to make a sale and nothing less; *nothing less.*"

Sam said a closer who has his game plan well organized and a positive mental attitude would be ready to actually meet the customer.

He told me one of the main things to remember in this lesson is that the closer is programming and controlling his customer from the very first eye contact until the sale is made; he is literally closing the customer throughout the whole sales presentation.

The Closer's Initial Approach To The Customer

1. Approach and handshake.

When a closer first sees his customer he should walk directly to him in a controlled, poised and confident manner. (Note: Never carry anything in hand when first approaching a customer, such as a pen, pencil, or any type of sales material. This will only put the customer on the defensive.) When the closer says his first greeting, he should give a quick look at every person in the customer's party, out of courtesy if nothing else.

The closer should shake hands firmly and pleasantly with the customer, and look him straight in the eye. Do not use any old handshake tricks. When one salesman friend of mine shakes hands he gives a slight pull toward himself, throwing customer a little off balance. He feels this maneuver gives him some edge of control over the customer from the beginning. It's a cute trick that works *sometimes,* but in most cases his customers are offended and suspect what he is trying to do.

If a closer is not sure about handshaking procedures for ladies, large groups of people, etc., or just basic manners, he should buy a book on etiquette and start learning. A closer must know these things if he wants to show class when selling, and class is professionalism.

After the handshake the most important thing to do is get the customer relaxed so he can feel comfortable and at ease around the closer. This *has* to be accomplished if the closer wants the customer to be attentive during his sales presentation.

2. Getting immediate control of the customer.

There is a vitally important moment after the first handshake when the closer can take direct and instant control of the customer, without the customer even realizing what is happening. That moment is crucially important to the success of the sale.

Right after the first handshake and general exchange of greeting, the closer must move his customer to another location — a different closing room, or even another desk. If a closer walks up to a customer, shakes hands and proceeds to give his initial sales pitch, he will lose control of the sales situation almost every time because the customer has picked his own battleground; he has decided where to stand or sit, either in his own home or in a sales office or on a sales lot. The customer has established his position, and is ready and waiting for the closer (at least he thinks he is).

If this sounds silly then you haven't sold much, because this is the way a customer actually feels. How many times have you seen a customer in one general location when talking to a closer. Just think about it. To the customer this is *his* territory and he feels secure there. When the closer moves the customer to a new location, the customer's game plan is thrown off balance. (He simply does not expect anyone to disturb him.) This relocation will confuse and disorient the customer for a minute — enough time for the closer to take charge.

This moving trick has to be done politely and courteously to work. The closer can relocate his customer by saying, "Let's find a better desk than this, it's too noisy here," or "This office is not private enough." Any excuse that shows concern for the customer will work.

Once the move is made the closer should make the customer feel comfortable and relaxed again, or he will be right back where he started, with a defensive and uncontrolled customer. Many closers have overlooked this controlling tactic and for that reason many sales have been lost. The closer must gain control of the customer from the beginning, and this maneuver will do it. (Note: The same principle works if a closer politely asks the customer to please move his car, for this reason or that. If this is done properly, the control factor will remain in the closer's favor.)

3. Seating the Customer (In a sales office environment) —

The closer should keep this rule in mind when seating his customer: Sit close. The greater the distance between customer and closer the less control the closer will have.

(Note: I'm not talking about a desk where the seating arrangement is obvious, but a closing table where the seating is flexible. It should be pointed out that all desks are barriers between the closer and the customer. The closer should try to eliminate that barrier by sitting at the side of the desk during parts of the sales presentation. This way the closer can get closer to the customer, every once in awhile, and make everyone feel more comfortable.)

There are two ways of seating customers and each way has good and bad points. The best way to study these two seating arrangements is to show an illustration and give respective information for each one. (Note: Seating arrangements for home sales presentations will be explained in the next chapter.)

Seating Illustration A

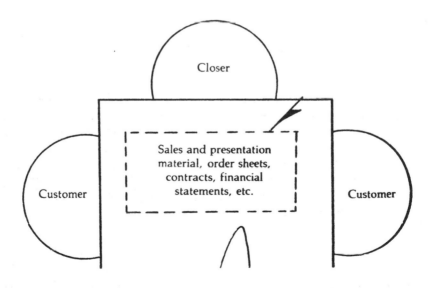

Closer

Customer

Sales and presentation material, order sheets, contracts, financial statements, etc.

Customer

I. In this seating plan the closer has a big advantage: The closer has placed himself in a central position where he automatically becomes a part of the customer's party — has joined their family. This seating arrangement also breaks up the bond between any customers (that feeling of strength from closeness) and weakens any pre-planned sales defense the customers have prepared.

II. Another advantage is that the closer can equally share his sales presentation, both verbally and on paper with both customers at the same time. The customers can read and examine sales materials from their positions and the closer can have physical contact with each customer simultaneously without looking awkward. (Example: Touching the forearm or hand of the customer, to keep them attentive and alert during the sales presentation.)

III. With this seating arrangement the closer can prevent the customers from communicating by secret contact with one another (whispering, a nudge). Without such gestures or signals between the customers, the closer will have much more control over the sales presentations, and keep the customers off balance (because now the customer's pre-conceived signals are useless). These advantages will work for the closer if he sits in the middle of the opponents' camp.

Seating Illustration B

I. The main advantage of this seating arrangement is that the closer can maintain eye contact with everyone in the customer's party, at just about the same time. This is the only legitimate excuse for sitting in this manner.

II. There are several disadvantages to this seating arrangement. For example: The customers can see what is going on behind the closer's back; that activity could kill a sale and the closer would never know why. The unseen distraction could not interfere with a party seated in Arrangement A because the closer will always have controlled eye contact, and can see everything the customers see.

III. In this seating plan the customers can nudge each other and make unseen contact, thus exchanging pre-planned signals the closer is totally unaware of.

IV. In Arrangement B the closer is not a part of the customer's family as he is in Arrangement A. In addition, the closing table becomes a barrier, putting more distance between the closer and the customers and creating a two-against-one environment. In other words, the closer is on one side of the table talking *to* the customers, not in between the customers talking *with* them. There is a big difference, and the closer had better realize it.

The closer plans his seating arrangement to allow him to have maximum visual and physical contact with the customers. The key rule is: "Distance is a barrier."

4. Three-step introduction

This is a great approach every closer should know. The technique will make the customers feel like old friends just minutes after the first greeting. Not many closers use this approach because they don't know about it, but it's fantastic and it works. This is how it is done.

Step 1. When you (the closer) meet your customers, after the handshake greeting and relocation maneuver, tell them you have to go check on something (a phone call, your inventory, etc.) and for them to relax and help themselves to some coffee. Then leave them for a few minutes.

(Note: Let the customers get their own coffee, never get the coffee for the customers unless they are elderly. If you get coffee for them you are putting yourself in a subservient position and the customers will feel they are in control.

Step 2. After you have been away from the customers for a few minutes, go back to them and sit down for a minute. Ask the customers a couple of easy, relaxed questions such as: "Where are you from?", "What kind of business are you in?", "Is this your whole family?" Listen to the answers with interest and excuse yourself again for some believable reason (you're going to get yourself some coffee, etc.) and leave. This ends your second meeting with the customer. (The second introduction completed.)

Step 3. After you have been away a minute or two — or even longer, if you think the customers need more time to relax or more time to get accustomed to the environment — go back to your customers and start the sales presentation. This will be your third meeting with the customers and they will actually feel as though they know you by this time. (The third introduction has been completed.)

Now to explain what took place during the three-step introduction. Initially customers are on guard and have built a defense shield around themselves to ward off any sales presentation (especially from a stranger). When the closer first excuses himself, letting the customers get some coffee and relax a little, that defensive shield starts to weaken because the expected sales pressure is not present.

In Step 2, the closer comes back to the customers and asks some general questions, and then leaves again. The customers' defensive shield is weakened even more because the customers get to know the closer from these brief conversations and have some breathing room in between.

By Step 3, when the closer approaches for the third time the customers have had time to observe the closer, close up and from a distance so they feel they now know the closer much better. (That protective defensive shield really starts to come down at this point.) The customers have also had time to digest what is going on and feel that the closer is their representative, responsible only to them.

Now the closer can make his sales presentation in a relaxed and comfortable manner, with an atmosphere that is pleasant both for himself, and for the customers.

The three-step introduction works if it is used properly. I have seen many closers start right in on their sales presentation without giving the customers any kind of breathing room. This loses sales. The closer has to defuse the customers and get that protective shield lowered if he wants a sale.

I have to say it one more time: The three-step introduction will do the job, everytime. (Note: When the closer is away from the customers he will have more time to analyze and observe them.) The three-step introduction works for the closer in the same manner it works for the customers.

5. First Meeting Closing Traps (Box-In-Questions)

There are some easy and fun ways to get a customer committed to buy, right from the very beginning of the conversation. These Box-In-Questions are traps that can make a sale before the closer even explains the product. The best way to describe them is to give examples:

A. "Mr. and Mrs. Customer, if I could show you how you could save X number of dollars a day or X number of dollars a month for so many months, and at the end of that period of time I gave you back all your money, plus some extra, would you be interested? Now, remember, no strings attached. If I could show you the way it worked, would you be interested?" (Note: The customers will give an answer, but first they will try to ask questions about any strings attached and what they have to do, etc. The closer should ignore these questions and keep saying, "Don't think about that now, but if I could show you the way it works, would you do it? Could you save that much a month to do it?")

The customers will nearly always say "Yes". Now the closer has received a commitment and can use this affirmative answer later against them if he has to. The customers will trap themselves almost every time, if this question is presented properly and with sincerity.

B. "Mr. and Mrs. Customer, let me ask you a question. If I could show you a way to insure your family's future and give you total peace of mind concerning your children's future education, would you be willing to save X number of dollars? If I could completely convince you, would you be interested?"

C. "Mr. and Mrs. Customer, would you like to have the very best product for the least amount of money possible? And to know in your heart that you're getting the best service with that product, would you be interested? Just tell me the truth — if it was that clean-cut and simple, would you?"

These three examples of initial Box-In-Questions illustrate a few of the avenues a closer can use to get the first affirmative commitment from the customers. They do work. But they have to be delivered lightly (soft, sincere and relaxed) so they don't scare the customers off. The affirmative answer will be light and easygoing also, but it can be turned into a terror later on by the closer. (Note: This will be explained later in the book.) The customers are not aware of the trap and will stay attentive during the sales pitch because they will be curious about the "Box-In-Question."

The closer's next move, after he has received an affirmative answer is to drop the subject (the Box-In-Question) and continue with his regular sales presentation.

A good way for the closer to get from the Box-In-Question back to his basic sales pitch is illustrated by this example:

"Mr. and Mrs. Customer, all right, let's forget about what I just said for right now and let me explain to you how it really works."

These traps are great tools to get the attention and involvement of the customers from the beginning. The closer can devise any kind of Box-In-Question he wants but he has to ask with softness, purpose and sincerity. This trap won't work if the customers think it is a joke.

Before we go on to our next topic concerning the first meeting, we should take a look at a summary chart that puts the initial approach to the customer into proper perspective.

1. THE FIRST APPROACH AND HANDSHAKE
2. GETTING IMMEDIATE CONTROL OF THE CUSTOMER BY RELOCATION
3. SEATING THE CUSTOMER
4. THE THREE-STEP INTRODUCTION
5. THE FIRST CLOSING TRAPS (BOX-IN-QUESTIONS)

These five steps are essential if a closer wants to be completely organized and have control over the customer from the very first. There are a lot of short-cuts a closer can use, but if he practices these steps he'll sell more than he ever has before.

Tips and Tactics That Work
(Candid Information to Use and Remember Regarding the First Meeting)

1. Basic Rule — Talk to the customer alone, then get by yourself for a few minutes to think about him and what he said. Analyze him as well as you can and use that information to determine your strategy.

2. The customer loves to hear his own accomplishments admired and his name mentioned over and over again. It's all music to his ears.

3. Every customer has a weakness or "hot button" somewhere in his make-up. The customer is well aware of it, so he will be over protective in this area (especially in the first meeting). Sometimes the closer must find this weakness to get any action out of a customer. A sudden increase in objections or excuses from the customer is an indication that the closer is about to touch on the customer's spot. The customer is really only fighting what he knows is his emotional "hot button;" when he feels the closer is getting too close he will put up his greatest resistance and try to throw every obstacle he can at the closer.

4. To make the customer feel more comfortable, the closer should speak clearly and pronounce his name distinctly — spell it if need be. This draws the customer closer to the closer. The closer should understand the customer's name also, and remember it. If the closer didn't hear the customer's name he should be polite and ask how to spell it. This is all very basic, but it has to be done correctly to get a sale.

(Note: There is a school of thought that says a first-name basis is *too* friendly; if the closer it too friendly he might let the customer off easily and lose a sale. This thinking does have some merit, but if the closer has built up a good rapport with the customer, first names should always be used. A lot more pressure can be applied to the customer by a closer who uses first names than by a closer who uses only last names.

5. The customer who talks all the time will eventually tell everything about himself, his family, his home life, business, etc. The closer should get the conversation going, then sit back and take mental notes. It's all ammunition.

6. The closer should treat every single customer as though he werethe last one he will ever get. The closer should always give a hundred and one percent to his own future, and that future lies in his customers.

7. When the initial conversation is going on between the closer and the customer, the closer should never let the customer's small talk go off toward some far and unknown horizon, or the closer will lose control. The closer should encourage small talk but he shouldn't let the customer talk too long — the sales presentation tends to vanish in the background somewhere.

8. When the closer first meets the customer he should be alert to any little thing the customer might say, that both the customer and closer could relate to. Example: "Mr. Customer, I understand you're from upstate New York. That's where I used to go fishing with my father; it's beautiful country you are from, I envy you." This kind of statement can work magic on the customer.

9. The closer should never say, "I'm going to be your representative," or "I'll be your salesman," to a customer. The customer already knows this and a stupid statement will only scare him more than he already is. The closer should meet the customer as an equal and then go to work. Both the closer and the customer will feel more comfortable. It's a sound idea not to broadcast "Master Closer" to the customer, but to project "a friend."

10. It takes only two individuals to make a sale, and both parties have to have trust, respect, understanding, and some love between them if any type of contract is going to be signed and honored. (Fact.)

11. If the customer is a referral from another customer, the closer should use a soft-sell approach, and go lightly until he understands the situation thoroughly. It's easy for a closer to trap himself if he

proceeds to give a sales presentation to a referral without finding out some facts first. (Referrals will be studied later in the book.)

12. If the closer has a team customer and only one member of the party is present (the husband or wife is absent; this is sometimes called a "one-legged unit") the closer should just give a brief and informative sales pitch. The closer should use a lot of personality and enthusiasm, touching the highlights of the product, always keeping it simple. This information should spark enough enthusiasm in the customer to make him carry the sales pitch to the absent party. At this point the closer should simply re-schedule the customer for another time, when both parties can be present for the full sales presentation.

(Note: This is very important for a closer to remember regarding a husband and wife customer team, when both parties are not present for a full sales presentation. The closer might be able to sell one of the parties, but the chances for a cancellation are tremendous. The reason for this is basic: When the buying party gets home and trys to explain the new purchase to the other party, tempers and friction usually materialize because the party at home didn't have a chance to get involved. So the buying party will try to cancel, just to have some peace at home. Basically the party left out of the buying decision wanted to give some opinion, or knew the family's financial situation better or didn't like the whole idea in the first place — all these negative reasons cause unrest and unwanted pressure until the buying party ends up calling the closer to cancel his contract.)

13. If the closer has a customer who has been drinking heavily or a customer who is in a big rush to go somewhere else, the closer should be polite and try to re-schedule a new meeting time. The closer should not waste his time when these negative factors are present.

Note: There is *no* certain time or set place in the sales presentation to actually close the customer. The Master Closer is continually (from the first second he says "Hello" to his customer, until the sale is made) going after the sale with every question and statement he can think of. The Master Closer knows that every single "Yes" or positive response he gets from his customer is a step that much closer to getting the sale consummated.

14. If a closer ever asks a customer to buy his product without first programming him, or giving enough product information — the answer will always, and I mean *always* be "No." The closer must channel the customer through the whole sales presentation, feeding him organized, understandable product information, to achieve a positive buying answer. All the little questions and tricks the closer uses will lead up to a great and well-delivered presentation. It's just like a staircase: to get where you want to go you can't miss one single step.

15. If the customer looks scared or overly nervous the closer can "break the ice," with one maneuver:

The closer should walk right up to the customer, look very serious, and say, "Which one do you want to buy?" or "How many do you want?" or "Did you call me?" This approach will throw the customer off balance for a second. The closer should immediately smile sincerely and say, "I'm just kidding, my name is Sam, may I help you?" or something to that effect. This approach works and will help break down that invisible defensive customer shield.

16. If a closer feels uncomfortable with his customer, for any reason, he should politely excuse himself, go somewhere alone for a few minutes and re-group. The closer should try to figure out the problem that exists, then return to the customer with a new and better attitude.

It is easy to get upset if a customer has a chip on his shoulder or is rude, but the closer has to control his feelings and show professional class if he wants to get this type of customer sold. (Note: Being a Master Closer isn't always easy.)

17. Another way for a closer to deal with a customer who makes him uncomfortable is this: The closer can frankly tell the customer that he feels somewhat awkward. Then the closer should ask the customer for his help in trying to resolve that feeling. For example: The closer can say in a nice, friendly manner, "You know I've never been around South Texas people before, and I'm not sure how to deal with you," or "This is the first time I've ever been in a coal mining community and it sure is different from where I'm from." Statements like these that fit the closer's situation will work wonders on the customer if delivered with a tone of voice that reflects, "I need your help." The customer will come to the aid of the closer every time. The customer will give local information, tell stories, talk about this or

that, and generally open up. (People love to help other people who sincerely ask for it.) The closer ought to use this approach whenever he can; it's a winner.

18. The closer should never be afraid of the customer. Remember, the customer needs the answers the closer has. Besides, the customer is just another ordinary man. The closer should approach the customer with self-confidence and belief in himself. The closer should walk right up to the customer with pride — pride not only in his product but in himself. Then the closer should look the customer straight in the eye and say to himself, "I'm going to get a sale, I'm going to win."

19. This is a great way to disarm the customer on the first meeting that is fun and easy. The closer should approach and greet the customer in a confused, disoriented manner. This attitude will confuse the customer because the customer expects a more serious and professional closer. All this "bit acting" on the closer's part will make the customer feel he is not threatened, and he will let his guard down. (It's the old "country fox" trick, but it works.)

20. When a closer first meets the customer he not only has to take the lead, but he has to give and understand more, he has to appreciate more, he has to think more and he has to love more.

This concluded my lesson covering the first meeting of the closer and his customer. Sam said I had just started to learn about sales closing in its actual form and this lesson was only the first step towards the final close.

Well, I knew one thing: I didn't want to stop learning at this point. I think Sam knew that too.

Chapter Seven

THE CLOSERS

THE SALES PRESENTATION
(Explaining, Showing and Demonstrating the Product)

A. The Pre-Demonstration Pitch, Part I
   (Programming the Customer)

B. Presenting the Product, Part II
   (Show-and-Tell Time)
   "The twelve product presentation steps"

C. In-Home Sales Presentation
   (The Do's and Don'ts)

D. Pressures, Tricks and Traps
   (Special Notes to Remember)

NOTES

Chapter 7
Part I

THE CLOSERS

THE SALES PRESENTATION

One morning Sam asked me if I was ready for another sales lesson. Since we had just studied "the first meeting" between the closer and the customer, he said we would now study the next important step, the actual sales presentation.

I told Sam that anytime he wanted to teach I was more than ready to listen and learn. Sam smiled and began to tell me about sales pitches and he didn't miss a trick.

Sam said the first thing a closer has to remember about his sales presentation or his product demonstration is that everything is brand new and unfamiliar to his customer. A customer may have heard a thousand sales pitches before, and may have purchased hundreds of different products, but it will be the very first time he has ever heard *this* closer's presentation. Therefore the closer must keep his sales pitch simple, understandable and well organized.

Note: There is *no* certain time or set place in the sales presentation to actually close the customer. The Master Closer is continually (from the first second he says "Hello" to his customer, until the sale is made) going after the sale with every question and statement he can think of. The Master Closer knows that every single "Yes" or positive response he gets from his customer is a step that much closer to getting the sale consummated.

The Pre-Demonstration Pitch
(Programming the Customer, Plus Creating Interest)

Before the closer jumps right into his basic show-and-tell presentation, he has to give a pre-demonstration pitch (also called a map-pitch, warm-up pitch, pre-map, point pitch, or qualifying pitch). This gives the closer some time to program his customer, get him more relaxed and less defensive. (Note: The customer is not aware of this programming process. It is accomplished through conversation, with the closer in complete control.)

Programming develops the customer's thinking in a way that the closer can channel and direct toward the final close. In other words, programming introduces the customer to the basic product information so the customer can keep this information in mind during the rest of the sales presentation. For a customer to remember any sales information, it has to be repeated several times during the sales presentation, and the pre-demonstration pitch does just that. (Important note: When speaking to a group of customers, the closer must involve every member of the party in the conversation. The closer cannot forget one single member in the party, or that member will be the pin for the closer's bubble. It happens everytime. No on likes to be left out and any member of the customer's party who feels that way will kill a sale.

To illustrate exactly how customer programming works, Sam outlined the following steps. These steps are flexible enough to adjust to different products and situations, but the basic pre-demonstration function is the same. (Note: I don't care what you sell or how you sell it, the customer *must* be programmed to buy.

1. Closer is Special —

The closer should not let the customer think that he is just another closer, or one of many in the sales office, because a customer doesn't want to do business with someone who is mediocre or average. To make any kind of special deal (and all customers want special deals) the average closer will have to go to someone else who is higher in the sales organization. Also the customer knows that he won't really be talking to the "top man" and will feel he isn't getting the attention he deserves.

The first thing a closer should do is tell the customer that he is in management, or that he is the top closer. (Note: Don't be arrogant, but humble and personable. The customers love it.) I am not suggesting the closer should lie to his customer, but he'd better be more than "just one of the boys" when he's pitching. A lot of closers don't realize how much this one small detail can hurt a sale. If the closer is someone special, people he deals with will feel special too. It's simple, and it's true. The customer will feel he is getting that little extra attention other customers miss. With this kind of thinking on the customer's part, the closer can sell as much to that customer as he wants.

(Note: I know closers who don't say they are the top closer, or whatever, but they build themselves up in other ways that have exactly the same effect. For example: The closer will say, "I've been with the company longer than anyone," or "The president of this company and I grew up together." All of these statements have the very same meaning to the customer — that this closer is someone special, someone a cut above the other closers.)

2. The Closer's Story —

The closer should tell the customer a little something about himself and his family. This brief background information should explain why the closer is working for his company and his future plans. This must be an interesting and unique story to keep the customer's attention and interest. The closer can make it a happy tale or a tragic one, whatever suits the situation. But it had better be believable and told with sincerity.

The main purpose of the story is to show the customer how positive the closer is about his own company or product. If a customer does not believe the closer would buy the product himself he won't buy either. I can guarantee that. The closer has to show emotion and try to interject parallel problems his customer might have. This will add a great deal to the closer-customer common bond, and help the customer feel more at home with the closer.

3. Trap Set-Up —

The following example is a good pre-demonstration trap pitch (trap set-up) for the customer.

"Mr. Customer, before I really start talking, before I try to give you a big sales pitch, let me say something. It might sound funny, I guess, but did you know that with our product, we would sell every single person we talked to, I mean every single one, if it weren't for three reasons. Some people don't understand what we're doing; some people don't believe what we're doing; and bless their hearts, some people just can't afford it. And that's it — we would sell everybody, if it weren't for those three reasons." (Note: Don't stop at this point. The closer can't break the train of thought he has just created or the trap won't work.)

"What I'm going to do, Mr. Customer, is this: I'm simply going to tell you what we've got, give you the very basics — not a big sales pitch, or anything. I'm going to show you the best deal in the house and I'm going to get it for you at the best price I can, better than anyone else. What do you think, is that fair enough?"

This down to earth pre-demonstration pitch will do several good things for the closer. The closer has told the customer if he doesn't buy he is stupid and can't understand, or he thinks the closer is a liar, or he just plain can't afford it. What kind of answer do you think the customer is going to give to the closer's question, "Is that fair enough?" The customer will (through programming) always say "Yes," and that is what the closer wants.

Something else happens that is also good for the closer: The customer understands he won't get some fancy, elaborate sales presentation, but rather a man-to-man, bottom-line, take-it-or-leave-it pitch. The closer has put the customer in a position of having to say "Yes" or "No," and has avoided the trap of "I'll think about it." This pre-pitch works if delivered properly, with sincerity, and believability.

4. Thought Questions

The closer should inject occasional "thought questions" as he moves closer to talking about the product. These questions have to be directed toward everyone in the customer's party, if there are more than one, so the feeling of equal participation exists. The closer can get to know the customer's make-up through the answers he receives, especially if he listens to the customer's children. Kids are a great way of getting information the adults want hidden. Two of these thought questions are illustrated here, so the closer can see how they work, and get a general idea of how they affect the customer's thinking.

"Mr. Customer, I want you and your family to think about something. Did you know that one thousand of your neighbors have already bought this product? Now there has to be something good about it, right? No one has a thousand idiot neighbors, do they?" (Note: The customer will laugh, thinking that statement is funny. At least he is thinking, and he knows he isn't the first "guinea pig" customer.)

"Mr. Customer, you know we've built this office and this huge complex, all the roads, the country clubs, the golf courses, swimming pools, houses, everything, without one penny from you. Do you know why we got you here if we've already done all of this? Well, I'll tell you. We know we can build roads, put up street lights, build lakes, swimming pools, clubs, the whole works. But we've tried and tried and tried and we can't yet build one of *you*, a person, and this is what our company is all about — people. It takes people to make our product work, and the better the people, the better it works. That's why we asked you to come, because we need you and your family. We are only as good as our people." (Note: The closer has just planted an ego seed in the customer's mind, plus he has involved the customer's whole party.)

There are hundreds of thought questions the closer can use to plant information and to activate the customer's mind. The main thing to remember is to use logic with personality and listen for the complete answer — don't ever try to second-guess a customer.

5. The Company and Product —

The closer must present his company and his product to the customer in the best possible light. The closer should tell the customer how many years the company has been in business, about its credit rating, financial standing and all the highlights that demonstrate the company's dependability. The closer should build his company and its product up with controlled enthusiasm and pride.

All this information will provide the customer with the basic facts necessary to make a buying decision. (Note: Too many facts and company brochures will only bore the customer. The point the closer wants to make is that he works with a proven, dedicated company.)

There is another goal — a personal one — the closer can achieve by pitching his company: self respect. (Note: In an earlier chapter I mentioned that the closer *is* the company, in the customer's mind.) The closer might be down, or depressed; he might be broke, or maybe he's just gone through a divorce — anything that's negative. The company product pitch can do wonders to help the closer get out of a negative attitude. All the closer has to do is promote his company with enthusiasm. The closer's company is successful and positive — it's big and on the way up. Since the closer is a part of that company, he is also successful. He's on his way up too. The closer is the company and his strength should spring from that fact. (Plus he has himself, the Lord, and the product he's pitching.)

There is no reason for the closer to show depression when his company is successful because that makes him successful; that success, coupled with self-confidence, and self respect, will show through to the customer everytime.

Sam said there is no time limit on the pre-demonstration pitch. He said sometimes a closer will ask one or two insignificant questions and then go right into a full-scale sales presentation. Then there are other times when the "pre-pitch" can last for an hour or more. It's all up to the closer, Sam said, to determine when his customer is attentive and interested.

The following is a brief summary of the five steps in a pre-demonstration pitch Sam taught me. (Note: The pre-demonstration pitch begins when the closer and the customer are seated and comfortable.)

Step 1. Closer is Special — The closer should tell the customer he is someone special; this makes the customer feel special also, and helps the closer achieve more control and authority.

Step 2. The Closer's Story — The closer should let the customer see some personal insight into himself, not only to establish trust and a common bond, but to find out personal information about the customer as well.

Step 3. Trap Set-Up — The closer needs to drop this kind of time bomb early in the "pre-pitch" to get an affirmative answer from the customer. This "pre-pitch trap" will work for the closer if he uses it properly.

Step 4. Thought Questions — The closer uses these little questions along the way to find out information, plant ideas, and maintain customer participation. These little thought questions will eventually build up to a big affirmative answer.

Step 5. The Company and Product — The closer needs to introduce the customer to the company and the product for the first time here. This orients the customer and provides a knowledgeable foundation for him so he can understand the sales presentation as it continues.

Sam showed me some notes on the pre-demonstration pitch. He said these reminders are important to the closer if he ever intends to use a pre-demonstration pitch.

Pre-Demonstration Pitch Notes

1. The closer should be able to pre-qualify (make a judgement about the customer's financial capabilities, personality make-up, and degree of product interest) the customer to some extent after he has talked to him for awhile. (The time period is up to the closer.) The closer should think about the right price range for the customer and set up his demonstration to encompass that "price area." The closer should always direct the customer to the smaller-priced product first in that "price area" and let the customer go up the price scale if he wants to. The closer should be able to adjust and re-figure his price range quickly if need be. (Note: The closer still has his basic game plan, but at the same time, it has to be flexible enough to incorporate any new information the customer himself might contribute.)

2. If a woman or girl in the customer's party is attractive, the closer should mention it. There is no need for embarrassment, or shyness on the closer's part. For example: "Mr. Customer, I hope you won't get angry with me, but with all respect, your wife (or daughter) is one of the prettiest ladies I've ever seen. My wife would kill me if she heard me say that, but I really mean it. You're a very lucky man." This kind of statement, if said sincerely, will get the closer a sale, period.

3. If the closer doesn't know an answer to a question — or sometimes even if he really does — he should tell the customer, "Mr. Customer, that's a good question. You're the first person who ever asked about that. I'd like to know the answer myself. Excuse me and let me go find out."

This will show the customer he doesn't have a know-it-all closer. It will also build trust and respect between the customer and closer. The customer will feel that the closer is honest by admitting he didn't know something, so the customer will tend to believe the closer's statements more during the sales presentation.

4. *Always* build self-confidence in the customer throughout the pre-demonstration pitch and the sales presentation. Work on his ego, his achievements, his family's future dreams — anything that builds positive strength. The customer will need this self confidence and fortitude to make a buying decision when the time comes and it's up to the closer to develop that quality in him. The closer should remember that all the little positive ego boosts along the way will do the trick. But they have to be delivered and developed by the closer with sincerity.

5. If the closer feels physically ill or has a hangover from the night before, he should simply tell his customer the truth. For example: "Mr. Customer, last night we had a company party and I feel terrible today, please forgive me." He will automatically think he caught the closer off guard and will, in turn, let his guard down.

This is the perfect place to use reverse psychology. The closer should give a negative pitch and ask for the customer's help (now and then), during the sales presentation. For example: "Here, Mr. Customer, would you please hold this material for me? I don't feel too good." or "Mr. Customer, did they just page me, did someone call me?" or "Mr. Customer, I apologize, but what did you say?"

The customer will join right in and become more involved than he meant to in the first place. Before anyone knows it the customer will be saying, "You know, this doesn't look like a bad deal after all." This maneuver is a great way to get the customer interested, and then sold — not through a great sales presentation, but because the closer let the customer feel like a team member.

6. The closer should show the strength of his company for the customer through facts, data, sales plaques, awards, sales material, etc.... There are times the closer has to use all the sales information he has to close a customer; other times he doesn't have to use any. The important thing for the closer to know and remember is how to use the facts when he has to.

7. The closer should tell his customer he is going to get some "inside information" other customers won't have.

The customer must know he gets this inside information and special treatment because the closer is "special" in some way (a staff member, top closer, manager, etc.). This draws the customer closer to the sales situation and makes him much more interested in what is going on. It's just one more step closer to the sale, compliments of the closer.

Note: There is *no* certain time or set place in the sales presentation to actually close the customer. The Master Closer is continually (from the first second he says "Hello" to his customer, until the sale is made) going after the sale with every question and statement he can think of. The Master Closer knows that every single "Yes" or positive response he gets from his customer is a step that much closer to getting the sale consummated.

8. The closer can get very close to some customers and just about guarantee himself a sale every time if he uses this "special approach statement":

"Mr. Customer, the reason *I'm* going to explain the product to you and not one of the other men, is because the regular salesmen didn't really want to spend any time with you. They think maybe you can't afford the product or something. I don't know and I don't care. All I know is that I would love to show you what we're doing and help you in any way I possibly can. So just forget about them, because now you are with me."

This kind of "special approach statement" should be used on the financially poor customers, the minority customers and the depressed-looking customers. This approach will usually get the customer angry — not with the helping closer, but with the other salesmen. But it will generate a sale, if there is any way the customer can afford the product. This approach has to be delivered with tact and a lot of understanding and sincerity.

9. Sam told me he once knew a closer who used to say, "Look 'em straight in the eye and lie your ass off." That's very cute and all, but the closer has to learn that the truth is a million times stronger than a lie. The truth can exert as much pressure on the customer as the closer needs. The closer can push a customer around, pound on him and beat him senseless with the truth; if the customer knows it's the truth, he will usually take the punishment. The truth is the only pure, one hundred per cent guaranteed closing weapon the Master Closer possesses and he'd better build on it, use it and honor it, if he wants to be the best. And that's the truth.

10. The closer should always change places with the customer, in his own mind, during the pre-demonstration pitch. By sharing the customer's viewpoint the closer will build a bond of common understanding.

11. The closer must become people-oriented. The closer should be aware and alert to all the obvious factors surrounding his customer. The customer will say things and do things that tell his whole story. The closer just has to watch, listen and think.

12. When the closer is giving his "pre-demonstration pitch" or sales presentation, he can't let someone else distract him. The closer ought to be aware of his customer's actions and reactions all the time. The closer should be able to tune in or tune out any outside elements, at his own discretion, but his main concern should only be his customer and a sale, not unrelated matters.

13. The closer has to acknowledge he will *always* have objections and excuses from each and every customer. There will always be more "No's" said than "Yes's" but it's all part of the game. These little hurdles make him a Master Closer instead of a salesman. If the closer didn't have to overcome objections, anyone could call himself a closer — even a mere salesman.

14. If the customer gets ahead of the closer with a question unrelated to what is being discussed at that moment, the closer can put the conversation back on the right track by saying, "Now, Mr. Customer, you just jumped to page seven and I'm only on page three. Please slow down and give me a chance to catch up — you're going too fast."

This will not anger or offend the customer — in fact, it will flatter his ego. A tactful way to maintain control.

15. All through the pre-demonstration pitch and the sales presentation the closer has to constantly build value for and in his product. This is the only true way the closer can justify the product's price tag. The closer has to establish this value through a slow and deliberate presentation, explaining the merits and potential of the product. When the customer finally hears what the product's price is, he won't have a heart attack. (This "value build-up" process will be explained later in this book.)

16. The closer should never depersonalize his "pre-demonstration pitch" or sales presentation, because the customer is not a number and never will be. He is a human being with feelings and any closer who forgets this, isn't even worth being called a man.

17. The complex matter of the sales presentation can be summarized in three simple steps: Firstly, build value in the product; secondly, compare the product with others in the same field; and thirdly, sell the product.

18. Suggestion: The closer can make some personal observations about his customer if he studies the customer's handwriting. There are many books on the market that teach handwriting analysis; some are good and some are bad, but it wouldn't hurt the closer to know a few basic ideas about this subject.

19. The Master Closer has a right to know if his sales presentation is being taped by a customer. If the closer feels he is being recorded he should politely ask the customer why. If the customer denies any such action or fails to give an answer, the closer can just walk away from the customer and laugh, or give a basic and factual presentation. The

Master closer is a professional with his own techniques and format; he has a right to protect those secrets from anyone, especially a customer carrying a tape recorder.

20. If the closer has delivered the pre-demonstration pitch correctly, he should be able to tell where he stands with his customer. The closer should be able to see how the customer relates to the product and also to him. The closer will also have a good idea of how far to proceed with the sales presentation before he starts closing in on the customer for the sale. All this information will be available to the closer if he just gives a good, comprehensible "pre-demonstration pitch."

Sam told me to remember that the pre-demonstration pitch is the beginning of the total sales presentation; it directs and channels the customer toward the actual product presentation. Sam said that since I had been introduced to the "pre-pitch," and I knew how the closer utilized it, I was ready to study the product presentation itself.

NOTES

PRESENTING THE PRODUCT
(Show-and-Tell Time)

Sam said the purpose of the sales presentation is to describe, demonstrate, explain and show the product in the most positive way possible, so the customer will want to buy it.

The total sales presentation has three basic parts, he said. The first part is the pre-demonstration pitch. The second part is when the actual product is being presented. The third part is when the closer asks the customer to buy the product.

I had just completed studying the pre-demonstration pitch (Part I), and Sam said it would be a good idea not to take a break at this point but to continue right into the actual product presentation itself.

To explain the product presentation properly, Sam chose an undeveloped square acre of land as an example product, presenting and showing it in "progressive steps." All the presentation maneuvers, techniques and tricks that will be illustrated and explained here can easily be adapted to other sales fields. All the closer has to do is understand the steps and procedures of product presentation, then incorporate them into his own sales field.

Sam said the most effective way to demonstrate the product presentation is to show how the steps work, individually, and then how they fit into the overall sales presentation. Each of the twelve steps are outlined in a progressive order leading to the final closing question.

Before studying the presentation steps Sam said there are two very basic rules (Fundamental Facts) a closer must understand to utilize the presentation steps.

The first is the "Rolls Royce Rule" (primarily for the closer's benefit); the second fact is the "Seeing is Believing Rule" (mostly for the customer's benefit). Without these two rules, a closer cannot expect to give a complete and successful sales presentation, much less get the sale.

The Rolls Royce Rule

This rule states that sales are made by closers, not by a company's advertising department.

Let's say a young ad executive thinks he has a "different" idea for selling. Instead of hiring closers to get the job done, he hires a number of sweet-talking, attractive women (professional models), dresses them in beautifully coordinated outfits and gives each one a Rolls Royce. Then the eager beaver exec assembles all the company's potential customers and sends them on a demonstration tour with these lovely women as guides. After the tour is complete, the beautiful tour guides bring the customers back to the company's sales office and hand them over to salesmen who ask them to buy the company's product.

This type of selling sounds good on paper, but in cold, hard reality it won't work because the good-looking tour guides are not *closers*. True, the tour guides give the customers some product information in the canned presentation pitch. But then this type of sales presentation starts to fall apart because the guides never get to know the customers personally. They can't take time to learn the customers' feelings, know their characters or listen to their dreams and ambitions. The beautiful guides don't have the opportunity to stay with the customers during the whole sales presentation, making it impossible to establish a one-on-one relationship. To the tour guides, customers tend to turn into numbers and not real people.

Selling in this manner can never match the basic one-on-one relationship that exists when the only parties involved are the closer and his customer. Fact. *Every customer needs personal attentiveness, individual acceptance and acknowledgment plus genuine interest.* The closer provides this whether it's real or just showmanship. The closer makes the customer feel appreciated and downright special. Without these positive elements the customer is nothing more than a percentage point on a piece of paper, someone's sales quota, or punched data in a computer. When that condition exists, the superior sales performances Master Closers can provide will not.

A company must hire closers instead of tour guides or plain salesmen to sell its product. The closer stays with his customer during the entire sales presentation; he knows his customer inside and out. The closer understands his customer's needs and realizes his buying capabilities. He develops a well-founded and trusting friendship with his customer.

All these feelings, thoughts and emotions that the closer establishes will affect the customer when the final buying question is asked. The Rolls Royce, the beautiful women and all the advertising gimmicks can't compete with a determined and confident closer, one who stays with his customer from the start of the presentation until the sale is finally made.

(Note: The next statement is not a contradiction of the example above. That illustration was given to make a strong point concerning the "one-on-one" closer-customer relationship.)

A "tour guide-closer" type of presentation *can* work *if* it is executed properly and in a professional manner. This type of "team-work" selling can be very effective if the tour guide and closer are well organized. The team has to educate the customer about each member's respective role in the total sales presentation. For example: One team member tells the customer that he will demonstrate the product and the other team member will explain the financing and paperwork involved. Each closer or team member specializes in a particular area of the overall sales presentation. This simple explanation will keep the customer from getting confused during the presentation, and give him some understanding of the team's working arrangement.

Note: There is *no* certain time or set place in the sales presentation to actually close the customer. The Master Closer is continually (from the first second he says "Hello" to his customer, until the sale is made) going after the sale with every question and statement he can think of. The Master Closer knows that every single "Yes" or positive response he gets from his customer is a step that much closer to getting the sale consummated.

This type of selling is not only fun but very powerful when used on a customer. Both team members get to support each other's statements and each member gives the other strength. The team can bounce the sales presentation back and forth between each other, with the customer always in the middle and off balance. This team action keeps everyone (including the customer) excited and enthused. The main thing to remember about team selling is: Each team member must know exactly what the other member is saying or going to say to the customer. If the team members don't have their game plan down pat and well organized, one member might say something to the customer that would overlap or contradict what the other member has said. This only leads to confusion and distrust on the customer's part, and ultimately a lost sale.

Seeing is Believing Rule

The closer must remember that the pre-demonstration pitch was the very first time the customer was exposed to the closer's company and to its product. In the presentation pitch the closer gave a simple overall picture to his customer of his product. The closer also set up a starting point or base foundation on which to build the rest of his sales presentation. (Note: The closer, and it cannot be expressed enough, has got to keep his sales presentation direct and simple, so the customer can follow it, understand it, and then take positive action in the form of a decision to buy the product.)

With the pre-demonstration pitch completed, the closer is now ready to go directly into the physical presentation of the product itself. In other words the closer lets the customer actually see, feel, smell and touch the product. The closer shows the product in its physical form and presence, with the customer involved in what now is a "seeing is believing" situation. All the "sales table" talk is finally being backed up through his visual and physical product presentation. Example: "Mr. Johnson, I've been telling you in the sales office how beautiful the view of the valley is from this particular piece of property. Now you can see for yourself — isn't that view magnificent?"

These two basic rules make up the foundation of the total sales presentation. With those under my belt, Sam said I was ready to study the "Twelve Product Presentation Steps," that lead to the pre-closing questions and the close (Chapter 8).

(Note: Remember that one square acre of undeveloped land will be used as the model product for the "Twelve Steps.")

Step 1. Setting the Stage (Getting the Customer Physically Oriented)

The closer should tell his customer interesting stories about the area surrounding the acre of undeveloped land. He should build narratives around special landmarks — lakes, streams, cliffs, caves, old houses, barns, or just beautiful views — anything the closer feels will spark the customer's imagination and interest.

The closer must present a comfortable and intriguing picture for the customer so he can begin to establish a personal attachment to the land (the product). The closer simply sets the stage; the customer himself will inject the product into his dreams and future plans. The customer's subconscious becomes actively involved and begins to consider the product (acre of land) as his own property, to some degree, before he has consciously decided to buy.

This type of showmanship on the closer's part will also help build the product's value in the eyes of the customer.

The closer should always make his stories thought-provoking, active and clear. He should show his product with controlled enthusiasm and excitement because the mental and physical activity he creates will produce some positive reactions in the customer. The closer's enthusiastic actions will keep the customer alert and attentive, and his adrenalin flowing. The closer should get the customer physically involved in the product presentation (walking the land, driving a demonstrator car, working a piece of machinery himself) so he becomes a part of the presentation. This makes the final closing question a little bit easier for the customer to answer.

Note: The closer must observe, listen to and learn from his customer continually throughout the total sales presentation to gather customer information. He will need that information later as ammunition against his customer when going in for the close (the Kill).

Step 2. Learn From the Customer

One of the best ways for the closer to establish a personal relationship with his customer during the product presentation is to learn, or at least act like he has learned, something important from his customer. (The information doesn't have to be related to the product although it would be beneficial if it were related. The customer must believe the closer has genuinely gained some new knowledge from him and that the information is sincerely appreciated.)

This kind of "appreciate the information" maneuver on the closer's part will build up confidence in the customer by flattering his ego and let the customer know his thoughts have merit and are respected by the closer. For example: "Mr. Customer, I didn't realize that, thank you for enligntening me," or "Mr. Customer, I've been trying to find that answer for a long time and you're the first person who could tell me — thank you."

The customer will become more attentive to the closer's product presentation, because he will feel his "new" information has put him on the same level as the closer. The customer won't feel as though he is just receiving information from the closer (a one-sided situation) but that he is actually assisting and contributing as well. The customer will feel he is a part of the closer's personal inner circle and not just a regular, ordinary customer.

Note: The closer must observe, listen to and learn from his customer continually throughout the total sales presentation to gather customer information. He will need that information later as ammunition against his customer when going in for the close (the Kill).

Step 3. Find Out Who Handles the Money (Who's the Leader or Who Wears the Pants)

The closer should determine who is the leader, the decision-maker and the money controller in the customer's party (husband and wife team). It could be the husband, the wife or both equally. But no matter who it is it's the closer's job to find out so he can direct his main sales attack (product presentation) toward that individual.

The same is true of large customer groups as well. For example: In a party of four couples there will nearly always be a leader. The closer has to know and recognize the central figure if he wants to get a sale, period. If the closer can't recognize the leader then he will pitch the wrong member of the team, and appear foolish — the customers know who their leader is, and they will lose respect for a closer who misjudges so badly. The closer must always be alert to avoid this fatal mistake.

There are several ways the closer can spot a leader. The following rules will be a basic guideline to help determine who handles the money.

Rule A. The person in the customer's party who asks the most questions, talks the most and seems to have the most interest in the product will most likely be the leader. The closer should keep in mind that this is not always and absolutely true. For example: In some parties, such as families, the oldest son will try to demonstrate his intelligence by asking a flood of product questions to try to impress the closer and his dad. In truth it will be the son's father, the fellow who is just sitting back and listening, who actually controls the family's money. He's the one who makes the final buying decision and not his action-packed son. This is also true of large customer groups. One member of the customer's party may do all the talking and appear to be the leader when in reality he is just trying to impress his friends. In many cases the talking and active customer turns out to be broke, and the silent, reserved customer is the one with the financial capability to purchase the product.

When the closer is confronted with this type of sales situation, he should ask himself, "Who is the most sincere or reserved or interested person in the whole group?" This little "self-question" will almost always point to the party's real leader. The closer knows he has to constantly read between the lines, defining and analyzing everything being said and done or not said and done.

Rule B. The closer can determine the customers' leader by observing the individual's physical actions. The closer should notice which members of the party are nervous, which ones are always looking around the sales office, which members are whispering to others. These little physical actions will tell a great deal about the members of the party. By observation the closer can pretty accurately identify the leader.

The leader is usually the one all the other members look at most. The members consciously and subconsciously look to him for guidance, direction and approval. Whether he is a silent type or a visible and verbal leader, the closer can identify him if he just observes and thinks.

Rule C. The closer can force his customers to identify their leader through the following two maneuvers:

(1) The closer should direct all important questions to one member of the customer's party. If that person turns out to be the leader, then everything is fine. But if he isn't then the person the closer is addressing will look to the leader for help sooner or later. The closer's questions will make that customer uncomfortable because he knows, in his own mind, he doesn't make the decisions, and will seek out the

stronger member for support. From that point on the closer will know exactly whom to talk to.

(2) The closer can jokingly ask the whole group, "All right, I give up — which one of you is the leader?" This question might sound silly, but it works. The closer isn't really looking for a sincere answer; but he is watching to see which member blushes, puts his head down, or gets embarrassed. Also, when that silly little question is asked, most of the members will look directly at the money man. It might only be for a split second, but they will look at him, just to see his reaction. The closer has to watch everyone's eyes and pay sharp attention or he might miss the clue.

By using these silly little questions the real leader can be discovered. Then it's up to the closer to follow his planned sales presentation, and direct it toward the real decision-maker.

Note: The closer must observe, listen to and learn from his customer continually throughout the total sales presentation to gather customer information. He will need that information later as ammunition against his customer when going in for the close (the Kill).

**Step 4. Tell the Customer You (The Closer) Own The Product,
        or Would Like To —**

A good way for the closer to make the customer feel more confident and secure about the product being sold is for the closer to tell the customer that he owns the product, or would like to buy it himself.

For example: "Mr. Customer, this property is the best and most beautiful piece of land I've seen in over two years. I'd buy it myself but I have my money tied up in some other property. I even tried to call my brother so he could buy it, but he was out of town and I couldn't reach him. If you really like the property and you're sincere, I'll let you have it for the same price I was going to quote my brother, and on the same terms. In other words, I'll let you buy it at the same price I could have gotten it for myself. But if you let anyone know about this, I'll tell everyone I don't know what you are talking about."

By telling the customer the closer couldn't afford the land, he shows the customer he is human too and has financial limitations. This pitch also demonstrates that the product is good enough for the closer himself to buy, thus making the customer feel more confident in it.

This speech must be delivered with total sincerity and sober showmanship on the closer's part or the customer will see right through it as soon as the closer opens his mouth. This statement will do wonders if the customer believes it, and it's up to the closer to make him believe.

Note: The closer must observe, listen to and learn from his customer continually throughout the total sales presentation to gather customer information. He will need that information later as ammunition against his customer when going in for the close (the Kill).

Step 5. Demonstrating the Product (The Actual Act)

When the closer actually touches and handles his product, he must have a genuine sense of respect and reverence for his product. This doesn't mean the closer should go overboard and treat a common rock as a perfectly cut diamond or a piece of steel as if it were a rare porcelain sculpture. But the closer should give his customer the best show he can muster.

The closer is now in the act of physically presenting his product to the customer, and that product has to be the best, the finest, and the greatest in the whole world. The closer cannot afford to show his customer anything less than the best. The customer must feel this specialness, this respectfulness that the closer radiates, because that feeling will excite him and make him realize he is seeing the best.

Even if the product is a bucket of mud, the closer should present it in a velvet cloth, saying, "It's the finest, richest and rarest mud in the entire world." The closer has to convince the customer the product is the finest that can be produced, period.

Here are some notes the closer has to remember when demonstrating the product:

(a) When a closer shows a car, or piece of machinery, etc., he should touch it or hold it gently, and avoid pointing at the product or slamming a hand on it. (Note: There are times when the closer has to handle the product roughly to demonstrate a point, but we are not talking about that now.) The product should be handled with kindness and shown respect; the customer will see the product is worthy of respect.

(b) The closer must show his product in a simple and easy-to-understand manner. The presentation should have a smooth tempo so the customer can pace with the closer. The closer should not talk or explain his presentation so fast that he loses the customer. This will only confuse the customer and force the closer to repeat himself, leading to more confusion and frustration for both the closer and customer.

(c) When the closer turns a dial on a vacuum sweeper or walks a piece of real estate or demonstrates a new car, he should do it slowly and deliberately, taking enough time to let the product soak into the customer's subconscious.

(d) The closer should point out the most impressive and surprising new features of the product last as a kind of "icing on the cake" for his customer. In other words, the customer has heard and seen all of the basic and familiar amenities of the product. But then, as a final touch, the customer learns about all the goodies, the deluxe extras, the specials that make this product the top of the line. The closer, by showing the extras last, has brought his product presentation up to an even higher level of interest — a level near the peak of the product presentation and the beginning of the closing questions.

When demonstrating his product the closer must show genuine pride. This pride and self-assurance the closer projects will be noticed and respected by the customer, and will sway the customer in a positive way. Through showmanship, enthusiasm and pride the closer can make both himself and his product the best in the world; the customer will see this attitude in a second, and appreciate it.

Note: There is *no* certain time or set place in the sales presentation to actually close the customer. The Master Closer is continually (from the first second he says "Hello" to his customer, until the sale is made) going after the sale with every question and statement he can think of. The Master Closer knows that every single "Yes" or positive response he gets from his customer is a step that much closer to getting the sale consummated.

For example: "Mr. Customer, just like I told you, back in the sales office, you will never see a more beautiful view, more majestic trees, or a more peaceful setting than this piece of property has to offer. I don't care if you look all around the country, this property is the finest and I think you can see that. Not only that, but the price will fit into your budget. Now you can see why I was so excited and enthused about showing you this acre of land."

Note: The closer must observe, listen to and learn from his customer continually throughout the total sales presentation to gather customer information. He will need that information later as ammunition against his customer when going in for the close (the Kill).

Step 6.   **(a) The Closer Should Get Physically Involved With His Product;**
                (b) How to Make the Customer Feel More Obligated

The closer can create interest in his product and more of an obligation to buy if he becomes physically involved with the product and "gets his hands dirty." When a closer shows his customer a product he should touch, pick up, pat, and hold it. If he projects a standoffish attitude concerning the product, so will his customer. The customer will think to himself, "If *he* doesn't want to get physically involved, then why should I?" And if that feeling exists there won't be any sale, period. The closer has to lead the customer to get him involved. He can't do it by sitting on the sidelines himself.

(b) "The extra mile trick" will get a customer more involved in the product presentation and create a feeling of obligation to buy. When the closer is involved with his product presentation physically, he should tear his shirt sleeve or step in some mud or "bump" his head or get some grease on his clothes — anything to get the sympathetic attention of the customer. He will see that the closer hurt himself or had some misfortune when he was presenting his product to him and will feel the closer went that extra personal mile for his (the customer's) benefit.

This product presentation trick is so simple it works, and it works wonders. Most customers will feel sorry for the closer because of the misfortune and become more deeply involved with the closer personally because of his concern. This will bring the closer and the customer closer together, creating the total customer-closer relationship the closer needs.

Note: The closer must observe, listen to and learn from his customer continually throughout the total sales presentation to gather customer information. He will need that information later as ammunition against his customer when going in for the close (the Kill).

Step 7. Planting Seeds of Imagination in the Customer's Mind

(Note: Steps 7 and 8 go hand in hand)

During the product presentation the closer should tell the customer where actual improvements (water mains, roads, street lights, etc.) are going to be built on the acre of land we are using as an example. The closer has to take the lead at this point and draw an attractive picture of the raw, undeveloped acre of land being sold. The closer will always have to plant "positive idea" and "possibility seeds" throughout the product presentation for the customer to feed on. (For example: "Mr. Customer, wouldn't the front of the property look beautiful when it's landscaped just the way you and your family have always dreamed?" or "Mr. Customer, wouldn't it be nice to build a sun deck over there to take advantage of that magnificent view?")

The customer will pick up this picture and paint it with his own multi-colored visions and dreams. The customer becomes more involved in the product presentation by the minute, both mentally and physically.

The closer has to constantly plant positive suggestions and stories about the product before the customer's imagination is truly activated. (Fact.)

A customer can imagine the thrill of owning a new car or swimming pool more vividly than the closer can convey. But the closer has to steer the customer's thoughts toward the product being sold and then show how the product would benefit the customer. Then the closer should sit back for a moment and watch how the customer will start closing *himself* through his own special and private dreams. It's an amazing reaction on the customer's part, and it works. But the closer must always use showmanship with enthusiasm when he is planting his "positive suggestion seeds."

Note: The closer must observe, listen to and learn from his customer continually throughout the total sales presentation to gather customer information. He will need that information later as ammunition against his customer when going in for the close (the Kill).

Step 8. Put the Customer in the "Driver's Seat," Get Him Involved Both Mentally and Physically

(Note: Steps 8 and 7 go hand in hand)

Throughout the total product presentation the closer must stimulate the customer to visualize himself as the owner of the product being sold. The closer has to describe the product's uses and advantages (but not in great detail, because it will only bore the customer) so his customer will "daydream" about how the product would fit into his life. The closer can spark this "customer self-envisionment" through the very basic sales procedures. For example: If a closer is selling cars, he should put his customer in the driver's seat and let the customer drive around, flattering the customer (working on that old ego) by telling him how sharp and natural he looks behind the wheel of that particular car. If a closer is selling a vacuum sweeper he has to use a convincing demonstration to show his customer the advantages of his product, and let the customer actually use the sweeper himself. If a closer is selling stocks and bonds, he needs to point out the return profits to be made and all the future potential of the investment. If a closer is selling home improvements, television time, shows or whatever, he must always show the best possible advantages of his product, plus all the benefits his customer can and should expect.

The closer has to build an understandable and positive picture for the customer to see; and he has to constantly work on the customer's never ending ego and future-ownership pride. All these things are basic and proven — sales wouldn't be made without them. Any rookie salesman knows them — they are rituals that have to be done to get a sale. These sales procedures are the groundwork for any product presentation, but this book is not going to dwell on or go into detail on these fundamentals. That information can be found in any ordinary sales book on the market.

This book goes beyond those fundamentals, as a closer goes beyond a regular salesman when giving a product presentation. The reader will see a magical happening, a closer's phenomenon called "customer self-envisionment" and understand how it works and how it is accomplished by the closer. The closer will actually get the customer involved, both mentally and physically, during the product presentation. That is a fact. But the closer will do something extra special, something salesmen don't know how to do or just don't do, and that is this: The closer will not only put his customer in the driver's seat and let him visualize himself there, but the closer will actually make the customer believe that he belongs there, and he deserves to be there. The closer will not only build a dream for his customer, but he will make his customer believe that dream with all of his heart. The closer makes the customer know for himself, deep down in his gut, that he not only would use the product being sold and would like the product being sold, but that he really needs the product being sold. The closer establishes this customer feeling in one simple way. He makes the customer believe in himself, feel confident about himself and like himself. The closer accomplishes this through compliments, courtesy, respect and a real and genuine interest in the customer. The closer demonstrates these feelings to the customer and the customer feels them and accepts them.

Note: The closer must observe, listen to and learn from his customer continually throughout the total sales presentation to gather customer information. He will need that information later as ammunition against his customer when going in for the close (the Kill).

Step 9. Playing the Older Customer Against the Younger Customer or People Against People

(Note: This is an example of just one of many thought-provoking statements the closer can use throughout the product presentation to plant "personal idea" and "selfishness" seeds in the customer's mind.)

The closer should use this "statement and question trick" on either the older customer or the younger customer, depending on who the closer is with, sometime (at the closer's own discretion) during the product presentation. This "statement and question trick" will actually trap (box in) the customer with his own answer. It's a "statement and question trick" that could be used as a closing question, but it would be much more useful and have more purpose if the closer delivers it during the product presentation. This is how the "old customer vs. the younger customer statement" works.

When the closer is demonstrating or showing his product to an older customer, he should casually mention, "Mr. Customer, you know I show this product to a lot of people and in doing so I've learned something very important: the younger customers — the folks who haven't been around much or haven't gone through all the hard times you have — don't really appreciate or understand my product and its advantages. I guess what I mean is, the younger customers just haven't grown up enough to really know what is good for them, or what's really beneficial for them. Mr. Older Customer, you know what I mean, don't you?" At this point the closer should shut up and wait for the older customer to answer (and he will). The older customer will, in most cases, automatically say "Yes, I sure do know what you are talking about." (Note: This spontaneous response comes from a natural feeling that exists in nearly all older people. The older customers tend to think most of the younger people don't have the same respect for certain things and responsibilities that they had when they were younger or that they have now. This is a common feeling on the older customer's part that is as old as time.)

By agreeing with the closer, the older customer has actually stated that the younger generation doesn't know all the things he does and they aren't smart enough to see a good deal when presented with one like he does, so. . . (Bang, Presto). The older customer, without even knowing it, has just trapped himself with his own answer — an answer that was set up and developed by the closer from the beginning. The older customer has given a positive answer to the closer which the closer can turn around and use against him when the closing process begins. (For example: "Mr. Older Customer, do you remember what you said earlier, about how younger customers don't appreciate this offer or product because they haven't been through too many hard times? And do you remember all the situations you've been through, the problems you've overcome that the younger people haven't ever had to face yet? Do you realize all the advantages you have over them, because you have already been through it and have the knowledge you have? Well, let me ask you this, with all of your background and know-how, surely you know the benefits of my product. I know that you can't sit there and tell me "no" you're not interested, when you actually know, deep down, the true potential of this product, am I right?")

The secret to this "statement and question trick" is for the closer to continue (without missing a beat) with his product presentation as soon as he hears the older customer's answer. In other words, the closer should never stop or pause after the older customer gives his answer, because this statement is only being used as a trap (a seed thought) for the older customer. In fact, after the older customer gives his positive "Yes" answer, he will start to think to himself "What in the world have I just said? What have I just done to myself?" But it will be too late, the closer has sprung the trap and the point has been made.

This "statement and question trick" will work exactly the same way on younger customers. The "statement" made by the closer simply has to be reversed, turned around. The closer should tell the younger customers how the older customers don't appreciate or know what is going on in today's world, and that the younger customers have the foresight and opportunity to take advantage of new offers or products, that older customers just don't understand. The closer should plant the "ego seed" the same way for the younger customer as he did for the older customer. This "statement and question trick" will work on either customer, older or younger; the only thing for the closer to remember is to continue on with his product presentation and let the customer's answer soak in and work on the customer's own mind, all by itself. (Note: The "statement and question trick" can be used to attack or compare people from different parts of the country, different backgrounds or from different ways of thinking.)

Note: The closer must observe, listen to and learn from his customer continually throughout the total sales presentation to gather customer information. He will need that information later as ammunition against his customer when going in for the close (the Kill).

Step 10. "The Plain Jane vs. The Top of the Line"

(Note: This is one of many example steps that can be used throughout the product presentation to explain the development of the closer's product and make the product's future potential and value easy for the customer to understand and relate to. This example can be easily adapted to any product.)

The closer should tell the customer he is on the ground floor (the best place and time to buy the product) in regards to the undeveloped acre of land. The closer should point out the advantages of purchasing the property before any improvements are put on it, so the customer will not only save money but make money after the property has been developed and goes up in value.

The closer can illustrate this point to the customer by using this example. "Mr. Customer, this undeveloped acre of land that we're looking at is exactly like a 'Plain Jane' car — it doesn't have any special equipment on it or any extras at all. That's why you can go down to your local car dealership and buy this automobile at the lowest possible price. Isn't that correct? All right let's say you take this 'Plain Jane' and you put steel belted tires on it. Then you put leather upholstery in it; you put a sun or moon roof on it, a tape deck, power steering and power brakes — the works. Now, all of a sudden, you don't have a stripped-down model car anymore, do you? Now you've got an expensive top-of-the-line model that costs a whole lot more than the 'Plain Jane' we started with, and it's still sitting on the very same 'Plain Jane' frame. Mr. Customer, this undeveloped acre of land is exactly the same thing as the 'Plain Jane' car. You can buy it at the lowest possible price, right now, because there aren't any improvements on the property at this time. But when there are water and sewer lines on the property, the terrain is landscaped and roads are built with curbs and gutters, then, Mr. Customer, you don't have an empty acre of land anymore, do you? No, not hardly. What you have is an improved piece of property that is worth a great deal more, and I'm talking about dollar and cents more. So, Mr. Customer, like I said: What we're looking at right now, when we look at this land, is simply a 'Plain Jane' car. All you have to do is use your imagination a little and I think you can visualize what this property will look like when it's improved, and at the same time, Mr. Customer, what the dollar value of this land will be. It's just that simple."

Note: The closer must observe, listen to and learn from his customer continually throughout the total sales presentation to gather customer information. He will need that information later as ammunition against his customer when going in for the close (the Kill).

Note: There is *no* certain time or set place in the sales presentation to actually close the customer. The Master Closer is continually (from the first second he says "Hello" to his customer, until the sale is made) going after the sale with every question and statement he can think of. The Master Closer knows that every single "Yes" or positive response he gets from his customer is a step that much closer to getting the sale consummated.

Step 11. Tell "Other-People Stories" and "Third-Party Stories"

The closer can pressure the customer, make a point to the customer, or explain a "good deal" (the right opportunity) to the customer by using people stories. For example (This is an "other-people story" used to explain a "good deal": "Mr. Customer, the reason this property is for sale at this unusually low price is because the people who bought it a few months ago had to make a sudden move to another part of the country due to a job transfer. The property hasn't been re-priced or appraised yet, so you can buy it at the same price the other family did. In other words, you can purchase the property for the original price." Or, "Mr. Customer, another family was going to buy this property two weeks ago, but they decided that they wanted more acreage. In all the confusion the land hasn't been put back on the market yet and you can get it without any new inventory price change."

The closer can use "third-party stories" to put added pressure on his customer. For example: "Mr. Customer, I had another customer just like you — in fact, you remind me of him. About one year ago he said that he wanted some property for his family so he could take them out in the country to go camping or maybe build a vacation home someday. You know, just get the family together. But first he said he had to look around and think things over and then he would let me know about the property. Well, I found out three weeks ago he never did buy any vacation or investment property — he died of a heart attack at a fairly young age. He never did have an opportunity to get close to his family like he was telling me, and I want you to know I feel that if I had pushed him a little harder or used more persuasive salesmanship I could have maybe helped him make his dream come true. But I didn't, and now it's too late. Mr. Customer, I hope that kind of sad ending doesn't happen to you and your family, because it could and that's the tragedy — it really could."

The customer generally feels the "third-party stories" or "other-people stories" the closer tells put the pressure and problems on someone else, not on him. But in reality the customer will see the parallel and start thinking. The closer can use this simple tactic all day long and get positive results.

But, third-party stories have to be told with complete sincerity and showmanship on the closer's part. The closer can't make the story seem ridiculous or silly. It has to make sense and be believed by the customer to have any effect. The closer can explain away objections, problems, incidents — just about everything, by using "third-party" and "other-people" stories — but he has to make doubly sure that they directly relate to his customer and the sales situation, and the closer had better make sure his customer gets the point (tactfully).

Note: The closer must observe, listen to and learn from his customer continually throughout the total sales presentation to gather customer information. He will need that information later as ammunition against his customer when going in for the close (the Kill).

Step 12. Tell Customers They Are the Best

Important: The closer should, at some point in the latter half of the product presentation, tell his customer that he is one of the finest people he has ever talked to. (Note: The closer should not make this statement during the closing part of the sales presentation because it will be too late to give out compliments at that point. Any complimentary statement at that time would only sound phony to the customer. In other words, it would only sound like a cheap shot to get a sale and in most cases it would be.) The closer should make a statement something like this: "Mr. Customer, what I'm about to say might sound like a sales pitch, and please forgive me for making it sound that way, but, in all sincerity, you and your family, whether you buy my product or not, are some of the best and most likeable people I've ever known. I really mean it. It's a pleasure to talk to folks like you. It makes my job a whole lot better."

After the closer makes this statement he should act a little embarrassed, so he can get the point of honesty across to the customer. Then the closer should continue with the rest of his product presentation, not waiting for any kind of response. The closer shouldn't dwell on the subject but simply let it linger and soak into the customer's mind. Then when it finally comes time for the closing questions the customer will think about this genuine compliment and react in a positive and receptive manner. (Note: Remember, no one can dislike someone who really likes them.) This complimentary statement the closer made will only make the sale that much closer. Customers tend to melt in the closer's hands if this statement is delivered by the closer with tactful sincerity and if the customer honestly believes it.

Note: The closer must observe, listen to and learn from his customer continually throughout the total sales presentation to gather customer information. He will need that information later as ammunition against his customer when going in for the close (the Kill).

Sam said this ended "the twelve product presentation steps," but before I began my study of the "in-home sales presentation" do's and don'ts there were three important notes I should remember concerning the "twelve presentation steps."

Note 1. **Taking the Customer's Temperature** — The closer should know exactly where he stands with his customer at any given time during the product presentation. He should also know how close his customer is to making a buying decision at any point during the presentation or demonstration. The closer can always find this type of information out by taking the customer's temperature. (Seeing how "hot" or close to the sale the customer actually is.) This is accomplished through questions directed straight at the customer. (Note: It's up to the closer's own discretion at what time during the product presentation he wants to take this temperature reading.) For example: "Mr. Customer, how do you like the fantastic view from the back of this property?" or "Mr. Customer, what kind of driveway would you build from the main road?" or "How would you landscape the property to take advantage of that huge old oak tree?" Any kind of question from the closer that requires a positive and involved answer on the customer's part will work. The customer will either give an interested and thoughtful answer or an indifferent and unconcerned answer. The thing for the closer to remember is that the answer the customer gives will tell, to some degree, how he feels about the product, and it will show how close he is to buying. (Note: The closer has to listen intently and be alert to any answer the customer gives. The closer has to read between the lines and pay strict attention not to miss a thing the customer says or the sale could be lost at that point. The closer can tell a great deal, not only by what the customer says but how he says it.)

The closer can, if he feels the customer's answer is positive enough and the customer is ready, go right into a closing question, to get the sale then. But by the same token, the closer can keep right on pitching if he feels the customer's answer wasn't that positive or if the customer wasn't quite ready for a closing question.

Taking the customer's temperature is an easy way to get the customer involved in the product and to find out where things stand at the same time. The closer has to use tact and sincerity when he throws out his temperature questions, but the answers he receives will give him the coordinates he needs to steer in the right direction to get the sale. To put it another way, the closer has to have his finger on the customer's pulse all the time.

Note 2. (a) **Customers Want What They Can't Have** — The closer should be aware of a basic purchasing phenomenon that is true of every customer: All customers want what they can't have or get. If a closer shows the customer a common or average acre of land and the customer sees another piece of property that is beautiful, but has already been sold or is unattainable for some reason or other, the customer will dwell on the sold property and say things like, "Now, I would buy that property if it was for sale," or "That property is just what I was looking for, it's too bad that it's already been sold." (Note: Remember, people are people and they want what they can't have. Example: Why does a lovely woman date an unattractive man? Forgetting about money as a factor, the reason is because the man played hard to get and most women love to be challenged.)

Note 2. (b) **How to Trap Customers by Using This Human Weakness** — The closer should set up traps for his customer by using this buying phenomenon. To illustrate this trap-setting maneuver, let's say a closer has a customer and he first shows the customer an acre of land that looks all right but is nothing spectacular or special. Then the closer shows the same customer another piece of property (because it's in the same vicinity or some other believable reason) but this land is beautiful, with a great panoramic view for the exact same price. Now the closer tells or suggests to the customer that the beautiful view property has already been sold (in truth it hasn't, it's still for sale) and that the first property they looked at is the next best thing to buy. This is when the customer starts making all of his positive and serious declarations and statements, saying that the view property is the only one he really wants and if it was for sale he would buy it immediately. This kind of statement is what the closer wanted to hear in the first place, because all the closer has to do at this point is give a mediocre presentation concerning the first property (the average one) but still keep referring to the view property in an off-the-cuff manner, such as "Mr. Customer, you know, that view is fantastic, no wonder it has already been sold. I just wish we could have been here sooner so you could have owned it."

From this point on the customer will think that he's off the closer's hook because the property he really likes is gone. So the customer will continue to rave about the view property, its potential, its character, and all of its possibilities, not knowing he is only getting himself boxed in and trapped deeper by the minute. After the product presentation is over the closer should excuse himself for a few minutes and go look at his property listings or inventory. Then with excitement and enthusiasm the closer should tell the customer that upon checking, he found out that the view property was indeed sold, but the owner had just traded his equity into a piece of lake property (or some other positive and believable reason). So now the customer can buy the property he wanted so badly at the price first quoted. The closer should simply start writing up the order, without waiting for any customer response or objections. The closer should assume the sale is made. (This will be studied in detail in Chapter 8.)

Note 3. Customers Talk to Customers — Some customers will always try to get with another closer's customer so that they can compare notes and information (whether it's in the restroom of a sales office, on the parking lot or at the refreshment center). Even if the customers don't know each other, they will try to talk to each other. The customer wants to know if the product presentation he is hearing from his closer is about the same as the presentation being given by another closer. Customers are basically skeptical and they think they need this type of reassurance or safety check on their closer. The closer has to keep his customer away from the other closer's customers, without his customer's being aware of what the closer is doing. The reason for this separation of customers on the closer's part is this: Customers will talk, exaggerate, and make up stories regarding their closer and the product to make themselves look knowledgeable about the whole sales situation in the eyes of the other customer. The customer wants and needs to give out an air of confidence and strength to the other customer (his new-found friend) because he can't show this type of attitude around his own closer, because the closer is in charge and in control. So the customer lets the pressure off by talking (tough or inquisitive) to the other customer and in doing so let's the other customer know little thises and thats. These little "thises and thats" comments between the customers can kill a sale for a closer faster than anything else, and the closer will never know what happened.

Any kind of statement from the customer that might contradict another customer's statement could blow out one of the sales or both.

The closer should keep his customer to himself and protect his own product presentation from outsiders. The closer must have total control; any adverse conversation or question from another customer could destroy the closer's control.

The customer separation can be achieved tactfully by the closer if he tells his customer he is not a regular closer, but is in management or on the staff, etc. . . , and that he (the customer) will be given special product presentation facts and prices other customers won't have and don't have to know about. The closer should then explain that because of that reason the best thing to do is for the customer to stay right with the closer and keep all the secret information to himself.

Since my lesson on the "twelve product presentation steps" was completed, Sam said I could proceed into my next subject of study: the "in-home sales presentation." Sam told me the best way to study the in-home presentation was to look at it in the form of a "do's and don'ts" list. The reason for this is because in closing sales, whether a closer is in his sales office or in the customer's home, the basics never change. The closer has only to adapt his presentation to fit the situation and environment. The most important positive factor the closer has going for him when he is in the customer's home is that he (the closer) can tell everything about the customer's lifestyle (the way a man lives will reflect the man) and adjust his presentation properly.

When the customer is in the closer's sales office, the closer has to judge the customer's lifestyle only from observing him personally without the advantages of seeing his normal and total living habits. The "in-home sales presentation" is educational because every house and every customer has something different to offer, and every simple call the closer makes only adds to his professional character and knowledge.

The closer knows the basics of closing — or at least he should — so the list of in-home sales presentation "do's and don'ts" will pretty well explain the closer's main responsibilities and duties for getting a sale in the customer's home. (Note: Remember, the closer is in the customer's home, not his own or his sales office, so he'd better treat that home with respect no matter what it looks like, because that home is the customer's castle.)

In-Home Presentation
(The Do's and Don'ts)

1. **Do: Go empty-handed.** The closer should always go to the customer's door empty-handed, without any of his sales material. If the closer took all his sales equipment with him and the customer peeks out the window from behind a curtain or just opens the door, the sight of a closer with all his sales paraphernalia would only scare the customer and make him more tense. (Note: When the closer goes to the door empty-handed, he looks more relaxed, unpressured and at ease, thus making the customer feel, to some degree, the same way. When the customer comes to the door, the closer should just give a simple, pleasant greeting, introduce himself, and then after an exchange of positive comments, excuse himself so that he can go back to his car and get the sales material he needs. For example: "Mr. Customer, good morning, my name is _____ and I'm with _____ company. I hope I'm not too early for our appointment. (response) My watch runs a little fast. By the way, you have a beautiful home and yard, I bet you spend a lot of time and work on it. (response) Would you excuse me for a minute and let me get my material out of my car?"

The closer should always use the "three-step introduction" and all the other basics he knows when greeting a customer, whether the presentation is in the customer's home or in the closer's sales office.

2. **Do: Get the customer involved.** For example, if the closer is selling steel siding, he should get the customer to help with some of the measuring of the house or get the customer outside so he can point out this or that about the house. This tends to get the customer enthused and more excited about the project.

Note: There is *no* certain time or set place in the sales presentation to actually close the customer. The Master Closer is continually (from the first second he says "Hello" to his customer, until the sale is made) going after the sale with every question and statement he can think of. The Master Closer knows that every single "Yes" or positive response he gets from his customer is a step that much closer to getting the sale consummated.

3. Don't: Go into the customer's home and try to get control by talking first and sitting in the customer's favorite chair. This is an old pro's trick and it stinks. The customer—I don't care who he is—will be offended and resent the closer. Plus the sales presentation will get off on the wrong foot. (How would you like for a stranger to come into your home and sit in your favorite chair?) The closer should ask politely where he can sit and then adjust his chair toward the customer so that a proper and understandable presentation can be given.

If the closer needs to use a different room for his presentation, or the kitchen table, or whatever, all he has to do is show some charm and ask the customer permission. And the customer in nearly every instance will go out of his way to help the closer.

4. Do: Look for objects in the home (bowling trophies, football awards, hunting rifles, etc.) that tell you something special and unique about the customer, and then, for goodness' sake, comment on them in a sincere, positive and inquisitive manner. The customer will be more than happy to explain them (to you).

5. Don't: Park your car right in front of the customer's house or behind someone else's car in the customer's driveway. By parking the car say, one house away, it gives you (the closer) time to straighten yourself up, (clothes, hair, etc.) before walking to the customer's home. (Note: If there is a newspaper in the customer's yard, pick it up for the customer and hand it to him.) Plus the customer won't see you coming, so he won't run and hide or not answer the door when you ring. Curiosity will make the customer answer the door and then there you are—surprise! The reason for not parking your car behind someone else's car in the customer's driveway is just to show class and courtesy. Some old pros say to block the driveway with your car, a "cute little control trick," (so the customer can't just leave during the presentation) but the closer will do a lot better and get more sales if he just thinks, "Now, how would I like to be treated?" and show some human-to-human respect. It works.

6. Do: If you're a white (caucasian) closer and you are in a black customer's home, ask for a drink of water from his kitchen. When you get the glass of water, drink it. This will immediately demonstrate to the black customer that there are no racial thoughts or uncomfortable feelings on your part. The sales presentation will be a whole lot better and go so much smoother if this one silent race question is killed on the front-end of the demonstration. This "drink the water" trick will do wonders and get the white closer more sales from the black customers than he ever imagined. (Fact.)

7. Do: If the customer needs help doing something around the house while you're there — if time allows — help the customer. For example, if the customer has a large piece of furniture he wants moved but can't do it himself, then help out; the sale will be that much closer and easier to get.

8. Do: When the sales presentation seems to be at a standstill or lull, ask the customer if you may use the phone and make a real or fake phone call to your office. Then act as though you have other appointments waiting and business is going fine. This little act will get the ball rolling again, stir up the conversation. This maneuver will be studied in detail in Chapter 8.

This "Do and Don'ts" list for the in-home sales presentation has to be coupled and worked in with the basic product presentation steps so that the closer feels just as comfortable in the customer's home as he does in his own sales office. (Note: The only difference is that in the sales office the customer is the closer's guest, and in the customer's home the closer is the guest. But with all the sales information the closer possesses he is always in control in both locations. That's why no matter where in the whole world the customer is waiting, the closer still gets the sale.)

Pressures, Tricks and Traps
(Special Notes to Remember)

1. The closer has to adjust his total sales presentation so it has a tempo that will be acceptable and understandable to his customer. The closer should keep the presentation sharp and crisp, but it has to be geared with the customer in mind. (For example: Older customer — slower and more deliberate; younger customer — excited with more enthusiasm; hard-of-hearing customer — a little louder and slower.)

2. Important — Sell the things the product will accomplish and do, more so than selling the product itself. It's easier to sell a dream than it is to sell a physical object. The closer should not only sell the product, but sell past the product itself and sell the future benefits the product can offer. (Note: The customer will do most of the dreaming once the closer plants the "imagination seed.")

3. When something special and exciting happens during the product presentation, comment on it, put it into the sales presentation. If while driving some customers to show them real estate, a deer runs out from the woods, the closer should point it out

and build a story around it; or if a closer is selling boats and he's out on a lake with his customer when a school of fish swim by, the closer should get excited and build a sales story around the school of fish. It all rubs off on the customer. (Fact.)

4. During the sales presentation, if the closer hits a lull, goes blank, or has a dry period (silence), he should ask the customer a question and let him do the talking for a while so the closer can regroup, think and rest. The closer should ask a question that he knows will take the customer some time to answer. This not only gives the closer a breather, it keeps the customer active and involved.

5. The closer can put another couple (who he personally knows) with his customer and act as if both parties are new customers. Then, when the closer is giving his sales presentation, the "customers" he knows personally can ask all the right questions and act as though they are buying the product. The real customer will most of the time follow suit and purchase also, never knowing that the whole presentation was staged. This practice isn't right but it works and it works well. (Note: Don't get caught.)

6. During the sales presentation the closer should drop hints about high inflation, a new price list coming out next week, the limited supply of the product, or anything that makes the customer know he can't wait forever to buy.

7. If a customer doesn't have time to hear a closer's complete sales presentation (a legitimate excuse), then the closer should simply reschedule the appointment and make another date. The closer's time is money and he shouldn't waste it on a customer who can't take the time to hear the whole nine yards.

8. When a closer is with his customer he should be friendly to everyone he meets. This will at least make his customer think that he is well-known and well-liked. Of course the closer should be friendly when he's alone too — it's only good sense and business.

9. The closer shouldn't make his sales presentation boring; he should tell interesting stories that help illustrate points he wants to make or describe, and stories people can relate to.

10. When a closer has a new customer with him and he sees one of his old and satisfied customers from the past, he should stop and say hello to him and see how he is doing while his new customer is present. This will make the new customer (the one who hasn't bought yet) feel more comfortable and at ease with the closer, because he will picture himself after he buys and feel better knowing that after the sale the closer doesn't just forget him.

11. When the closer is giving his sales presentation, he must pay attention to both members (husband and wife) of the customer's party. The closer has to be a perfect "balancer" when throwing out questions. That is, he (the closer) has to ask both husband and wife an equal number of questions and get an equal number of responses, so each customer member will feel equally involved in the presentation. If one member is feeling left out then the sales presentation is dead.

12. The closer has to nearly always lead the customer toward the product he (the closer) wants to sell. For example: "Mr. Customer, I think you really need this larger model to accommodate your entire family. Then everyone can enjoy the same benefits." The closer has to use some tact when he is leading so the customer winds up thinking it was his idea in the first place to choose that particular model. If the customer feels pushed into something the sale could be lost very easily.

13. When the closer is giving his sales presentation, he should ask the customer's kids questions and get them involved in the product also. Kids are great allies for the closer because they always slip up and tell secrets about their parents. These slips add to the closer's information warehouse about his customer, so when it becomes time to close the closer has all the ammunition he needs to get the sale.

14. The closer should never monopolize the sales presentation. It has to be divided with some conversation from the closer and some conversation from the customer, but not necessarily evenly. This will make the sales presentation a team effort and not one party against the other party.

15. The closer should always express positive thoughts when talking to the customer. For example: "Mr. Customer, now that color would look good on you," or "Mr. Customer, can you imagine what this product will do for your business? Why, you'll not only be the biggest supplier in the state, but most likely in the country."

16. The closer should always use the word "when" in talking to his customer, and not the word "if" or any other negative word. For example: "Mr. Customer, when you and your family build your vacation home on this acre of land, I promise you, that will be one of the proudest days of each member of your family's lives."

17. If the closer even once thinks about his sales commission during the sales presentation, he is dead. That greed and money sign will show right through to the customer, and the customer will read it like a book every time. (Fact.)

18. During the sales presentation the closer shouldn't downgrade his competition. The customer will not think much of this kind of sales procedure and it sure doesn't show much class on the closer's part. The best thing for the closer to do is to talk up his product and just put himself above the competition. The closer can even tell his customer that he respects his competition but their product isn't even in the same league. The customer will like that.

19. When the closer figures with a pen and paper, it actually has a type of hypnotic effect on the customer. The reason is that the customer doesn't know what final price or other piece of information the closer will finally come out with. So all the anticipation and thoughts are directed toward the closer's pen. The closer can use this tactic very effectively if he writes with deliberate strokes and smoothness, always keeping the customer guessing about the outcome of the figuring. (Note: This type of closing procedure will be explained in detail in Chapter 8.)

20. To lighten things up a bit say, "Mr. Customer, my product is absolutely free, but you had better pay attention because my sales presentation costs ten thousand dollars."

21. Remember, customers will always have champagne taste with a beer budget; the closer has to show the customer how he can obtain the champagne and still stay within his budget.

22. The closer has to take action first if he wants his customer to follow. For example, if a closer has a customer in his car and wants that customer to get out and walk across a piece of real estate, but the customer doesn't really want to get out of the car, the closer can get the customer out by simply saying, "Mr. Customer, let's get out and stretch our legs." The closer shouldn't mention the property at this time, but just "stretch our legs, it's been a long drive." The customer

will follow almost every time, and once the closer has him out of the car he can show him the property.

23. Remember — If the closer has sold the woman, in 98% of the cases the sale is made. The man will buy if his wife wants the product badly enough. (Fact.) The closer has to establish that want.

24. Throughout the sales presentation, the closer should ask the customer, "Mr. Customer, can you see the potential of my product?" The closer has to constantly be dropping imagination seeds.

25. The closer should always remember he is an actor and everything around him should support his sales presentation. All the tools he uses are only props so he can put on his performance in a professional way. That is the only way a sale will be made.

26. If a customer says he doesn't have time for full demonstration, the closer should tell his customer he wouldn't be doing him justice if he didn't give him the complete sales presentation, he deserves the best and he is going to give him the best.

Sam said this ended my lesson on the sales presentation, and I was now ready to study closing — the art of getting the sale. Sam said that before I continued, I should remember this one thing about sales presentations: When the closer is giving his product presentation he should always be constant in his delivery. In other words, the closer should arrange and organize his presentation so it continually moves towards closing question and the sale. The closer shouldn't "zig-zag" (sporadically jump from one subject to another) or confuse the customer with unrelated material and information. The closer should stick to his product presentation game plan, and divert only when he has to make a special point concerning the product. The product presentation has to make sense to the customer because the customer not only has to follow what is being said, but also understand it. If this basic "presentation reasoning" is not used by the closer, then he won't sell, period.

The product presentation is the factual proof (product information) given to the customer so he will have enough useful knowledge to make a buying decision. The product presentation also has to be well organized (Note: Not referring to a salesman's canned pitch) and have continuity, because all the product information is being formed, channeled and aimed at one final goal: a closing question that will get an affirmative answer.

Chapter Eight

THE CLOSERS

CLOSING THE CUSTOMER
(The Closer Strikes)

PART I

A. The Word "Close"
(What it means)

B. Regrouping the Customer After the Product
Presentation

C. Closer's and Customer's Attitudes
(What each one is thinking at this point)

PART II

D. The Closers, Pre-Closing Questions,
Statements and Actions
(Setting up the customer for the "close")

E. Closing (The Actual Act of Getting the
Customer to Say "Yes")
1. Going In For the Kill
(The closer asks the customer to buy his
product)
2. The Closer Handles and Completely
Conquers the Customer's Objections
(The closer "closes," and gets the sale)

PART III

F. The "Master Closer's Deadly Rules of
Closing"

G. Important "Closing Notes" to Remember

NOTES

Chapter 8

THE CLOSER

PART I
CLOSING THE CUSTOMER

It was the latter part of August and this particular morning was beautiful. Everyone at Green Vista Estates was in a great mood except for Sam. He seemed to be extra quiet and serious for some reason. I asked if everything was all right. He just smiled and said everything was fine. So I went on doing my duties and paid no more attention. Later that afternoon, Sam came up to me and told me he had something very serious he wanted to talk to me about, after work. This was unusual because Sam and I usually talked about sales and selling as well as other things during the working day, never after work. When I got off work, we got alone and sat down together on the old hotel's back porch steps that overlooked a beautiful valley which was part of Green Vista Estates.

Note: There is *no* certain time or set place in the sales presentation to actually close the customer. The Master Closer is continually (from the first second he says "Hello" to his customer, until the sale is made) going after the sale with every question and statement he can think of. The Master Closer knows that every single "Yes" or positive response he gets from his customer is a step that much closer to getting the sale consummated.

Sam asked me if I had understood all the lessons on sales closing he had taught me up to this point, and I said, "Yes, I think so," wondering to myself if he was going to start talking about the lesson on product presentations again. But he didn't. Instead, Sam pointed out to the valley and gave me some down-to-earth, old closer's philosophy. He told me that everything in this wonderful world has a special meaning. It has a beginning and an ending, a true reason for being.

Sam looked at me with tears in his eyes, and said that he was about to take me through the most important and serious sales lesson I would ever have. He said my next lesson would be the culmination, the very peak of everything I had learned so far. Sam said he would explain this lesson only one time, so I had better pay close attention and not miss a single thing. He also told me that this was the lesson most closers do not completely understand or take the time to study at all. He said this lesson would be the very heart and soul of all sales presentations, regardless of the product. Sam said that he thought I was now ready for this special lesson in sales.

So I sat there, as the sun was setting over that very peaceful valley, and listened to my old friend explain the lesson that controls, literally, everything in sales: the lesson "closing."

The Word "Close"
(What it means)

Sam said the very first thing to learn about closing, before actually going into the study of closing a customer, was to know and understand exactly what the word "close" means as it pertains to sales. The best way to know exactly what it denotes, he said, was to see it through an illustration that not only demonstrated how the word "close" works but also showed all the ingredients that go into the word to make it function.

NOTE: When illustrated, the meaning of the word "close" looks like a box with each side made up of all the ingredients that go into its construction. The closer builds this "trap box" completely around his customer during his sales presentation, just waiting for the right time to "close" the final door to the trap. Each side could be used as the closing or boxing-in door, but it takes all sides joined together tightly and united at exactly the same time to make the "trap box" work. In other words, getting the boxed-in customer to say "Yes" when asked to buy.

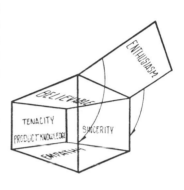

THE WORD "CLOSE" ILLUSTRATED
("THE TRAP BOX")

Sam said the word "close" simply means the final act of a closer, through the efforts of charm, persuasion, product knowledge and enthusiasm, to convince his customer to buy his product, right then and there, period. (Note: The closer "closes" when his customer says "Yes, I'll buy." The customer makes an affirmative decision.)

The "trap box" is exactly what the name implies. It's all the ingredients the closer needs and uses to get his customer into such a position that when he is asked for the final time to buy the product, he (the customer) has to say "Yes." The illustration showing the "trap box" makes it easier for a closer to understand how (by using all of his skills and knowledge) he can surround the customer with invincible and invisible walls, and when the time is right, close the final door to the "trap." At this point the closer's customer is sealed in, locked in, boxed in, sold.

The closer has to remember that all of the steps, from the first meeting, the sales presentation, the pre-closing questions, everything, have to be used to build the "trap box" around the customer. If any part is left out, the "trap box" won't be complete. Instead there would be an opening, a complete side of the "trap" missing for the customer to escape through. The closer has to think and plan his total sales presentation with precision and professionalism in order to construct the "trap box." This is a basic rule that cannot be stressed enough.

Everything in the sales presentation should point to and lead to the final "Yes, I'll buy" answer from the customer. The sales presentation has to be directed toward that final goal and nothing else. The closer, by thinking how the "trap box" works and how it is constructed, can direct the over-all sales presentation so it evolves and arrives at the point where the sale is made (the point where the customer is "closed").

(Note: Sam told me not to confuse the meaning of the words "closing" and "close." He said "closing" was getting your point across to another person and getting that person to agree with you. There was no time limit or time element involved in "closing" — it could take two minutes or all day. But to "close" was *the act*, the conclusion, the one point where the customer gives a positive response to the closer, a "Yes" answer when asked to buy the product.)

Regrouping the Customer After the Product Presentation

Sam said we should take a look and see how the closer regroups his customer after the product presentation is completed.

A. Regrouping the Customer — When the closer has finished his product presentation (the actual act of showing his product) and/or demonstration he should regroup and direct (gather his customer by his side, that oneness effect) and lead his customer to a comfortable and if possible quiet location. The reason for this movement is to get the customer away from the product and back to the closing table so the closer can sit down with his customer and get to the business of closing the sale. This maneuver can be accomplished by telling the customer he still has something to show him back in the sales office or tell him some realistic story so that he will follow him. For example, "Mr. Customer, now let's go back to the office and I'll show you what everything looks like on paper," or "Mr. Customer, let's go inside for a minute and let me show you something about the product that you won't believe," or "Mr. Customer, I have to check in with my sales manager for a minute, so come on in and have some coffee," or whatever the excuse is.

The closer must get his customer sitting down and back into a frame of mind geared for finances and paperwork instead of mentally and actively geared for the actual product. This "product presentation to the closing table" transition has to be a calm and nonchalant movement so the customer won't panic or start to feel trapped. If the customer feels he is about to be "boxed in," his defensive shield goes up in a second. The location could be a closing table or a desk in the sales office, or the kitchen table in a customer's home, or even the closer's car, parked under a shade tree — anyplace that will be conducive for the closer to continue with the rest of his sales presentation and then, without moving the customer again (the less confusion the better), go right into the pre-closing questions, and ultimately the close.

It has to be remembered that a closer could "close" the customer right in the middle of his product presentation, for example, when he is out in the middle of a field showing real estate, or driving around with his customer in a new car, or showing the customer how to operate a new piece of machinery. The customer can be "closed" any place and any time the closer feels he is ready to buy the product. But we're not talking about a sales situation like that at this point. What we are talking about is a sales situation where the closer, after finishing physically showing his product, takes his customer to a closing table, seats him, gets him coffee or refreshments and then goes on with his sales presentation, heading consistently and continually toward the "close." (Important — When the closer is seating the customer back in the sales office after his product presentation, he has to use the very same seating arrangements and control factors he used when he first met his customer as explained in Chapter 6. The reason for using the same control factors is two-fold: Firstly, it makes the closer's and the customer's movements, from the first meeting, Chapter 6, Step I [inside the sales office], to the product presentation, Chapter 7, Step II [that was outside the sales office], to the closing table, Chapter 8, Step III [back inside the sales office again], go smoother and easier thus making the customer feel more comfortable. Secondly, the closer's seating arrangement and his control factors still have the same programming effect on the customer they did in the first meeting, plus they still work to keep the closer in control.)

B. After the closer has seated his customers, he should ask them if they would like anything to drink and then get the refreshments himself, leaving the customers alone so that they have some time to themselves, and can get their thoughts together. (Note: There is a school of thought that says the closer should never leave his customers alone after showing them the product, because it would give them time to talk in private and figure out how they are going to get out of the sales office without buying, or how they can come up with a good excuse for not buying today, etc.... This school of thought has some merit, but it's not right. The closer should get up and leave the customers by themselves for a few minutes so they can ask each other questions and exchange ideas they wouldn't share in front of the closer. And they will like the closer a little more for showing this respect. The customers will discuss everything from their personal finances, to whether they believe the closer's product presentation story. It really doesn't matter what the customers talk about because the closer should not only be in control, but by this time he should have made friends with the customers and established a close relationship with them. The closer has to keep in mind that he's already two-thirds of the way through the total sales presentation (Chapter 6, Step I, and Chapter 7, Step II); the closer only has one-third of total sales presentation to go, (Chapter 8, Step III), and that's a little late in many cases to pull a friendship or close relationship "feeling" out of the hat.

C. When the closer is away from the closing table getting coffee, checking the inventory, or whatever, he should keep an eye on his customers to observe their actions, for example, to see if they are having a serious discussion or if they are just laughing and having a good time as though everything about the product presentation was a joke. The closer had better know where he stands with his customers when he comes back to the closing table, because that's the time to get down to the bottom line of getting the customers sold.

(Note: The closer can tell a lot about his customers from just watching them as they talk together and remembering the degrees of interest they showed during the product presentation, along with all the things that were said. The closer should know at this point what maneuver, approach or technique he is going to use to "close" his customers. He's had sufficient time to study the customers and analyze them during the pre-presentation pitch and the product presentation. The closer should have no problem determining their overall makeup and what weak points are vulnerable to his closing attack. That is, if the closer has been paying attention!)

D. When the closer returns with the refreshments to the closing table (where his customers are seated comfortably) he should present a look of confidence and self-assurance, thinking to himself, these customers are going to buy the product, period.

The Closer's and Customer's Attitude
(What each opponent, closer and customer, is secretly thinking at this point)

Sam said that the stage is set (back in the sales office with everyone seated) and the two opponents are getting ready to go into the final, deadly round (Step III) of the overall sales presentation. It would be a good idea to look at each opponent's attitude separately, to see exactly what each one is thinking privately to himself. Sam said I should take a look at the customer's attitude first and then the closer's.

1. The Customer's Attitude — *What the customer is thinking about and how he feels as he sits at the closing table waiting for the closer to continue with his sales presentation.*

The customer should have a sound overall picture of the closer's product, plus he should understand the product's advantages and benefits due to the closer's pre-demonstration pitch and his product presentation. The customer's general attitude at this point could be one of the following or a mixture of all.

A. The customer is sold on the product and wants to buy it immediately, but he doesn't know the price yet. He is anxiously waiting for the closer to tell him.

B. The customer wants to buy and he knows the price of the product, but he can't afford to pay cash at this time, or thinks he just plain can't afford it. So he is anxiously waiting for the closer to tell him about the financial terms and ways of purchasing that will or will not fit into his budget.

C. The customer is undecided. He doesn't know if he wants to buy or not; his mind isn't made up yet — in other words, he's not completely sold. So he sits there waiting for the closer to explain more about the product or he just sits there waiting for the closer to make his next move. (Note: In this case the customer could afford the product if he wanted it badly enough.)

D. This customer is not sold on the product. He doesn't like it and doesn't want it. He's simply waiting for the closer to hurry up and get his presentation over with so he can leave and go home. (Note: This customer can be sold, but that will be discussed later in this chapter.)

The closer has to acknowledge and understand one very important fact concerning customers and their attitudes: When sitting at the closing table and waiting for the closer to continue his sales presentation, all customers, no matter who they are, will have the very same basic thoughts and feelings. They are fear, anxiety, confusion and excitement. These four elements are present and bottled up inside of every customer that the closer will ever talk to at the closing table. Some of the feelings will be stronger than others, but it's a fact that every customer, whether rich or poor, will have these feelings when it's "sit down" time and "dealing time" with the closer.

Sam said the reason these common elements are found in all customers is easy to explain; at this point in the sales presentation the seated customer really doesn't know what to expect next. He doesn't know what the closer is going to say, or how or when he will ask him (the customer) to buy. The customer doesn't know if the closer is going to use some "closer's trick" or if he is going to bring in another closer — say, the sales manager — to help get the sale. The customer is somewhat tense with a number of thoughts running through his mind.

If the closer has done his job properly during the pre-demonstration pitch and the product presentation, the customer should be thinking seriously about buying the product, and some meaningful questions concerning the product. But if the closer didn't do his job and failed to create enough interest and desire in the customer to own the product, the customer will only be thinking of ways to say "No" and get out of the sales office. The customer's attitude and way of thinking depends on how the closer has done his job. It's also very important to remember that the customer, if not completely sold on the product (they don't really know if they will buy or not) will automatically be looking for reasons not to buy rather than reasons to buy. It's easier to say "No" and be uncommitted and unconcerned than it is to say "Yes, I'll buy," and then have to take on a new obligation or responsibility. The customer, in most cases when buying decisions are left to him alone, will want to take the easy way out, and that usually means a "No" answer.

The customer will be looking for and trying to come up with what he thinks are legitimate reasons not to buy, reasons for not having to spend his hard-earned money. The customer will want to be able to justify his "No" answer to the closer because he likes him and doesn't want to sound ungrateful or rude. The customer will also be trying to rationalize his "No" answer in his own eyes, so that he will feel that by not buying he didn't really miss out on anything.

The customer's attitude after the product presentation is very, very important. Not only because it shows the closer how close he is to getting the sale, but because it gives the closer customer information he needs to know so he can plan and direct his "closing" attack. This information is obtained by observing and listening to the customer's actions and statements, which are all derived and reflected from his general attitude.

Notes to Remember Concerning the Customer's Attitude

A. No matter how much a customer believes or likes the closer, he will somewhere in the back of his mind be somewhat skeptical and leery, because the customer has sometime in his own past put his trust in another closer and got hurt. (Fact.)

B. The customer is wondering to himself what exactly the closer is going to do next. So he automatically starts to build up his lead shield or guard again. The closer has to re-relax the customer at the closing table, so he is calmed down and not defensive.

C. If the customer is timid or unusually quiet compared to how he acted during the product presentation, it could be because he has a question to ask about the product and is embarrassed to ask it, thinking it sounds silly or that he got too excited about the product during the product presentation. He feels he showed too much emotion and now he realizes it's time to get down to the business of buying so he is reestablishing his defenses. To put it another way, the customer got carried away with enthusiasm when he was inspecting the product and showed too much of his hand to the closer, and now he has to act reserved and self-controlled so he won't look like an easy sale.

The closer can take care of both of these problems by merely getting the customer relaxed again, getting him talking again (asking questions), becoming his friend again and making him feel at ease at the closing table, and letting him know that nothing has changed from the first time they met and that no one is going to shoot him or break his leg if he decides not to buy. (Note: This relaxing process will be discussed in detail in Part D. "Setting up the customer" of this chapter.)

D. When the customer is sitting at the closing table, he ought to know enough about the closer's product to still be able to pay attention and know what the closer is talking about. If the customer doesn't understand something or missed something during the pre-demonstration pitch or the product presentation, that missing information could very easily kill the sale, just because the customer and closer didn't fully understand each other. There was a lack of communication. (Note: It's the closer's responsibility to make sure this doesn't happen.)

E. The customers will be thinking and talking between themselves (husband and wife team) about how they can afford the product. This discussion could cause a problem if one party is sold and the other party is not. One party won't want to spend their money and the other one will. The closer has to watch out for this husband and wife "money fight" and stop it, or the whole sale will be lost because the customers and the total sales situation got out of the closer's control. (Note: To avoid this type of problem and to keep control of the customers when talking about money, the reader should study Part E. "Closing" of this chapter.)

Note: There is *no* certain time or set place in the sales presentation to actually close the customer. The Master Closer is continually (from the first second he says "Hello" to his customer, until the sale is made) going after the sale with every question and statement he can think of. The Master Closer knows that every single "Yes" or positive response he gets from his customer is a step that much closer to getting the sale consummated.

F. The customer will tell just about everything about himself through his eyes. He doesn't have to say a word to the closer. For example: If the customer is looking around the sales office in sharp, short and jerky movements, the customer is scared to death and nervously waiting for the closer's next step; or, if the customer is looking out of the window or across the room with a kind of faraway look in his eyes, there is a good chance he is thinking about finances, the product, or its advantages. He will be daydreaming about everything the closer has shown him and said. The customer's eyes and facial expressions will pretty much tell the closer the story on how close the customer is to buying, after he has received and gone through the product presentation.

G. If the customer is sitting back in his chair and has pushed away from the closing table with his arms folded, not talking, or is nonchalantly chatting to other customer team members, the closer should know this customer is not sold. (Note: Customers have to have both feet squarely on the floor and arms on the table, showing interest in what the closer is saying or doing, if a sale is to be made.) The customer who has an attitude of "Okay, I've seen the product, what now?" is not sold, period. The closer has his work cut out for him but that's all right. If the closer does his job correctly the customer will buy.

H. The customer will be trying to regroup, to get back to his original game plan of "I'm not going to buy today." The customer is trying to get his thinking together, just the way he had it before he met the closer and was introduced to the product. But now it's more difficult because the customer likes the closer and he knows more about the product. He also found out that the product presentation wasn't as bad or rough as he had thought it was going to be. So now the customer is somewhat off balance in his thinking (off guard) and somewhat confused. The closer has tactfully broken through the customer's defenses and now the customer's original "no buy" policy is starting to fall apart. (Note: This is exactly what the customer's attitude should be after the closer's product presentation, if the customer hasn't bought the product already.)

2. The Closer's Attitude — *What the closer is thinking to himself and how he feels just after he has given his product presentation and just before he goes back to the closing table with coffee, to sit down with his customer.*

The closer has to know that his customer is sitting on pins and needles waiting for his return. He must calm the customer down before going into the pre-closing phase of the sales presentation. (Note: This will be discussed in Part D of this chapter).

Once the closer knows the customer's attitude he can plan for himself, getting his own attitude adjusted properly.

The closer should be thinking that he has the sale (if he gave a good product presentation). He has to assume the customer is going to buy. The reason for this is because the air of confidence that the closer shows will unconsciously rub off on the customer when the closer sits down with him. The customer will feel this self-assuredness and automatically become more secure and more positive in his own mind. The customer wants to do business with a winner, a champion, someone who shows that he is a professional and that his product is the best, not a runny-nosed little salesman who is afraid of the customer and afraid to ask for the sale. (Note: Some customers will resent the closer's assured attitude and will put up their defensive shield to protect themselves. The closer should be able to spot this "standoffishness" from the start and then through simple, non-committal, comfortable conversation and friendly charm get the message through to the customer that the confident attitude doesn't mean that he just assumes everyone buys, but that he believes in his product and he knows his product is the best. After the customer sees the closer's attitude is based on enthusiasm and not malice, his defenses will come down some.)

The closer also has to watch his customers' actions and notice who is talking or acting like he is not interested in the product, and could become a future problem for the closer (a member of the customer's party who is not sold yet and is trying to talk everyone else out of buying). The closer has to be alert and observant of all these things so that he can plan exactly how he wants to approach the seated customers, plus know exactly what he wants to say and to whom.

The closer should have the attitude that he has just shown his customer the best product in the world. He couldn't go out and buy a better product anywhere. The closer should take pride in the fact that he represents this product and that he is giving his customer the opportunity to buy it. The closer has to not only show this pride but *believe* it. (Note: This does not mean the closer should be arrogant or snobbish, but rather he should display an attitude that radiates the feelings of being on a winning team, or a "Mr. Customer, my product is in a league by itself, it's the top of the line" type of attitude.)

This kind of thinking on the closer's part will get more sales than one can imagine, plus it makes the customer feel more comfortable knowing that he is with a professional, someone who knows what he is doing.

Notes to Remember Concerning the Closer's Attitude

A. The closer should take the attitude that reflects this statement: "What would really happen if the customer says "No." The closer has to realize that a "No" is not the end of the world, but only the beginning of his job. He should go in to close his customer with nothing to fear whatsoever. If the customer doesn't buy, then it's his loss, not the closer's. That's not a bad attitude.

The closer has to remember that he is the one who has to get the customer over his fear-of-buying feeling and the closer can't accomplish that if he shows the fear of asking him to buy himself. Two fears sure don't make a buying decision. (Fact.)

B. The closer has to get himself mentally prepared to go in and sit down with the customer, leaving only after the sale has been made. To do this, the first thing the closer has to do is clear his mind of everything except his customer and his product. He can't be thinking about his wife, the commission he's about to make, the party he's going to later, or anything else. The closer has to be totally dedicated and committed to get the sale. If he lets his mind wander when he sits down with the customer, it will show and the customer will get the feeling that if the closer doesn't care enough to show complete interest then why should he, and a sale will be lost. (Note: We're not talking about a planned negative closing maneuver at this time, where the "I really don't care if you buy or not" attitude exists. We're talking about the closer who gets lazy and doesn't want to go the extra yard that just might get the sale.)

C. The closer must realize that to get the sale he has to use the power of emotions on his customer. To get himself ready for this "final act" in overall sales presentation, the closer should go someplace alone and psyche himself up for this closing process. (Note: He should use the mirror technique and get serious with himself.) The closer should know by this time the weak points in the customer's makeup and plan an emotional attack for that sensitive area. (For example, the customer's weaknesses (vulnerable points) could be his future dreams for his children or his commitment to a particular group or church.) Anything that when "speared" by a closing question or statement will get the customer activated, excited, and thinking.

D. The closer has to realize that this is his final approach, his last shot to deal with the customer and get the sale. The closer has to be mentally ready for a long and drawn-out battle with the customer, if necessary. The closer has got to know how to use and handle tenacity, period.

E. A closer should understand one thing about "closing" a customer: The act of getting a customer to buy the product, of getting him to make a decision that is good and right for him, isn't always nice and pretty. The closer sometimes has to use strong, intense pressure on the customer. The kind of pressure that not only produces tears but many other forms of emotions, to get the sale. There are many sales books and schools of thought that look down on tough, hard, cold, heart-tearing pressure. That's their privilege. Sam agrees; he said this kind of closing practice shouldn't ever be the normal procedure a closer uses. But he did say that it is a very necessary tactic for the closer to utilize when he must.

This kind of pressure closing exists, it's alive and well and it will always exist; any closer who is not using it when necessary is missing many, many sales. (Examples of this high-pressure closing tactic can be seen later in this chapter and also in Chapter Nine.) The closer should remember he has to be mentally prepared for this type of "close" if he expects to be a top closer. (Fact.)

Chapter 8

PART II

CLOSER VS. CUSTOMER
(Show Time)

PART II
THE CLOSERS, PRE-CLOSING QUESTIONS, STATEMENTS AND ACTIONS
(Setting the Customer Up for the "Close")

Sam felt I was ready to study the next most important thing to actually "closing" the customer, and that was how to get the customer set up, get him prepared through product reeducation and programming (trial close) for the final closing question when the closer asks the customer to buy his product.

To understand the pre-closing procedure, Sam said that first I had to know and remember one very important fact: The customer has just finished the actual inspection of the product (the product presentation) and a lot of the information that he heard in the pre-presentation pitch has been most likely forgotten. (Note: Customers cannot remember everything they've seen and heard during the total sales presentation.)

So when the closer sits down at the closing table with the customer after completing the product presentation, he has to reeducate, reorient, reoutline and reprogram him. (Note: The closer shouldn't bore the customer with a complete detailed recap of everything; instead summarize, hitting only important product facts that will help persuade the customer to buy.) In other words, the closer has to put all of the parts of the puzzle (the overall sales presentation) back

179

together again, in proper perspective for the customer. Then the customer can make an easy and unconfusing decision when asked to buy the product. (Note: Remember the rule, "If you confuse 'em, you lose 'em.")

Sam said the best way to explain and show this process of customer and reorientation and programming was to give examples in three orderly and progressive steps. These three steps will start from the first words a closer speaks up until it is time (in the eyes of the closer) for the customer to be asked to buy the product. (Note: At this point the closer has given the customer coffee and is sitting at the closing table with him, waiting for the closer's next move.)

Step 1. Get the Customer Relaxed — The customer is waiting for the closer to drop the hammer (ask him to buy) so the customer is defensive and tense, trying to be prepared for anything that might happen. The best thing the closer can do to ease this feeling is to first ask a question or make a statement that doesn't even relate to the product at all. This will get the customer talking about another subject and he will start to feel more at ease and less defensive. The closing table, the sales office, and the other closers in the general area, will tend to scare a customer every time. The reason is that when the customer first met the closer in the sales office there was no obligation on the customer's part at all — he was a free, independent "looker" or window shopper. Then when the customer was out of the sales office actually inspecting the product (example: an automobile) he was still feeling free, because he was out of doors and could walk away if he wished. It was just himself and closer on equal ground (at least the customer thought so). But once back inside the sales office surrounded by a lot of sales material and product paraphernalia, the customer starts to feel the obligation and pressure build up because he has taken up the closer's time. The closer, through his product presentation, has indeed invested his energy into the customer and the customer feels all these things pressing in and simply gets nervous.

This is an example of how the get the customer talking, thus leading to some relaxation on his part: "Mr. Customer, you said earlier that you were in the home construction business. Have you ever built large commercial buildings before?" or "Mr. Customer, your kids said they like to ride horses. Do you have some horses back home or is there a special place the family goes to ride?"

Unrelated questions like these will get the customer's mind off the product for a few seconds and he will start to calm down. It's important for the customer to be at ease because if he isn't, then he won't hear a word the closer says. (Fact.)

Step 2. Reeducate the customer about the product. (Summarize the product presentation to a small degree with "trial closes".) The closer has to get and keep everyone in the customer's party involved in this conversation. Remember, it's fatal to a sale if one member feels left out.

This is the step in the pre-closing process that lets the customer again hear some of the product information the closer had related earlier in the pre-presentation pitch and during the product presentation. This is the "refresher outline" that enables the customer to comprehend the total product and its benefits, so he has enough product knowledge to base his buying decision on when the time comes.

Here is an example of summarizing for the customer using a square acre of land as the model product. (Note: The closer could do this step on paper or verbally or both, it all depends on the time and sales situation.) "Mr. Customer, let me show you, for just a minute, exactly where we've been and where that property was I showed you. [The closer is pointing to a map at this time.] Mr. Customer, I told you that the property was only one-quarter mile from the ski slopes. Remember I said that our company was going to build a new country club right on the other side of that mountain we were standing on. Well, [pointing to the map] that's the location where the club will be built, and we were standing right about here — pretty close and convenient, isn't it?" etc....

Note: There is *no* certain time or set place in the sales presentation to actually close the customer. The Master Closer is continually (from the first second he says "Hello" to his customer, until the sale is made) going after the sale with every question and statement he can think of. The Master Closer knows that every single "Yes" or positive response he gets from his customer is a step that much closer to getting the sale consummated.

This kind of showing and telling maneuver, the backing up of facts and statements with maps, sales material, and verbal summaries, reassures and reinforces the customer's belief in the closer and the product. (Note: Even though an acre of land is being used as the product model in some of these examples, the basic reeducationing process and rules can apply to any product, in any sales fields.)

Another example of summarizing: "Mr. Customer, now that you have seen the property and everything that my company is doing to improve it, wouldn't you say it has potential? If you buy the property and wait two years for all the improvements to get in, can you imagine what that land will be worth at that time? You know, every little thing that we do, every amenity, every street light, everything that's put in, makes that property worth more. Remember that you and your family could come here and use the club, the swimming pool, the lake — use everything for practically nothing and at the same time own property. We are in the process of doing everything I've told you we were going to do, and you saw it. You were right there with me. Mr. Customer, when we first got together I told you I was going to prove everything I was going to tell you about my product, and I have. I think you'll agree that when we say it's going to be done or something is going to happen, you can count on it. Wouldn't you say so? My product is great but it's nothing without you and your family, because the better the property owners are, the better our whole surrounding area is, and that's a fact. Mr. Customer, you can see the potential here and you know it, right? Now tell me the truth, I've been honest with you." or "Mr. Customer, let me put everything back together for you. Remember when we first met, I told you that my company knows what it's doing, and that we have the best product anywhere. Well now, I think you can see and understand what I was talking about. Not only have you looked at all the benefits of my product on paper, but you've actually seen them with your own eyes during the demonstration. Wouldn't you agree that my product has a lot of fantastic potential?" or "Mr. Customer, I told you that the property was beautiful, didn't I? And remember, I told you that my company was putting in underground cables to the property, didn't I? And didn't I say you could see the lake from that property? Well, you could, couldn't you?" etc. . . .

The closer has to keep in mind that he's continually bringing the customer up to a point, a peak, where the customer is excited and enthused enough to be asked to buy the product. (Note: The timing and precise point of asking for the order depends on the closer. There is no set rule.)

In this type of conversation, the closer is also forming and programming the customer's thinking, so that it is actually being funneled (directed) toward a positive buying decision.

With a team customer the closer has to keep everyone at the closing table involved in these outlining and summarizing questions and statements. (Note: This cannot be said enough — total participation on the customer's point is required to make a unifying and positive buying decision.)

Step 3. Summarizing up to a point — It's a fact that the closer has to know when to stop reeducating the customer about the product and know when to ask him to buy. The reason is simple. If a closer doesn't know exactly when to ask for the order and keeps right on summarizing while his customer is ready to buy the product then and there, the closer could lose a sale because he walked right past the "magical buying point" where the customer's attitude, emotions and feelings were exactly right and ready to buy. This "magical buying point" is such a fine speck at first, that it takes super concentration on the closer's part to see it. But that "magical buying point" grows, it gets stronger and bigger the more the customer is sold, thus making it a little easier for the closer to see. Finally that "magical buying point" is so huge it's right smack in front of the closer's face. If he still doesn't see it and continues summarizing, the "magical buying point" will become less visible and weaker until it finally vanishes, and the closer is left wondering how he missed the sale. He thought he had a deal all the way. Well, he did, the stupid idiot. But he was so professional, so matter-of-fact, so detailed in his pre-closing and closing statements and questions that he lost it and never knew why. (Note: In Part E., "Closing", of this chapter, the 'magical buying point' [recognizing the customer's buying signs and signals] will be explained.

The closer has to understand that at this point he is on the very final approach to getting a sale. The only thing left to do after getting the customer reprogrammed is to ask him to buy the product, and then if he has objections the closer has to overcome them and again ask the customer to buy. And again, and again.

When the closer is summarizing he should remember in what direction he is heading and the object of the whole outline. It is all designed to point the customer toward a positive buying answer and nothing more.

The closer's pre-demonstration pitch, his product presentation, the pre-closing conversation — the whole package — has one common goal, and that is to "close" the customer.

Sam said the main factors to remember about the closer's pre-closing questions were to first relax the customer, second, to get him reoriented, and programmed and third, pay attention not to go right past a "closing" opportunity.

Tips and Notes on Pre-Closing Questions

1. Always get the customer to agree with you all along. Use only positive ideas, illustrations or examples when giving a product presentation summation.

2. Set the customer up (get him ready) for the "close" with deliberate and sharply directed questions throughout the pre-closing question and statement process. For example: "Do you see the potential?", "Wouldn't this be nice to own?", "Can you imagine how proud you will be?", "Won't your kids love it?"

3. Remember that every customer has a bit of larceny in him. The closer should plant "greed seeds" and "self-indulgence seeds" throughout the pre-closing process, if necessary. It all depends on the customer. But if the customer is the type who'll act on these seeds then the closer should plan them, without much hesitation.

4. When the closer is reiterating the main positive points of the product he has to be aware of the customer's interest level. If the customer is not maintaining the same enthusiasm he had during the product presentation, or if the customer starts looking around and not paying as much attention to the closer as he should, the closer has to bring the customer back into the pre-closing process with "shock questions." For instance, "Mr. Customer, what did you say? Oh, I do apologize, I thought you said something." The closer has got to get the customer's attention and keep it, to get a sale. (Note: Do it tactfully; if you make the customer too angry, the sale will be lost.)

5. The closer can build his pre-closing statement on either fear, greed or love. Any one of the three will get the job done.

6. If the customer doesn't believe the closer it's because the closer doesn't believe himself. (Fact.)

7. The closer can lead a horse to water but he can't make him drink. Leading him to water is the pre-closing questions and statements; making him drink is the "close." Sam liked this one.

8. A good saying for closers to remember is this: "If you love the customer, you understand the customer, you become as one with the customer. Then you will sell the customer. All you have to do is be sincere."

"Closing" (The Art of Getting the Customer to Say "Yes")

Sam said the time had finally come to study and learn about the delicate art called "closing," *"REAL CLOSING."* He told me that in this very specialized lesson I wouldn't just be hearing all of the same old closing processes or procedures that many so-called sales books talk about and continually repeat. (For example: Teaching what they think are the basic techniques of "closing," while still tip-toeing around the very heart and soul of "closing" itself. See the following closing Fact A.) Sam said I would learn the exact and detailed maneuvers, manipulations, tricks and traps that go into "REAL CLOSING." The type of closing practice that leaves a customer not only enthused about the product, but with a signed contract that states he owns the product, period.

I was told that before I went any further on the lesson "closing," there were four "closing" statements I had to know. These statements would help me understand the basic foundation of "closing," plus help me realize what goes into "closing" to make it work correctly.

Closing Statement (A) The Customer's Emotion Factor

The main element and most important thing to remember throughout the lesson "closing" was the secret key: "CUSTOMER EMOTIONS." Sam said "CUSTOMER EMOTIONS" were the heart and soul of "closing," the very nucleus of what takes place in any closing situation. He said logic, comprehension, money and product benefits all have their merits and contributions to "closing," but they could never in any way equal the "CUSTOMER EMOTION" factor when it becomes time to make a buying decision.

A good thought for a closer to always keep in mind is this: The emotions of a customer will buy more products or turn down more buying opportunities than any one human could ever comprehend.

Closing Statement (B) The Closing Attack, Illustrated

I was told one of the first things to do before studying "closing" was to mentally picture a closer's "closing attack" that was aimed at his customer. Sam said the reason for this was so I could refer to that mental image whenever I needed, and better understand what was actually taking place while he was explaining "closing." The best way to show that mental picture is to put it into an illustration.

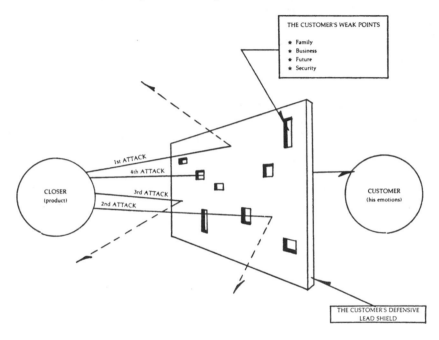

THE CUSTOMER'S WEAK POINTS

★ Family
★ Business
★ Future
★ Security

1st ATTACK
4th ATTACK
3rd ATTACK
2nd ATTACK

CLOSER
(product)

CUSTOMER
(his emotions)

THE CUSTOMER'S DEFENSIVE
LEAD SHIELD

This drawing demonstrates how a closer has to use many "closes" of different avenues of approach to finally penetrate the customer's protective and defensive shield. When the closer accomplishes his closing attack and successfully spears the customer (hits his emotional button, his "hot point"), the customer will react almost immediately and become not only more attentive, but more aggressive (either positive or negative) in his thinking and his actions. It's totally up to the closer to control this reaction and steer it (positively) toward a "close." If the closer does not handle the customer's reaction properly and professionally, it could not only kill the sale, but get the closer a black eye. Of course this all depends on how strongly the closer speared his customer.

Closing Statement (C) Timing, When to Ask the Customer to Buy

Sam said "closing" had everything to do with timing. He said there never has been and never will be a set law or time-honored rule that states the exact point or time in a closer's total sales presentation for him to ask the customer to buy the product. But he did say a closer could follow certain "guideline hints" concerning the best time to "close," and be right on the money, nearly every time.

He told me to remember throughout the total sales presentation the word "timing" was important, because it represented the closer's tempo — how he geared his presentation so it ran smoothly and coherently for the customer.

But when talking about "closing" the word "timing" means a great deal more. It means the very point where the closer asks the customer to buy the product. To find this point, this exact "time" in the sales presentation, Sam said to follow these "guideline hints."

The best way for a closer to know exactly when to ask for the order is to first, know in his own heart that the customer actually knows enough about the product and really comprehends what he knows to make a valid buying decision. If the customer has just been agreeing with the closer, without completely understanding everything that has been said, then he can't buy, he's not ready. (Note: If the customer buys the product without totally understanding it, there is a good chance he will go home and cancel later.) When the closer knows for sure that the customer understands the whole product presentation, it's time for the closer to start looking for a good opening (an opportunity) to ask him to buy. This opening (chance) can be noticed, felt, discovered or revealed by watching the customer's actions and facial expressions.

Here are some customer give-away signs and signals that will always let the closer know when to strike (ask for the order).

(a) The Customer is Ready —

When the closer gets through explaining to the customer a detail concerning the product or how financial arrangements are handled and he looks up and sees the customer looking serious and thinking deeply at what has just been said (the customer is silent). Then the closer should, in a positive "normal-soft" pleasant voice say, "Mr. Customer, why don't you give my product a try?" Then of course the closer should be quiet, shut up and wait for the customer's answer. If it's an objection then the closer has to overcome that hurdle and ask the customer again to "give it a try." (Note: Remember the person who talks first loses. That will be explained later in detail in this chapter.)

(b) The Customer is Ready —

After the closer has shown some fact about the product and the customer looks at his team member (husband or wife) silently and raises his eyebrows or has a "What do you think about it?" look on his face, the closer should wait to hear the other customer's answer, and then go from there to "close." Ask them to "Give the product a try?" : If the wife says "Well, honey, it's up to you, I'll do whatever you say," the closer had better interrupt (jump right in) and bring the wife back into the conversation, by saying, "Now, Mrs. Customer, remember when you got married everything was fifty-fifty. It's up to you, too." This statement on the closer's part will get a small laugh from both members, but it will get the wife interested and back into the decision-making conversation. (Note: Remember, no one can feel left out, or the sale could be lost.)

(c) The Customer is Ready —

When the customer leans back for a few seconds in his chair, looks at his wife, shuffles his feet and has that "Well, what should we do?" look about him, the closer had better lean forward, getting closer to him and ask him to "Give it a try."

Note: Remember, distance between the closer and customer is a selling problem. The closer has to keep close to the customer so he maintains that "oneness" effect. This way the customer doesn't feel alone in his decision-making (he's got his friend the closer right there with him).

Note: There is *no* certain time or set place in the sales presentation to actually close the customer. The Master Closer is continually (from the first second he says "Hello" to his customer, until the sale is made) going after the sale with every question and statement he can think of. The Master Closer knows that every single "Yes" or positive response he gets from his customer is a step that much closer to getting the sale consummated.

(d) The Customer is Ready —

When the closer is finished showing something concerning the product and the customer puts his hands on the table and starts tapping his fingers, he is thinking about buying. The closer had better ask him to buy right then. "Mr. Customer, we need people like you, so why don't you give it a try?"

(e) The Customer is Ready —

After the closer makes a statement, if everything is completely silent in the room, and the customer gives a slight sigh and looks down at the closing table, the closer should right then ask him to "Give it a try."

(f) The Customer is Ready —

When the customer acts nervous (for example, wetting his lips, wringing his hands, scooting around in his chair, playing with his hair or a cigarette, continually clearing his throat, pulling on his ear lobe, or whatever) he is actually thinking about the answer or objection he is going to give the closer when asked to buy. (Note: The customer knows the closer is going to ask him to buy any time now.) So the closer had better do what this nervous customer expects him to do, and that is go ahead and ask him to "Give it a try."

(g) The Customer is Ready —

When the customer asks a question about something the closer has said already, for example: "Mr. Closer, now exactly how wide is the front of that property?" Then he's not only interested, he is ready to buy. The closer should answer his question, then look directly at the customer, and ask him to "Give it a try."

(h) The Customer is Ready —

When the customer has a certain alertness, a certain sparkle, a bright, excited look in his eyes (the same look that a young boy has when he gets a new bicycle — the kind of look a closer can't miss) then the customer is ready to be asked to buy.

(i) The Customer is Ready —

When the customer looks downward and scratches his head and turns it a little to one side with a "Well, I don't really know" look on his face, he is ready for the closer to ask him to buy.

(j) The Customer is Ready —

When the customer starts talking more, leans heavily on the closing table with his arms, gets more involved in what is being said and what is taking place, tells his kids to be quiet so he can hear better, tells the closer to show him how the financing is arranged, asks the closer if he can get some coffee — anything that shows a more sincere and genuine interest on the customer's part means he is ready to be asked to buy the product.

Sam said there were many, many buying signs and signals the customer will unconsciously show to the closer similar to the ones mentioned. It's the closer's responsibility to be alert and notice them, or he could lose a sale. It's that simple. When the customer wants to buy the product the closer can't miss the enthused, excited and eager expression on his face and the light that radiates from his eyes. It's a dead giveaway.

ATTENTION:

In the examples just given the reason the "closing process" didn't continue on was because we were talking about "timing" only. When "closing" is studied later in this chapter the total "closing process" will be explained.

ATTENTION:

In the examples just given the closer always asked the customer to "Give the product a try," not "Buy it, Mr. Customer." The reason for this, Sam explained, was that when a closer makes it easy and uncomplicated for the customer to buy the product, he will get more sales. The word "try" is a great word to use, because it makes the customer kind of feel he is just trying or using the product for awhile and not really stuck with it for years and years. (Although, he really knows that he is.) The word "try" and other trick words will be looked at in detail later in this chapter.

Sam said to always know and understand that timing is a tempo, the pacing of a closer's sales presentation, but when applied to "closing" it's the moment, that very special opportunity the closer finds and uses (stopping whatever else he's doing) to ask the customer to buy.

IMPORTANT: NOTE: There is an "old pro's saying" that states you can't ask the customer to buy the product soon enough. In other words, the sooner the closer asks the customer to buy, the better. That statement is not true. A closer has to deliberately program and direct his customer toward the "close." He has to continually feed the customer product knowledge, plant imagination and owner-benefit seeds, throughout the complete sales presentation, if the closer expects to sell. Without the right amount of product information and total understanding of the product's advantages, the customer cannot make a proper buying decision when asked to, simply because the customer just doesn't know enough about the product. (Fact.)

If a closer does ask the customer to buy too soon in the sales presentation, that could quite possibly make the customer angry or upset, thus making him put up more of a rigid defense than he had intended. The customer will feel the closer is not only pushy but to some degree, arrogant, and this will only make it that much harder for the closer to actually "close." By asking the customer to purchase early in the presentation, the closer has only created problems and objections that were unnecessary in the first place.

The "old pro's saying," even though it is not correct, was designed for a purpose: By asking the customer to buy early, the customer will or might give the closer an objection. Then the closer could overcome that objection and work from there toward the "close." In other words, the customer's answer and/or objection to the closer's early "close" tactic would give the closer an insight into what the customer is feeling and thinking at that point. This would enable the closer to redirect and replan (if necessary) the rest of his sales presentation. The presentation would then be in accord with the customer's wants and thoughts. This early "close" tactic saves the closer some time (the customer might buy when first asked) and allows him ample time to pinpoint and concentrate on the customer's objections early in the sales presentation, rather than learning the real objection at the tail end of the presentation, and having to handle (solve) it then.

A closer can discover the same thing that the "old pro's saying" of "ask them early" was designed to uncover, without causing customer problems. By simply taking the customer's temperature and listening to him talk, the closer can use small trial closes (pre-closing questions), make positive statements about the product and how it would benefit him, and continually get the customer to agree with what is being said.

This type of sales practice will not anger or upset the customer, as the "old pro's saying" could. The fact is, it will not only achieve the goal of finding out what the customer is thinking and what his wants are, but this practice gives the closer the time he needs to educate and program the customer, so when he asks for the order, the customer will be able to make an intelligent and positive decision.

FACT: If one closer used the "old pro's" method during his sales presentation and another closer of equal talent used the method of taking the customer's temperature while giving a complete, positive, and well organized sales presentation, the closer who used the "temperature" method would outsell the "old pro's" closer, ten to one.

Closing Statement (D) Basic Do's and Don'ts of "Closing"

(a) **DO:** The closer should always listen to what the customer has to say. He has to hear the customer out completely when he is asking the closer a question or giving an objection.

DON'T: Pre-guess. The closer should never read between the lines or "short stop" the customer's remarks when he is talking. The customer just might say or ask something that is the complete opposite of what the closer is thinking. For example: The customer will say, "Mr. Closer, I don't think that the real estate we looked at is exactly..." And the closer jumps in saying, "Mr. Customer, I know it's not what you were looking for." Then the customer says, "No, that's not it, what I was going to say is that the property isn't exactly what I had in mind, but I really like it and I'm interested."

The closer, by cutting in, could not only jeopardize the sale but produce problems or objections that didn't have to exist at all. The closer should always listen and show the customer that respect. Remember, customers "ain't stupid."

(b) **DO:** The closer doesn't only have to listen to the customer, he also has to understand (comprehend) what the customer is saying and trying to say. The closer has to know exactly what the customer is talking about so he can get the sale. The closer and the customer have to have a "meeting of the minds" (complete understanding of what each one is saying).

DON'T: The closer shouldn't act like he understands the customer's remarks or statements if he really doesn't. This misunderstanding has killed many, many sales. The closer, by not completely knowing what the customer is saying or asking could very easily misdirect his sales presentation and completely miss the customer's main objection to buying the product. Plus the customer will see through this "act" and develop the feeling that the closer doesn't care enough about him to find out what he is saying. The customer will say to himself, "If he (the closer) doesn't care enough, neither do I," and another sale will be lost.

To overcome this sales situation the closer should politely and sincerely say, "Mr. Customer, excuse me, but I'm not exactly sure of what you're saying. Now what exactly did you mean?" The customer will not only respect this statement but will feel the closer genuinely cares enough to answer thoughtfully. This builds more trust and closeness between customer and closer. (Two important ingredients needed by the closer to "close.")

(c) **DO**: The closer must be aware of everything that is going on around him and his customer during the "closing" process.

The closer has to not only watch his customers' (husband and wife team) eyes (giving silent signals to each other) but, he has to be aware of other customers, closers, surrounding circumstances and happenings that might or might not affect the outcome of his sales presentation and "close." If the closer is alert and prepared for some incident or activity he can also protect or prepare his customer for the same, thus avoiding problems or objections that are unnecessary. For example: The closer is getting his customer prepared to buy and he notices another closer, who is within earshot and on the verge of a verbal battle with his customer. The first closer should tactfully get his customer away and out of hearing range so his sale won't be lost due to the second closer and his stupidity. (Note: Closers should always be courteous and respectful to another closer when he is with his customer, *always.*)

DON'T: The closer should never try to avoid or ignore any kind of (positive or negative) activity that exists around him and his customer, especially if he knows his customer is aware of it also. If the closer trys to overlook this activity and acts as though it didn't happen or wasn't important, it could create thoughts (unanswered questions) in the customer's mind, making the "close" that much more difficult. For example: The customer of closer number one sees the customer of closer number two get up angrily from a closing table, rip up a contract and storm out of the sales office. This kind of negative activity certainly won't help closer number one. So he (closer number one) should say something positive and get his customer settled down and calm again. If he doesn't convincingly explain to his customer exactly what happened, then closer number one could easily lose a sale. To get out of this unpleasant situation, closer number one should say something like, "Mr. Customer, did you see what just happened? Let me tell you the real story behind that." etc. and give the customer the most believable and understandable explanation possible. (Note: Closer number one must make the explanation positive and then drop it, so he can get back to work and "close" his own customer. If he dwells on the negative happening the customer will also, and this could lead to a lost sale.)

(d) **DO:** When asking the customer to buy the product, the closer should always say, "Mr. Customer, why don't you give it [the product] a try?" or "Mr. Customer, let's try it" or "Why don't we try it?" The closer has to make the customer feel comfortable and relaxed, not alone or isolated in his decision-making. The customer has to feel secure and unafraid when he is going to give his answer to the closer; if he doesn't feel that way, he won't buy. It's that simple.

The little magic words, "let's," "when," "try," "we," "our," can't be praised enough by closers. These magic words make the total sales presentation easy and uncomplicated for the customer. These magic words don't offend the customer, push him, intimidate or pressure him. All they do is offer the customer a pleasant buying opportunity. (At least it sounds like it when coming from the closer.)

DON'T: When the closer is asking the customer for the order he should never say, "Mr. Customer, why don't you buy it?" or "Buy it today," or "If it were yours." Any of these kinds of statements tend to make the customer put up that defensive lead shield again. The customer will not only feel cornered and threatened by these statements, he will feel somewhat distant and unconcerned about having to make a buying decision immediately. The reason is this: If a closer says, "Mr. Customer, if you buy this property, etc...." the customer will automatically think to himself, "Well, if I do..." That thought, "If I do" will subconsciously lead the customer to "sometime," and "sometime" will mean in the future. So the closer sits without a sale that day because he programmed and educated his customer through his "if" and "buy" words to purchase later on. It's completely the closer's fault for losing the sale.

Sam said the closer has to always keep everything he has learned in the overall and complete sales presentation process in proper order and in total perspective. Closers have to remember all the points, steps and ingredients that go in and contribute to the three main phases of "closing" (The First Meeting, Ch. 6; The Sales Presentation, Ch. 7; and Closing the Customer, Ch. 8) to be able to master the exact art of "closing." These three phases, Sam explained, are in precise and perfect order. If they are sincerely utilized, memorized and then exercised, they can and will make any salesman in the world a Master Closer. (FACT.)

He told me that before I begin to learn about "where the closer goes in for the kill," I should realize one very, very important point ... The closer has to make his customer (gradually and deliberately, during every step and throughout every phase of the total sales presentation) want his product so much that he (the customer) would do most anything, within reason, to purchase it.

The closer, if he wants to be called a Master Closer (a top producer) has to cut right into the very emotions and feelings of the customer. He has to examine what he finds, form a professional game plan ("closing attack") and then go in for the "close," the kill.

The closer's opponent is the customer and it's the closer's job to get a sale. The closer has to use all his gut feelings, imagination and all his knowledge to accomplish that job. (Excluding lying and fraud, of course.) If the closer used anything less, he will get fewer sales; if he gets fewer sales, he will be less than a closer.

Note: There is *no* certain time or set place in the sales presentation to actually close the customer. The Master Closer is continually (from the first second he says "Hello" to his customer, until the sale is made) going after the sale with every question and statement he can think of. The Master Closer knows that every single "Yes" or positive response he gets from his customer is a step that much closer to getting the sale consummated.

"Closing Points"
(Pre-"Going in for the Kill" notes to keep in mind)

1. A good old rule: The closer should never listen to or pay much attention to a customer's first "No," or negative answer (response) to his buying ("Give it a try?") question, until the customer gives his fifth answer. The reason is that a customer will usually throw out stupid, silly and unimportant objections when first asked to buy the product. These negative "No, I won't buy" responses don't really mean much because they are just weak excuses on the customer's part, so he won't look like an easy sale to the closer. (Note: Bless his heart, even the customer who really and truly wants the product has to put up some form of resistance just to make himself feel better.)

2. After the "close" and the contract is signed the closer should say to the customer, "Mr. Customer, remember I'm your man, if you ever need anything — anything at all. You call me first and I'll take care of it personally." (This not only makes the customer feel better and more reassured, but if the closer ever has any problem with the customer he will hear the news first and have the best chance to solve any matter before other nosey sales office personnel get involved and blow everything out of proportion.)

3. The closer should never settle for less than all he can possibly do. It won't work and it doesn't pay. If a closer doesn't want to be a top closer then he should get out of the profession. He's not needed. (FACT.)

4. "When all is lost, ask for the order one more time."

5. The closer can always give the customer some pointed "thought and emotion attacks" when the customer is dormant and there seems to be no headway being made in the "closing procedure." "Attacks" such as these will at least get the customer moving in one direction or the other. For example: "Mr. Customer, at least do it for the love and future of your family," or "Mr. Customer, you don't build your future on dreams, you build it on actions, your actions."

6. The closer should try to put himself, mentally, in the customer's situation and then try to solve his problem from that angle.

7. The closer is only fooling himself if he thinks he has a deal but has nothing on paper, or doesn't have a check.

8. The closer has to remember that when "closing," money will be the major objection, 96.9 percent of the time. Customers will never tell the closer the true reason until it has to be finally brought out. But if the closer has done his job and the customer won't buy, then money is nearly always the reason.

9. When "closing" (asking for the order) the closer should lower his voice and "kind of" whisper, giving the "main event" an air of seriousness and almost reverence. Customers love to hear secrets or quiet statements and a closer's whisper of "Give it a try?" will do the trick. The customer has to listen closely to hear the closer and this is what was wanted in the first place.

10. The closer has to keep in mind that his total sales presentation — all three phases — is over and finished only when he says it is, *not* when the customer says.

11. If a customer really believes in something, then the best thing a closer can do is to add something (an idea, a suggestion, etc.) to it, and then steer that belief toward a "close." The closer can, if he does it properly, put the customer's dream (his belief) into a compatible relationship with the product, thus producing a sale. For example: "Mr. Customer, that home you always wanted for your family could literally be yours, very easily, because we have our own financing and there is no problem whatsoever." (Note: The closer should never shatter a customer's dream or he's dead.)

12. When the customer tells the closer, after everything (the total sales presentation) has been completed, that he wants to look at all of the product information on paper, or see a brochure to take home with him, then the closer better start his sales presentation all over with this customer, because he's not sold and is simply looking for a way out. (FACT.)

13. If the customer makes any kind of silly offer or tries to pull off a bluff (for example: The customer offers $10,000 for a $25,000 piece of property) the closer should go right ahead, if he feels all else is lost, and take a check. This will either shock the customer into giving the closer the real excuse as to why he won't buy (the customer will start "crawdadding," and thinking up a lot of fantastic defenses — which is good because it gives the closer objections to overcome and get the sale). Or, the closer could get a sale by submitting the check to the sales office, and when the deal is turned down, go back to the bluffing

customer without the check and tell him that management will negotiate. (Note: Don't let the customer see the check or he will grab it and tear it up. Checks have a terrible tendency to remind customers what just happened.) Then go in for the kill again, explaining why the property is really worth $25,000 and not the $10,000 the customer gave the closer. If the closer keeps working on the customer he will get the sale because the customer is already partly there with his verbal commitment as well as some of his money.

14. To totally "close" a customer the closer has to explain and justify the price of his product. The reason for this is that the customer, in his own mind, has to know that all of his labor, time, sweat and inconvience was really worth purchasing the product. Sam said, "The price of the product has to equal the trouble of making the money to buy it."

15. The closer, when he has "closed" a customer who doesn't really have much money (in his pocket or in a bank), the closer should take the minimum amount necessary to get the sale financed or approved. The closer should never take all of this customer's money, because if he does then the customer will resent it and might possibly cancel later thinking that all the closer really wanted was his money. If the closer leaves this customer a little pocket money or something extra, not only will the customer appreciate it but he will be a super customer later on down the road, because the closer understood the problem, helped him out and was also his friend.

16. If the closer loses the sale, whether it's his fault or not, then he shouldn't "burn" or anger his customer; he should make sure that he (in his "closing" attempt) has planted at least a seed of thought. If customers leave the sales office grinning or laughing to each other (husband and wife team) then the closer can rest assured that they thought he was a joke and they never really took his product seriously. But if the closer plants a seed then the worst thing that could happen is when this "lost sale customer" goes and talks to another closer he will not only be a lot more alert but a little more reserved in his attitude. (Note: This is one little way that one closer can help another.)

17. The old saying, "Whenever the closer asks the customer to buy the product he should immediately *shut up*, not say another word and wait for the customer to answer him (talk first)," is correct. When the closer asks for the order and then is silent that silence puts pressure on the customer. In this situation the statement "silence is golden" is

very true. The customer will feel this "silent pressure" and he will feel it strongly. Then when he answers, he talks first. (Note: "Whoever talks first loses" is true also, because the person, closer or customer, that does speak first has "broken" first or given in, so to speak. This is a subconscious reaction that works on either party's mind, whether it's the closer or the customer. This reaction works in the same manner that arm wrestling does. Someone is going to have to give in (lose) and that is basically what happens when the first person talks — he loses, he broke that deadly silence first, he couldn't take it.) The closer will not only know the customer feels the pressure but he will hear what the customer has to say, whether it's an objection, statement or whatever, and be able to respond and handle it. The closer just has to keep quiet and let the pressure mount up, even if it takes five hours for the customer to answer. The wait will be worth it. (Note: If the closer thinks the customer cannot on his own initiative say the first word, then the closer should quietly and calmly say to the customer, "Mr. Customer, give it a try?" The closer should simply repeat himself and *shut up*, then wait again for the customer to talk. The closer should never make a habit of talking first, but in some delicate situations it's exactly what's needed to get the customer to answer.)

18. After the closer has completed the total sales presentation and tried to "close" the customer as many times as he thought was necessary and still failed to get the sale but, the customer won't leave the sales office or he is just standing around, then the chances are very good that he still has some unanswered or unexplained questions on his mind. He's still interested in the product. The closer should give him a few minutes by himself and then go up to him and politely try to sell him again, by asking if there was anything he wanted to know or could be helped with. This usually makes the customer feel the closer truly cares (by showing that extra concern), plus it gives the closer another shot at getting a sale.

19. If the closer is selling a product that has a legal recession, time period (cooling off period) attached to it — for instance, a three-business-working-days-right-to-cancel contract, after he has purchased it — then the closer had better not use that recession clause to sell the product. (Period.) The reason is that the customer will sign the contract just to get away from the closer and then go home and cancel. The closer who sells recession will have more cancellations than anyone can imagine. (FACT) When a closer sells he had better lock the sale in at the time the contract is signed and sealed. That way his

cancellation percentage will be very low. (Note: This type of "closing" procedure, how to hold the customer in, will be discussed later in this chapter.)

20. The closer always has to be in control of himself and his customer. He must show firm belief in his product and know what he is talking about. He has to show and give the customer a feeling of confidence at all times. The closer is the only person in the world who is going to put the customer with the product so he had better bond that coupling with professionalism (class) and nothing less.

1. Going In For The Kill
(The closer asks the customer to buy his product)

Sam said it was time to learn how the Master Closer asks the customer for the order. He said that if I put everything I had learned so far together with what I was about to learn, then there wasn't a customer alive I couldn't sell (close). Since my first sales talks with Sam, this was the very lesson I had really been waiting for.

NOTE I — SETTING THE STAGE — At this point in the overall sales presentation picture, the closer and the customer are both sitting down at the closing table. They have already gone through a summarization, "the pre-closing questions," of the pre-demonstration, pitch and the sales presentation. Now the time is right for the closer to ask the customer to buy his product. It should be kept in mind that the customer knows enough product information at this point to make a buying decision when asked.

NOTE II — It also has to be understood that the customer might or might not know the price of the product at this time. If he does know the product's price, he found out during the other phases of the sales presentation, and can make a buying decision by being shown some of the financial arrangements that are open to him, if that is necessary. For example: The customer can't pay cash for the product, so he has to put down a down payment and then finance the balance. The closer shows the customer the paperwork and then the closer asks for the order. He goes in for the kill.

Now, on the other hand, let's say the customer doesn't know the price of the product or any of the financial arrangements. The closer has been holding that information until last, to use as a "closing" tool. If that is the case then the closer will simply tell the customer the amount of money involved and the procedure for buying, then go in for the kill (ask for the order).

Both of these sales situations — knowing the price early and not knowing the price until the "closing process" — can be treated in about the same manner. But what's important is that the closer has to ask for the order at some point and get a response out of the customer; then overcome that response, if it is negative, and turn around and ask the customer to buy the product, "give it a try" again, until the customer gives a positive answer and buys. That is the bottom line. Attention: Both situations, knowing and not knowing the price of the product, will be illustrated in this book.

It has to be remembered that a sale can be made anywhere or at anytime during the total sales presentation, but for this lesson on "closing" the closer is sitting at the closing table and his customer is right there with him. The customer knows the price of the product but the buying terms or financial arrangements haven't been discussed yet. The closer is saving that information for last.

Sam said the formula for "asking for the order" was so simple that many closers not only overlook it, but try to make it more difficult than it really is when trying to sell a customer.

The formula for "asking for the order" is: FEELINGS (EMOTIONS) + TIMING = THE RIGHT OPPORTUNITY. (That special, precise moment when the closer asks the customer to buy and the customer is ready.) The "asking for the order" formula can be explained in this manner:

A. FEELINGS (EMOTIONS) — they are made up from the deepest and most personal thoughts and dreams a customer possesses. For instance, when the customer is asking to himself exactly what the closer's product can do for him and how he will benefit from owning it, whether for selfish reasons or not, he is in a world all by himself. The customer is thinking about his family and how they will use the product. He is daydreaming about how he will look owning the product. He is analyzing the product and all of its possibilities and how they will enhance him and be advantageous to him. The customer is in a serious and realistic mood at this point; he basically wants to think about the product positively and creatively. (Note: This is how the customer should be thinking if the closer has executed the rest of his sales presentation properly. If the closer hasn't given an organized and positive sales presentation beforehand he can still get the sale, but it will be a little more difficult. We will see how this is handled later in this chapter.)

B. TIMING — This subject has been explained earlier in this chapter, but Sam said it wouldn't hurt to take a quick look, just once more, so the closer doesn't forget. Timing is when the closer recognizes that special unintentional expression of contentment and satisfaction on the customer's face. The customer subconsciously radiates this physical expression not only through his eyes (they kind of sparkle) but the edges of his mouth will start to show a faint "satisfied smile." It can't be helped, it's normal, it's the same expression a person has when he knows the answer to a question about to be asked. It's that kind of anticipated exciting expression of anticipation the customer is trying to conceal. The closer, if he is alert and paying attention to the customer, can't miss it. This is timing that special moment, when the customer is waiting for the closer to ask him to buy the product because the customer feels he's ready to buy. He likes what he has seen and he wants it (the product). The customer will have a facial expression that says, "I understood what you told me about the product, Mr. Closer. Now what do we do?"

C. THE RIGHT OPPORTUNITY — This is when the closer thinks the customer's FEELINGS (EMOTIONS) are right and the TIMING is right. Then, at that second, the closer asks the customer to buy the product. For the closer this is just like jumping off a high diving board for the first time, in the sense that he feels butterflies, some excitement deep down inside when he asks for the order. It doesn't matter if the closer is an old pro or a new man, that feeling will be there — guaranteed. (Note: If that feeling of excitement is not there the closer ought to get out of the selling business because he's had it. Excitement and enthusiasm are the backbones of any Master Closer and a Master Closer cannot function without them.)

Note: There is *no* certain time or set place in the sales presentation to actually close the customer. The Master Closer is continually (from the first second he says "Hello" to his customer, until the sale is made) going after the sale with every question and statement he can think of. The Master Closer knows that every single "Yes" or positive response he gets from his customer is a step that much closer to getting the sale consummated.

Sam told me that right before the closer asks the customer to buy his product (give it a try) he has to mentally go over a "last minute check list" to make sure he hasn't forgotten anything and everything is in proper order. By doing this exercise the closer is far more likely to receive a positive response from the customer than a negative one.

CHECK — Intimidation, if the closer has to use it, then he should be prepared to use it. For example: "Mr. Customer, you've seen all the advantages of my product, and you know they're sound and good; I mean a one-eyed baboon can see that. Why don't you give it a try?"

CHECK — When the closer asks the customer to buy the product (giving it a try) he should make it sound like a "simple, friendly, concerned question," a question asked with some tenderness and sincerity, not a buying question that makes everything look like a big monstrous deal. This will only scare the customer. The closer's buying question should pierce (hit) the customer like a quiet and subtle dart gun, not a loud and frightening cannon. For example: The closer should say: "Mr. Customer, if the monthly payments fit into your budget — and I know that they do — why not give it a try?" The closer should not say, "Mr. Customer, if you can afford it, buy it now."

CHECK — No matter how many objections the customer gives, when the closer answers them satisfactorily, he has to ask the customer to buy the product again (one more time). The closer has to answer every *real* objection one hundred percent to the customer's complete satisfaction and understanding. (Note: Some objections don't have to be answered by the closer. These objections are just silly statements the customer nervously makes and doesn't think about when he says them. All the closer has to do is look at the customer, with the facial expression of "Now, you know the answer to that," and keep right on "closing," paying no more attention to that meaningless objection.)

CHECK — If the customer, after he gives an objection and it is answered by the closer, still has another objection, he is simply not yet sold on the product. (FACT) The closer has to find the real reason why the customer won't buy and overcome that reason (objection) before the sale can be made. Sometimes the closer has to go through ten to fifteen objections before he finally finds out what the *real* bottom-line objection is. But when that real objection is conquered and the closer gets the sale, then all the valuable time spent by the closer to find out what the real objection was tends to be worth it.

CHECK — The closer has to understand he is going to have to stick with the customer, stay right in there until he "closes" him. He has to learn that tenacity is his middle name if he ever wants to be a Master Closer. It's not easy and sometimes it sure isn't fun, but a closer should never give up if he thinks the customer could possibly buy the product. (Note: That is, if the product is beneficial to the customer.)

CHECK — The closer should know that when he has the opportunity to "close" then he should "close." When the chance to "close" arrives the closer should drop everything he's doing and take it, ask for the order. (FACT)

CHECK — The closer has to remember to never overreact to anything the customer says in response to his buying question. The closer shouldn't get angry, upset, or too excited, but always show control and calm. No matter if the customer's response is positive or negative. For example (Negative): The closer says, "Mr. Customer, why don't you give it a try?" and the customer says, "Are you kidding? Do you think I would buy this stuff?" Or (Positive): The customer says, "I don't think I'll take one, I'll take four." The closer has to use "over-emotional restraint" most of the time when he is closing. It makes the customer feel more comfortable in his buying decision and in his relationship with the closer. (Note: Sometimes it's good for the closer to get very emotional and excited when he is "closing," if it's used to make a point and the customer gets that point. For example: The customer says that the product costs too much, and in response the closer says, "Mr. Customer, when was the last time you looked at real estate? Do you realize how much it goes up every year? Would you sell your house now, for exactly the same price you bought it for twenty years ago? Now, you tell me what you'd do. I don't think that you really understand what's going on in today's world. I'm telling you the truth about this property, so you'd better listen!"

CHECK — The closer has to make it easy for the customer to buy the product (PERIOD). In other words the closer has to make the customer think if he buys "it's no big deal," it's not the end of the world, or instant bankruptcy. The customer has to feel calm and reassured in his buying decision. (FACT) This "customer calmness" can be accomplished by the closer through his positive statements and his close relationship with the customer. The closer's overall concern and attentiveness toward the customer will pay off when it becomes time for the customer to make his buying decision. (FACT.)

(Reminder: The closer's and customer's close relationship, a "oneness relationship," began when they first met and gradually developed throughout the entire sales presentation.)

CHECK — The closer should never put off or procrastinate his buying question or "asking for the order" question. That will only drag the sales presentation out and make it boring and confusing for the customer. The closer should take the first right opportunity he sees and act on it. The sooner he hears the customer's objection and overcomes it, the sooner he can get the sale. The closer should act (ask for the order) on his first impulse that the time is right; that first impulse is usually correct. (FACT) (Note: This is not a contradiction to the "old pro" saying of "ask 'em early," because that saying didn't have a thing to do with timing [the right opportunity]. This "check-statement" has everything to do with timing, because the closer is asking for the order when he feels the time is exactly right and not just asking for the order to get some kind of objection out of the customer. There is a big difference.)

CHECK — The closer has to keep in mind that the customer of today is a lot smarter and more consumer-oriented than he was ten or twenty years ago. The customer of today knows more about his rights and responsibilities than can be imagined. But there is one thing about a customer that will never change, and that is that he wants, and will always want, to be better off, have more, and be more successful than the next guy. The customer loves himself. (FACT) (Note: There are, of course, exceptions, but very few.) So it doesn't matter how much today's customer knows about this or that in the sales industry, just as long as the closer works on his ego and gets the customer motivated on himself (through compliments). The closer will not only make a friend, but get a sale, every time. (FACT)

Asking For the Order

Sam told me there are *three* distinct "degree-of-interest levels" that customers fall into when they are about to be asked to buy the product. The "first-degree customer" is the easiest one of the three for the closer to handle. This customer is "hot" — he's ready to be asked to buy the product, PERIOD. The "second-degree customer" is the customer who knows all about the product, but still needs that one last-minute bit of product information, that little extra positive statement from the closer, before he's ready to be asked to purchase.

And then there is the "third-degree customer." He's the toughest one of all three. He is the customer who understands the product and acknowledges all of its benefits, but still needs some time to be left alone so that he can decipher and digest all of the information the closer has told him before he is ready to be asked to buy the product.

Sam said the closer has to handle each one of the three "degree-of-interest level" customers differently. The reason for this is so that the closer can eventually get all three "degree customers" in the right and same kind of frame of mind (open, responsive, and receptive), just before they are asked to buy the product. (Note: It should be understood that the "first-degree customer" is already in the right frame of mind to be asked to buy, but the "second- and third-degree customers" still need some extra programming before they are ready. Now when the closer accomplishes this extra programming exercise, getting the "second- and third-degree customers" in the right frame of mind, he can then treat all three "degree customers" in exactly the same manner, and go ahead and ask the bottom line question of, "Give my product a try?"

Sam explained that the best way to see how the closer programs and then directs the three "degree-of-interest level customers" into the right "frame of mind" for the buying questions, is to look at each "degree customer's" situation separately. When the three different "degree customers" were on the same open-minded and receptive level, Sam said he would show how the closer asks the customer to "give the product a try?"

A. The First-Degree Customer:

This customer is either already sold on the product or is nearly sold on it. He is ready for the closer to ask him to buy. This customer might have one or two little objections about this or that concerning the product, but these objections won't be any real problem for the closer. This customer is ready to be "closed" now.

B. The Second-Degree Customer:

This customer has been alert and attentive during the total sales presentation; he knows what the advantages of the product are and he understands the total product concept. This customer is seriously thinking about the pros and cons of purchasing the product — he's still open-minded. But this customer is not quite ready to be asked to buy the product. The closer can tell this by the customer's facial expression. For example: The customer has a "Well, I don't really know" look about his or he has a "questioning or confused look" in his eyes. (Note: These facial expressions or concerned looks can be easily seen by the closer if the closer just pays attention. It's practically impossible to misread these expressions. (The closer can also tell that this customer isn't ready to be asked to buy yet by the way he is acting (standoffish and aloof). This customer is not as enthused or as excited as some other customer normally would be at this point in the sales presentation. This customer either needs a little more last minute product information, extra guidance or some positive "thought statements" from the closer before he is ready to be asked to buy. The reason for these last minute "miniconversations" is to make the customer feel a little more involved in the product, plus make him feel more united and secure with the closer. This not only gives the customer the added strength and courage he needs to face and be comfortable with the closer's buying question of "Give it a try?" but it also makes the circumstances easier for the closer to ask for the order. (Note: The "miniconversation" is that something extra the closer does or says right before he asks the customer to buy the product. It not only works, but will do wonders as we will see in this lesson.)

MINICONVERSATIONS: When the closer sees the customer isn't quite ready to be asked to buy, when he knows deep in his heart that if he did ask the customer to buy, the only answer he would receive would be a flat "No," the closer should take one more minute before asking for the order to give this customer some positive and informative statements (through a "mini conversation"). The "mini conversation" has to be deliberately designed to bring the customer in closer (away from his aloofness to the sales conversation) so he will be ready to receive the closer's buying question of "give it a try?" with an open mind. The best way to show these "mini conversations" along with the buying question, is to give the following examples.

1. "Mr. Customer, this product is an investment. It's just like a little train: the longer you stay on it (or with it), the farther you go. You can jump off anytime you want to — that's your decision — but first you have to get started, you've got to get on board. So why don't you "give my product a try?" (Note: The closer should shut up and wait for the customer's response.)

2. "Mr. Customer, you know the best thing to do before you say, 'I'll pay cash or I'll do this or that,' is to look at my product as though it were a new pair of shoes. What you need to do is try it on for awhile, walk around, and see how it fits. Then, if it doesn't fit right or

it feels uncomfortable to you, you can always liquidate your investment and get out. It's that simple. The worst thing that could happen to you while you are trying the product out is that it makes you a little bit of money. So why don't you give it a try?" (Note: The closer should shut up and wait for the customer's response.)

3. "Mr. Customer, you know you can either go first class or second class. It's all up to you. What you really want for your family is your decision. All that I can do is give you the opportunity. So why don't you give it a try?" (Note: The closer should shut up and wait for the customer's response.)

4. "Mr. Customer, when people buy my product, most don't pay cash. What they do is put a little bit of money down and pay so much a month. That way if they ever decide to sell the product, they wouldn't have that much of their own money tied up in it. Now later on, if they wanted to keep the product, they could just go ahead and pay cash without any interest penalty. It's just like going swimming in a big lake: You don't stand on a cliff and decide to jump right in because the lake might be too shallow or there might be a tree stump or something in the water that could break your leg when you jump. What you do is go down to the edge of the lake first and gradually wade in and see exactly how deep and safe it is; then if you want to go up to the cliff and dive in you can, knowing the water is safe. When you buy my product it's the same thing — just put a little bit of money in it and watch it grow. Mr. Customer, give it a try?" (Note: The closer should shut up and wait for the customer's response.)

5. "Mr. Customer, let me ask you something. Since you know all about the product and its benefits and advantages, plus you have all the facts because you've seen the product yourself — you wouldn't let anyone else who hasn't seen the product as you have shake your opinion of the product, would you?" (When the customer answers "No," and in 99 percent of the cases he will, the closer should continue with his buying question, then "give it a try?") Note: The closer should shut up and wait for the customer's response first.

6. "Mr. Customer, let me tell you something, just man to man. If I were in the same financial situation you told me earlier you are in, and I had the same opportunity to buy this product, knowing in fact that it wouldn't do anything but help me, then there is nothing in the world that would stop me from buying, and that's the truth. So why don't you give it a try?" (Note: The closer should shut up and wait for the customer's response.)

7. "Mr. Customer, did you know that you're just like everyone else who comes into this sales office? People come in here with no intention whatsoever of buying my product. But do you know what happens? After they've seen the product, understand and know the facts about the product, find out who my company is and what we've accomplished in the past, every person makes an honest and sincere business decision to buy. That's a fact. It's that simple, you're not alone. So why don't you give it a try?" (Note: The closer should shut up and wait for the customer's response.)

8. "Mr. Customer, if you feel I've been using some pressure on you throughout this sales presentation or that I might seem to be too pushy or excited about my product, well, you're right. I have been, and the reason is because my product is that good. If it weren't that good, believe me I wouldn't be making a nuisance of myself. I've got a family that wants to be proud of their Dad too. All I want you to do is exactly what I did, plus three thousand other people, and that is give it a try" (Note: The closer should shut up and wait for the customer's response.)

9. "Mr. Customer, I'm sure that you want more for your children than you had for yourself when you were growing up, and I know that you want them to have a good future — a chance, a good start in life. You know, you can give them the very things you've dreamed of and help them, the way someday they'll help their kids, if you own this product. So why don't you give it a try?" (Note: The closer should shut up and wait for the customer's response.)

Note: There is *no* certain time or set place in the sales presentation to actually close the customer. The Master Closer is continually (from the first second he says "Hello" to his customer, until the sale is made) going after the sale with every question and statement he can think of. The Master Closer knows that every single "Yes" or positive response he gets from his customer is a step that much closer to getting the sale consummated.

10. "Mr. Customer, remember earlier you told me your son was going to be an architect. You know, if you got him to help you build your vacation home on that property we were looking at, not only would he appreciate it, but it would help build the father-son bond that maybe because of his schooling and your business somehow isn't as strong as it should be. You only get one shot at life, Mr. Customer, and a man's family should be close (pause for three seconds). So why don't you give it a try?" (Note: The closer should shut up and wait for the customer's response.)

C. The Third-Degree Customer:

This customer is the hardest one of the three "degree-of-interest-level customers" to handle. The reason is because this customer could very easily go either way (sale or no sale) at this point in time. He could get up from the closing table and walk out of the sales office or he could sit there all day and act as though he's not interested in the product at all, and then buy at the last minute. This customer knows and understands the product and has been basically attentive, but he hasn't shown very much emotion or any real excitement during the sales presentation. He is reserved and tends to make the closer feel somewhat awkward (out of place). This customer needs some time alone so he can get his thoughts together before the closer asks him to buy the product. The best thing the closer can do with this customer to not only keep control of the situation (doesn't have the customer walk out on him) but get this customer in the right frame of mind for the buying question, is this: When the closer is sitting at the closing table with this type of customer, and knows that this customer might at any minute say "Well, I've seen enough of the product, I'll get back to you (Note: The closer can also recognize this "I'll get back to you" attitude from the customer, not only by his uninterested air, but by his lack of questions about the product and his unwillingness to have direct and real eye contact with the closer. This customer generally won't pay attention and can be easily distracted.), the closer should just get up from the closing table (while the customer is still sitting and before he has had a chance to say "I'll be back," even before he's been asked to buy) and say to the customer, "Mr. Customer, why don't you cuss and discuss the product, think of some questions about it and I'll be back in a minute. I've got to check on something." (Note: Many customers want to leave before they have been asked to buy the product. This reaction is normal for them because they are afraid of pressure from the closer.)

After making this statement, the closer should immediately walk away before the customer has a chance to stop him and try to give some stupid reason for not staying seated or for not staying in the sales office. (Note: Customers tend to feel obligated to remain seated in the sales office at the closing table until the closer returns and lets them go, "cuts them loose, says good-bye." This works to the closer's advantage because the customer loses the chance to walk away after the sales demonstration was completed and is still in the sales office surrounded by all of the product's promotions and sales material.

(Sam said that even time and exposure couldn't hurt at this point on this type of "third-degree customer.")

When the closer is away from the closing table he should keep an eye on the customer and watch his actions. If the customer is starting to talk seriously about the product, there is a good chance he's interested in buying. The closer should be alert and pay close attention to the customer at all times.

When the closer feels he has been away from the customer long enough (about five or eight minutes, it all depends on the customer and the situation) he should go back to the closing table, sit down and say, "Any questions?" (Note: Again the closer has to shut up and wait for the customer to speak first.) This customer usually responds with an objection, and that is exactly what the closer wanted in the first place.

The closer should never go back to the closing table and say, after sitting down, "Well, what do you think?", because the customers will most likely say, "Well, we talked about it while you were gone and we're going to pass on it this time," or the customers will say, "We'll let you know later on, thank you for your time." The closer left himself wide open for this type of response because the question "Well, what do you think?" means exactly the same as "Are you going to buy the product or not, Mr. Customer?" The closer programmed and forced the customer to automatically say "No." The customer didn't have any maneuvering room. The question didn't give him a way out, so he has to say "No," if he's not totally sold at that point. But "Any questions?" leaves the customer some room to talk and think; it doesn't offend the customer and sounds [to the customer] like a noncommittal question that can be simply answered.)

After the closer has asked, "Any questions?" and receives an answer or objection, he can proceed to ask the customer to buy his product. (Note: The closer, by walking away from the seated "third-degree customer" and giving him time alone to think and then by coming back and asking for "Any questions?" has actually programmed the "third-degree customer" into the same receptive frame of mind that the "first- and second-degree customers" have.) the closer can now ask the "third-degree customer" to "give his product a try" in the same manner that he asked the first- and second-degree customers. And that manner was easy, uncomplicated and comfortable.

Sam said that once all three "degree-of-interest-level customers" are in the right frame of mind (due to the closer's efforts) to be asked to buy the product, we could continue on and see exactly how the closer asks the customer for the order.

Money Information:

The closer can either tell his customer the price of the product, at some point during the total sales presentation (at the closer's discretion, when he thinks the time is right), or the closer can wait to tell the customer the product's price at the end of the sales presentation (when he asks the customer to "give his product a try").

If the closer tells the customer the price of the product sometime during the sales presentation, he has to summarize and repeat the price and financial arrangements to the customer again at the end of the sales presentation, right before he asks for the order to make sure the customer knows exactly how much money the closer is talking about. There cannot be any misunderstanding of the money matter or the sale could very easily be lost.

No matter when the closer tells his customer the price of the product, when he (the closer) is discussing the financial arrangements with the customer he'd better do it smoothly, calmly, comfortably and simply. The reason is this: At this late point in the sales presentation the closer can't afford to upset or frighten the customer, or the sale could be lost. For example: If the closer makes the financing look complicated and too technical for the customer to understand, the customer will simply put up his protective lead shield and not hear another word the closer has to say. (FACT) The closer has to make the price and the finances of the product look as uncomplicated and elementary for the customer as possible so the customer can make a simple and comfortable buying decision when asked to purchase the product.

The best way to show how the closer explains the finances and then asks the customer to buy is to give an example. (Note: This example takes place at the end of the sales presentation, with the closer and customer sitting down at the closing table.) "Mr. Customer, that piece of property we were looking at costs .... thousand dollars. Now my company will do all of the financing itself. We'll take ..... percent down payment or .... dollars and then we will finance the rest at ...... percent interest for ...... years. That would make the monthly payments exactly ...... Let me ask you this: Would the monthly payments fit into your budget?" (The closer should shut up and wait for the customer's answer.) (Note: The closer should always ask the customer if the payments are comfortable for him first, before he asks about the down payment, simply because the monthly payments don't represent nearly as much money to the customer as the down payment, thus making it easier for the customer to answer a question that is directed toward the lesser amount of money. In other words, from the customer's standpoint, the smaller amount of money is the same as a smaller obligation, and a smaller obligation is easier to take on than a large one. So the "monthly payment question" is easier for the customer to answer.)

If he's even half-way sold on the product, the customer will nearly always say, "Well, the monthly payments aren't any problem." The closer should then immediately say, "What about the down payment?" If the customer says, "I could handle that," then the closer had better say, "Then give it a try," and wait for an objection or answer. But if the customer says, "Now, the down payment — that would be a problem," the closer should say, "Don't worry about that, I can take care of the down payment. We don't have to have it all right now, we can work with you on that. But just let me ask you this: If I could make the finances fit into your budget, would you give it a try?" Again the closer should shut up and wait for the customer's response. By using the above example, the closer can get a response and/or commitment out of the customer every time. Then the closer can continue on and go in for the kill ("close").

The closer should always remember when talking about financing, to ask the customer if he can handle the monthly payments first, then the down payment. If the closer asks the customer if he can handle the down payment before talking about the monthly payments, the customer (if he thinks he cannot make the down payment) will automatically put up his defensive guard and think or say "No" to the closer, thus creating a big objection right on the first "customer close" go-round. So now the closer has not only received a negative answer from the customer by asking about the down payment first, but he didn't even get any kind of commitment as he would have if he had asked the customer about the monthly payments first. The closer must get the customer committed and then and only then go in and "close."

Pen Information:

The writing pen is not only the closer's right arm, but it's the ever-present "hypnotic closing instrument." (See the following note.) The closer has to get the customer accustomed to seeing the pen. (Fact: Customers tend to think the closer's pen is their enemy; it's against them because if they pick it up or touch it, they're that much closer to signing a contract with it. Customers think that if the pen wasn't there, a contract couldn't be signed and they'd be safe. Customers, for this reason, are scared of the closer's pen.) The closer also has to get the pen into the customer's hand so when it becomes time for the customer to write his name on the order (contract, working paper, etc.) he can.

The closer can get the pen into the customer's hand by using three methods. First the closer can, when he wants the customer to have the pen, gently lay it down on the closing table in front of the customer with the writing end pointing away from the customer; or, the closer can calmly hand the pen to the customer, with the writing end pointing down and away from the customer; or (the trickiest way), is for the closer to purposely drop the pen on the floor near the customer. The customer will think it was an accident and automatically pick it up for the closer. Bingo, the pen is in the customer's hand. The closer should keep right on talking and never take back or ask for the pen again — let the customer keep it. (Note: When the closer gets ready to ask the customer to buy the product, he'd better be prepared to write the order. The closer should have his pen and working paper or any other sales material he needs at hand, because if he doesn't, and the customer says that he'll buy the product now, the closer will have to take extra and valuable time away from the customer to look for his sales material; that wasted time could be all the time necessary for the customer to cool off and change his mind. The sale is dead, plus the customer will think to himself, "Now if the closer is that unorganized about his paperwork, how in the world can he possibly be organized and dependable for me, one of his customers?" This one thought alone could kill a sale. The closer has to be prepared to start writing when he starts asking the customer to "give it a try.")

The closer can actually use his pen to hypnotize the customer to some degree. This hypnosis can be accomplished if the closer uses his pen not only for writing but as a pointer throughout the total sales presentation. By using the pen as a pointer, the customer gets accustomed to seeing the pen all the time and will start to unconsciously follow the pen and focus on it when the closer is using it to point out facts, figures and product information. The customer will be watching the small writing instrument as it turns, swirls and moves continually around, thus making the customer's mind and eyes adjust to the pen's movements and positions all the time. This constant adjustment has a hypnotic effect on the customer, and the closer can use that effect to steer the customer more easily toward the "close."

The Closer Asks:

When the closer asks the customer to buy the product ("give it a try") there should be dead silence, pure stillness and total concentration on the closer's part. The closer should have both of his feet flat on the floor. He should have his chair pulled up to the closing table and both hands on the table. The closer should lean slightly toward the customer, look him seriously and positively straight in the eye, without blinking once, while thinking, "I love this customer, I know he's going to buy the product." (Note: If this mental exercise sounds silly to the closer, he should try it first before criticizing it, because it works wonders. FACT), and with a controlled and soft voice say, "Mr. Customer, you know everything about the product that I can tell you. This is the best opportunity you are ever going to have to buy this product at this price, and that's a fact. All I want you and your family to do is give my product a try, just that and nothing more — give it a try?" then, of course, the closer should shut up and wait for the customer to reply. When he does hear the customer's reply the closer should immediately go in and "close."

The closer should, right after he has asked the customer to buy the product, look directly and continually into the customer's eyes without blinking or looking away even once, and say over and over to himself, (smoothly and calmly) "Buy it...buy it...buy it...buy it...." (Note: Positive thought *can* make positive things happen. FACT.) The closer should say this to himself repeatedly while he is waiting for the customer to answer him, all the time looking striaght into the customer's eyes.

This type of determined mind control exercise works. (FACT) The reason it works is this: the customer will actually feel the closer's intense eye contact, and that contact will put real pressure on the customer to act (talk) whether it's an objection or another question. The "eye contact pressure" will not only make the customer feel uneasy, but obligated to say or do something. This eye contact will also, because the closer is thinking positive thoughts to himself like "Buy it, buy it," radiate through the closer's eyes, a sense of positive anticipation and a feeling of positive security to the customer. The customer will see this in the closer's facial expression as well and will be more tempted to give the closer a positive (Yes) answer to his buying question. Knowing the product is good and seeing the closer with that positive look about him, full of enthusiasm, it's very hard for a customer to look straight at a closer who has just sincerely asked for the order and say "No, I won't buy it."

When the closer asks the customer to "give it a try" it should be so quiet that a pin could be heard when dropped. The closer shouldn't make a sound, he shouldn't clear his throat, tap his foot, move his hand — the closer shouldn't do *anything* until the customer moves and says something first. The closer has to have total and complete control at this time. (Note: Nothing should break the concentration between the closer and the customer.) The closer should realize this concentrated silence is only going to be broken when the customer looks away, coughs, or says something. Once the closer hears the customer's response he should immediately acknowledge it and conquer it — "close."

2. The Closer Handles and Completely Conquers the Customer's Objections
(The closer "closes" and gets the sale)

Sam said that at this point in the overall sales presentation, the closer has to be highly sensitive and mentally alert to everything the customer says and does. He said this was the final meeting between the closer and customer and one of the two opponents had to lose. The closer has to use all of the information he has learned about the customer at this time and has to utilize all of his "closing" knowledge to win the final battle (get the sale). The closer has to use the customer's emotions and every little advantage he can think of to overcome and persuade the customer to buy the product. The customer will try to outwit, lie and dodge the closer's attempt to get the sale, but it's still the closer's responsibility to get the job done and "close." The customer will be a faithful and worthy opponent for the closer, but the closer is the professional. He'll win.

Before seeing how the closer handles the customer's objections and then conquers them, making a sale, there are six important "closing" facts that have to be reviewed. These facts will show how the closer looks at the customer's objections, and decides how to handle them. They will show what a closer must know about customers' objections if he expects to "close" every customer he talks to.

CLOSING FACT 1: The closer has to pin down the customer with the customer's own ammunition when it becomes time to "close." In other words, the closer has to trap the customer with his own words. The customer has been telling on himself all during the sales presentation (stories about his family, his business and his personal interests) and the closer shouldn't have forgotten a thing. When it becomes time to close the customer, the closer should, if necessary, bring up an aforementioned family fact or design a story around the customer's personal interest that would "spear" the customer right through one of his emotional weak points.

CLOSING FACT 2: The closer has to realize that when the customer says "No" to a buying question, it only means that he is not *yet* sold on the product. He still has questions. It's true that the lack of money could be the real factor (condition), but if it's not, there is no reason for the closer not to sell the customer. The closer should never take "No" as the final answer, unless he wants to for some lazy reason. (Note: A "No" answer usually means that the customer doesn't believe the closer's story.)

Note: There is *no* certain time or set place in the sales presentation to actually close the customer. The Master Closer is continually (from the first second he says "Hello" to his customer, until the sale is made) going after the sale with every question and statement he can think of. The Master Closer knows that every single "Yes" or positive response he gets from his customer is a step that much closer to getting the sale consummated.

CLOSING FACT 3: When the customer is asking a simple and obviously silly question, the closer, instead of getting frustrated with the customer, should turn around and ask the customer (nicely) what he would do or how he would answer that question. By making the customer answer his own question, the customer will be able to most likely solve it. This way the closer not only keeps control, but he can flatter the customer and say to him after he answers, "Mr. Customer, that is exactly what we are going to do," or "Mr. Customer, my company feels exactly the same way." (Note: If the closer slaps the customer with one hand, he had better be shaking hands with the other. The closer has to keep the customer in perfect balance all during the "closing process.")

CLOSING FACT 4: The closer must remember that more often than not he is the one who has to make the buying decision for the customer. The closer has to take the lead and proceed to write up the contract. If the customer doesn't stop him, then the closer has a sale. (Note: This will be illustrated later in this lesson.)

CLOSING FACT 5: The closer should know that when the customer says he has to "think about it," he is simply not sold on the product yet. The closer should realize the excuse "I have to think about it," is not a true objection which the closer must overcome, but rather a bunch of words that don't add up to anything in particular. The closer needs a solid objection he can wrestle with and conquer. The excuse "I have to mull it over," isn't that kind of objection. (Note: The "I have to think it over" problem will be explained and solved in detail in Chapter Nine.)

CLOSING FACT 6: The closer, if he feels he has to, could use the power of embarrassment to get the customer "closed." If the customer feels embarrassed badly enough, he will do about anything to get out of that situation, including signing a contract.

To embarrass the customer the closer could use his family as leverage against him along with intimidation. For example: "Mr. Customer, do you mean to tell me, right here in front of your own children, that you don't even make enough money to put some aside for their future education? What in the world are you working for anyway? You can't go on from pay check to pay check, always worrying about tomorrow — that's not fair for you or your family. At least in my product you will have an investment, something saved for the future. That's what you should be striving for, so why don't you look at things realistically and give my product a try?"

The Three Customer Responses

Sam told me that when the closer asks the customer to give his product a try, there are only three basic responses the customer could give. The "first response" is to answer the closer's buying question with a positive "I'm sold on the product" answer. For example, the customer will say, "All right, I'll take it" or "I'll give it a try," or "Well, I like it — you've got yourself a deal." This type of customer is sold on the product, says he'll purchase it when the closer asks him to buy the very first time.

The second kind of response the customer could give would be an objective "nearly sold" response. For example: The customer will say "I'm not sure, that sounds like too much money you're asking for the product. I just don't know. I like the product, but I still have some looking around to do first," or "I'll tell you what: Let me sleep on it and I'll let you know later." This kind of customer will put up some good objections, but he can be "closed" without too much difficulty.

The third kind of response the customer could give would be a flat negative "No, I'm not sold." For example: The customer will tell the closer "No, I don't think so, I'm going to pass on it. I don't want it, you are just wasting your time," or "It's not for me. No, I don't need it." This customer will not only put up strong objections, but in reality he is simply not yet sold on the product in his own mind. This customer's response is the hardest one of all three customer responses to conquer and "close." The closer has his work cut out for him when it comes to this kind of negative response.

To see how the closer deals with each of these three customer responses and eventually "closes" all of them, Sam said I should study each response separately.

The First "I'm Sold" Response: plus
The Closer's "Precise Steps" for Writing Up the Order

When the closer asks his customer to "give his product a try" the very first time, the customers (husband and wife team) will usually look at each other and one of them will say something like, "I think it's a pretty good deal, do you want to give it a try?" When the other customer team member agrees, the closer has a sale. (Note: This type of customer will have a couple of last minute questions or one or two light objections, but he is really sold on the product. The questions or objections won't mean much and can easily be conquered by the closer. All the closer has to do is keep a positive attitude and answer the customer, then start writing the sale up.)

The customer could also simply say, "I like it — I'll take it." When the closer gets this kind of positive response from the customer, the closer should above all keep his professional composure and not act too excited or overjoyed. (Step One.)

STEP ONE: If the closer does show too much enthusiasm when the customer says he will buy the product, that kind of overreaction could very easily scare the customer and possibly kill the sale. The customer might think to himself, "Gosh, if the closer is this thrilled that I'm buying his product then maybe I'm the only person in a long time that has bought. It could be I'm the only sucker around. There might be something wrong with this product I don't know about. I think I'd better reconsider before I sign anything." The closer has to realize that showing too much excitement and overreacting when the customer says he will try it, is just as dangerous to a sale as a closer who gives a dull and unenthusiastic sales presentation.

STEP TWO: The second thing the closer should do immediately after he hears the customer say he will buy the product is to look the customer straight in the eye, and with a genuinely happy "Thank you" smile on his face, give the customer a firm and receptive handshake. (Note: If the closer is working with a husband and wife customer team, it is perfectly all right for the closer to shake the woman's hand also. This little maneuver helps make the wife feel more involved in the buying decision. FACT.) The closer has to again remember not to get carried away with excitement when he shakes hands, but to stay calm and professional. When the closer is shaking hands (congratulating the customer for making the right decision to buy) with the customer, he should say something like "Welcome aboard," "Welcome to the club," "Congratulations, we're glad to have you," or a simple "Thank you." (Note: The reason the closer has to immediately shake the customer's hand after he says he will buy is because that handshake will act as a "locking in" measure for the closer. In other words, the customer will immediately feel both personally and morally obligated to buy, because of the "a man's word is his bond" handshake. The handshake has just about as much power in it as the actual act of having the customer sign his name on the contract. FACT. The customer, by shaking the closer's hand right after saying he will purchase the product, will be far less tempted to back off, cool off or change his mind during the "delicate time period" it takes for the closer to do the paperwork.)

STEP THREE: The third thing the closer has to do is to stop talking about the product and start writing up the order. After he shakes the customer's hand the closer has to change subjects (as tactfully as possible) and get away from talking about the product anymore. The closer should ask about the customer's job, his home town, his hobbies, anything, as long as it's not about the product. *Unless* the customer deliberately asks a specific question the closer cannot avoid.

If the closer has to answer a customer's question, he should do it calmly and simply, then go right back to asking the customer questions about his personal life, or whatever. The closer has to do the best he can to keep the customer's mind off of the paperwork so he won't start getting cold feet. When the closer answers a customer's question he should think first and make sure the question isn't one that is a trick or trap and get himself "boxed in." For example: The customer will try to trap the closer by asking a question the closer has already answered, just to make sure he gives the same answer.

The reason for the change of subject (from the product to something else) is to first get the customer's thoughts away from the sales transaction. This way the customer won't be tempted to second-guess his buying decision. The second reason is so the closer won't go right on talking about the product and accidentally bring up a point the customer didn't happen to think about, or a point of interest the customer doesn't like about the product. By continuing to talk about

---

Note: There is *no* certain time or set place in the sales presentation to actually close the customer. The Master Closer is continually (from the first second he says "Hello" to his customer, until the sale is made) going after the sale with every question and statement he can think of. The Master Closer knows that every single "Yes" or positive response he gets from his customer is a step that much closer to getting the sale consummated.

the product the closer could easily create unwanted and unneeded problems, thus possibly killing a sale, even after the customer has said he will buy. For example: The closer could say this: "Congratulations, Mr. Customer, welcome aboard. Do you know that the property you got is only one block away from a brand new grade school?" The customer might say, "School? I didn't know there was a school so close. I don't like kids running up and down the sidewalk screaming and hollering all the time. I like peace and quiet. If that's the case then that property is not for me." The closer has to be on his toes all the time at this point in the closing process and keep the customer happy, relaxed, calm and comfortable, so the working paper or financial statement can be filled out and the contract signed in a smooth and uncomplicated manner.

STEP FOUR: The fourth thing the closer has to do is calmly and in a professional manner start filling out the working paper (order slip, sales slip, contract, agreement, etc.). This is a very delicate and sometimes frustrating time, not only for the closer but also for the customer, because the paperwork process is usually very routine and dull exercise, compared to the overall sales presentation and the "close." The closer has to make the paperwork and "check getting" as compatible and positively enthusiastic as possible (without going overboard) with the rest of the sales presentation.

There shouldn't ever be a big noticeable difference or change of pace in the closer's tempo or timing from his sales presentation into his "check getting" and working paper process. The reason being that if the closer does go sporadically from a crisp enthusiastic and sharp presentation to a slow and humdrum paperworking process the change of pace will only tend to make the overall sales presentation seem disorganized and confusing to the customer. And the confusion could very possibly kill the sale. FACT.

The closer (if he is filling out the work order) should make the paper work as simple and understandable as possible for the customer. If the closer is asking the customer questions — for instance his full name, how he wants it on the contract, or his correct home address and so forth — he should make the "question-asking process" into a casual conversation. For example: The closer could say, "Mr. Customer, now you said earlier that you lived on North Palm Avenue. Isn't that close to a new hospital that's being built?" or "Mr. Customer, you have the same middle name that my dad has, you know that isn't a very common name. Is it an old family name?" This kind of "casual conversation" on the closer's part (while the closer is actually filling out the order sheet) will have a definite calming effect on the customer and tend to make the "time span" (period of time it takes to fill out all of the paperwork) go by faster, and will also make the customer feel more comfortable and relaxed with the closer. The customer and closer are now sharing personal stories and getting to be basically better acquainted, so the two opponents can now relax a little, due to the fact that the buying decision has been made (the pressure is off) and the closer and customer can talk as friends rather than opponents.

GETTING THE CUSTOMER'S CHECK: After and *only* after the paperwork is filled out, the first working paper and not the final contract, the closer should ask the customer, in a very normal, unconcerned way, "Mr. Customer, just make the check out to my company." The closer doesn't even have to see the customer's check book, all he has to do is make a simple, unassuming, positive statement while fiddling with the paperwork, a pen or something unrelated to money on the closing table. This unconcerned attitude will make the customer feel the closer doesn't just want his money, and that's all. The customer will immediately feel some hostility toward the closer if he asks for the check right after the customer says he will buy the product. The closer has to first fill out the working paper and (if it's the case or if it's possible) have the customer sign it before he signs the check or the final contract. The reason for this is that the customer will subconsciously feel, even though the order sheet is not the real contract, that by signing the order sheet, he has actually signed the contract. Then when it becomes time for the real contract to be reviewed and signed, that exercise won't scare or concern the customer.

When the customer has signed the order sheet and the closer casually asks for the customer's check and gets it in his hands, he has to tactfully hide the check within a few seconds. The reason is that the statement, "Out of sight, out of mind," is true in this situation. If the closer doesn't hide the customer's check (putting it under some paperwork or in his pocket, unnoticed) the customer would be sitting there at the closing table just after making a buying decision, looking at his own personal check on the table. That kind of "check exposure" is very tempting for the customer to change his mind. The customer might have last second "buyer's remorse" thoughts and simply reach over and grab his check and tear it up right in front of the closer and everybody. Then, boom — a sale is killed. If the check is hidden and out of sight then that can't possibly happen. The closer has to handle the hidden check trick with calm and tactful professionalism. Above all, the closer has to act like the check or its amount is not a big deal, but just an ordinary, everyday business transaction, that the closer is genuinely thankful for.

The closer should ask the customer, after he has the check (money) and the paperwork is filled out and turned in to the sales office for processing, if he wants some refreshment or coffee, etc., anything the closer can think of that will keep the customer in a relaxed, positive and receptive mood. The time it takes for the paperwork to be finished and the contract or agreement to be finally signed is very critical. The closer has to keep the customer's mind not only on other topics of conversation besides the product, but he has to make "casual conversation" light, agreeable and acceptable for the customer.

The closer has to keep the customer's spirits up so he won't start thinking negatively or backing out mentally on the sale, before he has even signed the final contract. (Note: If the closer is in a sales situation where he doesn't have to wait for any type of paperwork to be processed or have the customer fill out a financial statement, he can simply get the order along with the customer's check and politely shake hands with the customer, thanking him and part company. This type of sales procedure will be discussed later in this chapter.)

When the contract is finally typed up and ready for the customer to sign, the closer should sit down "comfortably close" to the customer (creating that "oneness" effect) and hold the contract himself so everyone involved in the sale can easily read and see it. (Note: When the closer holds the contract himself, he is still maintaining his control over the customer; at this point in the sales presentation, that control is very, very important because the closer doesn't have the customer's signature on the contract yet. The closer has to realize that the "closing process" isn't quite over until all the papers and contracts are signed, sealed and delivered. FACT).

Then the closer should go over the contract in a simple, precise manner, and with his pen as a pointer, point out only the important facts (the "high notes") in the contract. The closer should never read or explain every single word in the contract, because not only will the customer usually not understand the contract's language but the customer will tend to get bored and frustrated. (Note: The customer will be thinking to himself, "Boy, is this contract signing going to take all day?") The closer has to make the "contract reviewing process" look crisp and uncomplicated, like an ordinary everyday exercise.

The best way for the closer to develop this easy-going attitude, so the customer won't be thinking of the contract signing as a "life or death" operation, is to speak distinctly, calmly with control and self-assuredness. The closer has to talk softer and somewhat quieter than his normal voice with a pleasant but serious delivery.

If the closer is nervous or excited (which is normal) and his hand is shaking, he should rest his hand on the closing table while holding the contract. The table will act as a brace so the closer won't be shaking the contract around and getting the customer nervous too.

When the closer has gone over the contract with the customer and the customer understands it or seems to, then the closer (if he has to sign the contract too, along with the customer) should take his pen and *first*, before the customer signs, sign his own name on the contract, while simultaneously saying "Mr. Customer, now my name goes right here." When the closer has signed his name he should immediately without pausing for a breath turn the contract over to the customer and say, "Mr. Customer, I need your name right here with mine."

There is an "old pro's saying" that states a closer should never ask for the customer's signature (John Hancock or John Henry), but instead say something like "Mr. Customer, I need your initials right here," or "Mr. Customer, will you approve this," or Mr. Customer, I need your okay right here." This "old pro's saying" is all right to use and is correct, especially when it states not to use the John Hancock or John Henry method of asking for the customer's signature. But the closer can, if he does it with class, ask the customer for his signature in this fashion: "Mr. Customer, I'll need your signature right here," or "Mr. Customer, I need your name right here." When the closer asks the customer for his signature on the contract in this manner, the customer knows the contract and the closer are serious. The customer, if the closer asks him politely, won't be offended when he hears the word "name" or "signature." The closer can use this method all day long and have better results than he would if he asked the customer for his "okay" or "approval." The reason is that the customer isn't as stupid as many closers think, and when a closer asks for his "initials" or "approval" that kind of "asking" sounds like it came right out of rookie sales book. FACT.

The closer can get just as good or better results by asking for the customer's "name" or "signature" if the closer asks in a calm, polite and professional way. It has to be understood that when the closer says to the customer, "I need your name right here with mine," and when the closer signs his name first, these two maneuvers make the closer and customer more of a team, a unified body. This can and does strengthen the total closer-customer relationship. By signing the contract first, the closer has shown the customer there is nothing to be afraid of, plus it makes the customer feel he is not alone in his buying decision.

After the contract is signed the closer should again shake hands with the customer and sincerely thank him. (Note: The final process of saying goodbye, plus giving the paperwork to the customer, will be discussed later in this chapter.)

ATTENTION: If the closer has a customer who wants to physically hold the contract and read every word of it for himself, the closer should let him — that is, to a degree. (Note: In the first place, most customers can't understand a contract, and secondly, they are just trying to act the role of an intelligent buyer, either for the closer's benefit or for some other person in the customer's party.) For example: The closer, after he has handed the contract to the customer, keeps right on talking to one of the other members in the customer's team about his home town, his hobbies or any kind of light conversation. This talking will tend to interrupt and distract the customer who is doing the reading; it won't take much time for the customer to get frustrated and ask the closer where to sign the contract.

This little trick works 99 percent of the time because the customer usually won't understand what he is reading and the closer's constant, polite, and tactful conversation will irritate the customer's subconscious so much he will think to himself, "What the heck, where do I sign?" and then the closer can get his hands back on the contract again. Thus the customer will be more satisfied because he at least looked at the whole contract for a few minutes. He didn't lose face in front of the closer, his family or his friends.

The closer has to keep in mind that the first "I'm sold" response customer is the easiest of the three response customers to sell. This customer has been positively programmed all the way through the total sales presentation by the closer, so when it becomes time for the closer to ask this customer to give the product a try, the customer will do just that and buy the product.

Sam said the second "I'm nearly sold" response customer wasn't anything like the first response customer. He told me the closer has to start earning his keep with this next customer.

The Second "I'm Nearly Sold" Response

This customer isn't quite sold on the product, *yet*. He needs more convincing, more persuasion, from the closer before he is ready to buy. This customer isn't negative in his thinking toward the product, but he sure isn't positive. The closer has given this type of customer a good, solid, understandable and professional sales presentation up to this point, but when asked to buy the product the customer is hesitant and puts up objections left and right. (Note: The closer has to remember the main reason customers don't buy when they basically want to and really like the product, is the lack of money.)

The closer has done his job so far; all he has to do is "close" this customer. The closer has found the right opportunity to ask this customer to give his product a try and now the customer just sits there at the closing table and makes statements like, "I don't know if I'll ever use your product," or "I have to think about it." The closer — and it is a fact — can "close" this wishy-washy customer if he just has tenacity, while logically, emotionally and convincingly pointing out to the customer how he can have his cake and eat it too (own the product with the least amount of money involved from the customer's pocket). This customer will buy every time if he genuinely feels satisfied in his own mind that the product is advantageous for him and his family, and that he can afford to purchase it. (Note: This customer usually doesn't have the guts to make a buying decision on his own. He needs the power of the closer's positive forcefulness to direct him toward the sale and help him make up his undecided mind.) All the closer has to do is convince this customer that these two buying factors (benefits plus affordability) are of no consequence (show the customer these two factors aren't life or death problems) and that he can make a sound buying decision (with a little help from the closer).

To convince this type of customer that the product is good for him the closer has to repeat (summarize) some of the product facts not only to make sure that the customer understands them but to make sure the customer didn't miss any important product information during the earlier part of the sales presentation — some information that could very possibly sway the customer closer to buying. The closer has to also work on this customer's ego and tell him how important he is to the world and his family. The closer has to build this type of customer up so he will have the strength and self-confidence to make a positive buying decision. This customer wants to be better off than he is presently and wants more for his family. The closer just has to make this customer see how, by owning the product, he can achieve his goals in life a little sooner and a little better than if he didn't own the product at all. The closer has to use a lot of emotional "closing" techniques when he is dealing with this kind of response customer if he intends to get a sale. (Note: The closer has to be persistent and at times politely forceful with this type of customer.)

Customers' objections and the closers' responses will be studied in detail in Chapter Ten. To show how the closer "closes" this second "I'm nearly sold" response customer and consistently asks him to give the product a try, it's a good idea to look at some closer vs. customer conversations and statements. (Note: The closer, after he conquers an objection, should again ask the customer for the order, and again shut up and wait for the customer to answer.)

ATTENTION: Sam said the best way to show how a closer "closes" this type of customer is to look at some of the closer's responses to the customer's objections. The responses shown will give the reader an idea of how to handle this customer and "close" him. (Note: When the closer delivers these responses he is dead serious.)

Note: There is *no* certain time or set place in the sales presentation to actually close the customer. The Master Closer is continually (from the first second he says "Hello" to his customer, until the sale is made) going after the sale with every question and statement he can think of. The Master Closer knows that every single "Yes" or positive response he gets from his customer is a step that much closer to getting the sale consummated.

SETTING THE STAGE: The closer has asked this customer to give his product a try and now, with both opponents (closer and customer) sitting at the closing table, the customer is throwing out objections and telling the closer why he shouldn't buy. (Note: This customer in this illustration could afford to purchase the product if he really wanted to.) The customer looks at the closer sheepishly after he hears the closer ask him to give his product a try and (feeling the closer's pressure of "dead silence") the customer answers with a statement similar to this: "Mr. Closer, I don't really know. I'm just not sure it would be in my best interest to own your product." Now it is time for the closer to go to work on "closing" him.

The Closer's Responses

(With the customer's family present, if possible)

1. "Mr. Customer, you've seen my product and you know it is good, plus you know that you can afford it if you want to. Now let's be honest with ourselves. You've spent all your life working for your family's future, and I mean working hard; it shows — you're a good provider. But don't you think it's about time to give yourself the things you've always wanted? What are you living for if you can't enjoy life? You work to make money, don't you? So why not invest your money to make more money; plus, you can enjoy my product at the same time. Doesn't that make sense? Why don't you give it a try?"

2. "Mr. Customer, right now you have the opportunity to purchase my product at the lowest price possible due to our close-out sale. You'll never have a chance like this again, and that's a fact. All I want you to do is save some of your money and give my product a try. I know you like it — how about giving it a try?"

3. "Mr. Customer, did you know there are only four ways a person can really make serious money? The first way is to earn it, work for it, and you know in today's economy that is practically impossible. The second way is to inherit it from a rich relative, and how many times does that happen? The third way to make money is to steal it, but sooner or later you'll get caught and have to go to jail and that sure wouldn't be worth it. And then there is the fourth and final way to make money, and that is to invest in something. Mr. Customer, believe it or not, my product is just that kind of solid investment, and that's a fact. You know it and I know it, so why don't you give it a try?"

4. "Mr. Customer, if you don't want to buy the product for yourself, at least get it for your wife and children. They depend on you for their future, their lives are literally in your hands, just as my family depends on me. Why don't you give it a try, at least for them?"

5. "Mr. Customer, talking to you man to man, you know that sometime in every man's life he has to make a decision about his future, his goals. He has to take up the challenge himself. Mr. Customer, don't — like so many people who fail — run away from the opportunity to have something, accomplish something, make a decision. This product is exactly what you need and deep down you know it, so why don't you give it a try?"

The second-response customer can be sold if the closer uses emotional and hard-hitting responses on him, over and over again, continually conquering every objection. After every single customer objection is overcome, the closer has to ask the customer to give his product a try. Then shut up and wait for the customer's response. This customer, if he has the money and understands the benefits of the product, cannot take emotional pressure from the closer. This customer will eventually back down and surrender — he will purchase the product. If this customer doesn't really have the financial ability to buy the product, then the closer, by using pressure plus emotions, can find this true and factual condition and go from there to try to get the sale by saying something like (in a soft and sincere voice) "Mr. Customer, what we are really talking about here is money, isn't it? Let me ask you this: Do the monthly payments fit into your budget?" If the customer answers in the affirmative, the closer should keep "closing" as explained earlier. But if the customer says, "No, I can't afford the monthly payments," the closer can do one of two things: Either let the customer go, or try to "close" him harder from another angle — a new game plan. The closer can "close" any customer if he gets him emotionally and sincerely involved enough in the product. FACT. (Note: It can't be stated enough that the only reason a customer won't buy the product, if he is really sold on it, is because of the lack of money.)

ATTENTION: After the closer has "closed" and gotten this second-response customer to say he will buy the product, the closer should follow the same "follow-up steps" that were described in the first-response customer's illustration.

The Third "I'm Not Sold" Response

This customer is the hardest of all three types of customers to "close." FACT. This customer isn't sold on the product, or he isn't sold on the closer. Either way this customer tells the closer he's not interested and won't buy the product. The closer has to realize that this customer, like all other customers, has to be programmed to buy the product from the very first phase of the total sales presentation. If a customer is not sold during the overall sales presentation it is the closer's responsibility to put on the pressure at the closing table and use all his tricks, traps and ammunition to get the sale ("close").

The closer has to not only use reverse psychology, but intimidation and plenty of positive (and determined) force. This "I'm not sold" customer will put up a grand and resourceful argument with the closer. This battle of wits can go on for thirty minutes or five hours. It all depends on which opponent (closer or customer) gives up first and loses. (NOTE: By using the word "lose" it is not to be interpreted that the customer, by purchasing the closer's product, got a bad deal. Instead, the closer either overcomes and conquers the customer's objections and gets a sale or the closer goes without a sale and loses. The closer has to remember not to get angry with his customer or make him angry. The closer can use all the tactful pressure he needs to get the customer "closed." But if he upsets the customer too much, then no matter how powerful the closer is, he could very easily kill a sale.)

(NOTE: The closer has to remember that if a product isn't beneficial to the customer he shouldn't in any way try to pressure the customer into buying, much less sell the product himself. In the long run it doesn't pay off, either for the customer or the closer.)

When this type of third response customer says he isn't sold on the product, that could only mean one of four basic things: The customer doesn't like the product; he doesn't believe the closer; he doesn't have the money to buy the product; or there is some unknown problem, objection or condition that only the customer knows about that keeps him from purchasing. The closer has to discover the real objection and then go in for a serious "closing" effort. The closer can find out this information by asking questions, picking up on nonchalant statements that the customer has made throughout the sales presentation, and by listening to the customer's children and friends. Much information can be gained by reading between the lines. If the closer does all these things, he can put together an overall picture of the customer and use everything he's got to go in for the "close."

This customer can be closed if the closer knows his product inside and out, and if the closer has the guts and self-confidence to stand up to his customer and fight for what he believes in (his product). The closer has to show enthusiasm, and always a positive attitude. The closer can't let this type of customer get him down and make him feel intimidated or ashamed of his product. The closer has to show class, be polite and not get nervous or lose control during this confrontation with the customer. Above all other things, this customer will fall, he will purchase, no matter how tough he is, if the closer shows genuine interest and respect for him. It doesn't matter how hardened this customer is, he cannot take kindness and true sincerity from a closer over too long a period of time. The customer will start to "melt" and will let his defensive shield down. (NOTE: A customer like this usually isn't accustomed to someone being nice to him, so when the closer keeps acting polite that tends to put this customer off balance.) When the closer senses this "relaxing of the defenses" on the part of the customer, the closer can tactfully and vigorously go in for the kill (close). Slowly the customer will give in and buy the product. But the closer has to be prepared for a hard and sometimes long and drawn-out fight.

To illustrate how the closer handles this kind of customer with emotions, reverse psychology, and intimidation, Sam said the best thing to do was to study examples of what the closer says to the customer.

For example: After the closer has asked him to give a product a try, the customer might say something like this, "Mr. Closer, I'm not really interested. I just came out here to see what you have and I can see it's not for me." The closer again goes to work, and part of that work is to "hit" the customer's "hot button" to get him activated and start him thinking about the product in a positive manner. NOTE: The closer has to remember that when he listens to a customer objection, he first has to completely hear the customer out and then and only then give a serious and conquering response. When the closer is talking to the customer he has to look him straight in the eye and have a positive, confident expression on his face. There isn't a person anywhere in the world who hasn't at one time or another purchased a product from a closer. The closer has to acknowledge this and visualize himself getting the sale and knowing it is worth the effort he put into selling it, if he expects to show the customer the genuine and sincere enthusiasm that he, the closer, should be radiating.

The Closer's Responses
(With the customer's family present, if possible)

1. "You know, Mr. Customer, that some people are dreamers, some are lookers, and there are others who are doers. Mr. Customer, you and I might not be able to change the world, but I can guarantee you that we can change ourselves and help our families. I have already bought this product and my family is enjoying it right now. Why don't you do the same for your family and give my product a try?"

2. "Mr. Customer, let me ask you a very candid question. If I just turned around and gave you my product free, would you take it? Now tell me the truth." If the customer answers in the affirmative then the closer should realize that "money" (affordability) is the key to the solution. On the other hand, if the customer answers the closer's question with a negative response, for instance, "No, I still wouldn't take it," then the closer should look slightly surprised and ask, "Why?" The customer will either give the closer an answer that the closer can work with to "close," or the customer will start acting kind of silly (nervous laugh) and not really answer the closer. The reason for this customer behaviour is because the closer caught the customer off guard. The customer doesn't have a ready answer. The closer should again ask the customer, "Why?" until the customer finally answers. Then the closer can go ahead and proceed to "close" the customer's objection by asking him to give the product a try.

3. "Mr. Customer, you and I won't live forever. Someday we are going to die. Tell me what is going to happen to your family five or ten years after you're gone. Mr. Customer, hindsight is twenty-twenty, but foresight is different. It only takes a little planning, a little thought, and the future will be secure and comfortable for you and your family, without looking backwards to the past all of the time. Why don't you give it a try?"

4. "Mr. Customer, you know the sad thing in my profession is that no matter how good a product I have or how much I explain about all of the product's benefits, some people try to make the buying decision harder and more complicated than it really is. Please, Mr. Customer, don't make the same mistake. If you can afford my product, if the payment fits into your budget, then give it a try."

5. "Mr. Customer, you get exactly what you pay for. If the product is of good quality — like my product — then that's exactly what you get for your money. Remember, it is up to you, Mr. Customer. You have to live with and put your confidence into the product that you buy. Doesn't it make sense to purchase quality? Why don't you give it a try?"

6. "Mr. Customer, do you want a guarantee? All right, I will give you one. I can guarantee you that my product will make you money, if you can guarantee me that you will be around (alive) to collect it. I'll put that guarantee in writing if you like. Now, let's be realistic — why don't you give my product a try?"

The closer can "close" this customer if he just keeps after him and doesn't listen to his first five "No" responses to the closer's buying questions. (NOTE: The first five objections usually don't mean much, so the closer shouldn't let them get him down.) This customer is a *pushover* if he *likes the closer and believes him.* (NOTE: When the closer has used a lot of pressure on this customer and finally "closes" him, the closer should apologize to the customer in a friendly manner and say something like: "Mr. Customer, believe me, if my product wasn't as good as I've told you, I wouldn't have tried as hard to get you and your family involved. So I apologize if I said anything wrong. I'm happy to have you as a new owner and I know you will be an asset to our company." The reason the closer has to apologize to the customer — that is, if he feels he needs to due to the use of excess pressure — is because after the customer signs the contract and goes home he will start thinking about how he was treated (pressured) and could very easily cancel the contract. The closer has to always protect his interest and his sales presentation.)

After the closer has "closed" the third-response customer by repeatedly conquering and overcoming his objections, plus making this customer like him, the closer should go ahead and follow the very same "follow-up steps" described in the first-response customer's illustration. The closer should remember what Sam said, "You can attract more sales with honey than with vinegar, no matter how troublesome the customer is." (Silly but very TRUE.)

Sam said the closer has to keep in mind that when he's dealing with all three different types of customer responses, each type of customer will nearly always give objections but they will each in their own way be either "so close" to, or "so far" away from, purchasing. In all three cases the closer has to stick to the basics, use different degrees of pressure and constantly "close" throughout the entire sales presentation. When the closer has to close on the tail end of the presentation, at the closing table, then he'd better know what he is doing and know his product. If the closer can win the confidence of the customer, bingo, he's got a sale.

"Little" Closing Tricks to Know

A. When the customer says he will try it (buy the product), then no matter where the closer is located he should as quickly and calmly as possible get the customer to sign a working paper, an agreement, (not a check or partial down payment) anything that obligates and commits the customer (physically and in writing). This way the customer will be less likely to back out of his verbal agreement to purchase the product.

B. When a customer leaves the sales office and the closer somehow didn't "close" him, the closer should (if possible) give the "missed customer" some kind of brochure or literature. This way any new customer the closer hasn't talked to yet will see this "missed customer" leave with some paperwork. Thus when the closer gets with the new customer he can tell him or make him think the previous "missed customer" bought. The new customer will automatically feel a little more curious and relaxed (knowing someone else thinks the product is good) toward the closer's product.

C. The closer should (if he can) carry on his person five one-hundred-dollar bills. The reason for this is when the closer is explaining money or investments to a customer during the sales presentation he can take out the five hundred dollars and thus better illustrate just how much money he is talking about. This "flashing" of money trick will get the attention of the customer and will bring home the closer's point. The closer can physically show the customer how much money he would either save or lose (depending on the sales pitch) by not buying the product immediately.

D. The closer can make this nonchalant statement just about any place in the sale presentation and it will get the customer thinking: "Mr. Customer, some folks will buy this product and some won't and the only real difference between the two folks is money. But that's a personal matter, everyone knows their personal business better than anyone else, right?" The customer will automatically, without thinking say, "Right." Now the closer has planted a "thought seed" for the customer to meditate on.

NOTE: If a closer needs help in "closing" a customer he shouldn't be so foolish as not to ask another closer for help. Between the two closers a sale can be made. It's part of the business.

Note: There is *no* certain time or set place in the sales presentation to actually close the customer. The Master Closer is continually (from the first second he says "Hello" to his customer, until the sale is made) going after the sale with every question and statement he can think of. The Master Closer knows that every single "Yes" or positive response he gets from his customer is a step that much closer to getting the sale consummated.

"Button-Up" Information
(The closer wraps the "closing process" up)

Sam told me it was time to see how the closer finishes up a sale (buttons it up). He told me a closer has to treat the customer with just as much respect, courtesy and enthusiasm *after* the sale is made as he did when he first met the customer. The customer needs all the friendship and assurance the closer can provide after the sale, so he (the customer) won't get cold feet or feel as though he made a bad decision by purchasing the product. The closer's responsibility when buttoning up a sale is to keep the customer not only happy but calm and confident, thus helping him know he has made an intelligent and productive decision for himself and his family.

Sam explained that it would be a good idea if I remembered three "Button-Up" suggestions that demonstrate how the closer wraps up the "closing process" and bids the customer (the owner of the product) a pleasant good day.

A. The closer has to remember that after he has sold (closed) the customer, he has to bring the customer back down to earth, calm him down. The reason is that everyone (closer and customer) secretly inside are excited and enthused. The closer has to be the "settling-down" force for this kind of sales "close" situation. This calming down of the customer can be accomplished by the closer if he changes subjects (away from the product) and has a simple enjoyable conversation with the customer.

B. When the closer "closes" the customer and the contract is signed (everything is finished), the closer should say "goodbye" to the customer not only with a simple "Thank you" but with a "double handshake" to make sure the customer feels appreciated. (Note: The "double handshake" is when the closer takes both of his hands and shakes the one hand of the new customer (without going overboard) welcoming him "to the club." This type of appreciation on the closer's part will make the customer feel more welcome and wanted.

C. If at all possible, the closer should walk the customer to his car after he has sold him. The reason for this is that the time and effort it takes to accompany the customer will make him feel that the closer didn't just want to get the sale and then get rid of him. In other words, the customer will feel the closer appreciates his business more if he takes that extra minute of time to see him to his car and safely on his way home. FACT.

PART III

The "Master Closer's Deadly Rules of Closing"

1. MAKE THE CUSTOMER LOVE YOU

2. ASK THE CUSTOMER QUESTIONS ABOUT HIMSELF

3. STAY CLOSE TO THE CUSTOMER (Create Unity)

4. TELL THE CUSTOMER A SECRET ABOUT THE PRODUCT (Make him think he knows something special about the product that other customers don't know)

5. EARN THE CUSTOMER'S RESPECT BY SHOWING CLASS

6. REFUSE TO ACCEPT "NO"

7. CARE ABOUT THE CUSTOMER'S NEEDS

8. LISTEN TO THE CUSTOMER

9. OBSERVE EVERYTHING ABOUT THE CUSTOMER

10. SHOW THE CUSTOMER YOU CARE AND APPRECIATE HIM

11. EMOTIONS ARE THE KEY TO "CLOSING"

12. REMEMBER TO THANK THE CUSTOMER FOR THE SALE

Important "Closing Notes" to Remember

1. The closer has to be aware of how (in what manner, frame of mind) the customer answers his buying questions. For instance, the customer could say he's not interested in the product either seriously or jokingly. The closer has to pay attention so he will know the customer's true attitudes when the customer responds to the closer's questions. If the closer doesn't "read" the customer's answers and attitudes correctly he could easily misjudge the situation, and this could lead to a missed sale.

2. The closer should never, never beg the customer for a sale. Not only will the closer fail to get the sale (because the customer won't respect that type of desperate sales approach), but he will wind up not liking himself or his style very much.

3. The closer should remember that when he thinks he has lost the sale (has that kind of negative attitude), then in most cases he has.

4. A closer can know all of the tricks and "closes" in the world and still miss a sale. If the closer doesn't "close" continually throughout the total sales presentation and keep every sales step in its respective order, flowing towards a final goal (the last "closing" question), then the customer will become confused and disoriented, and the sale will be lost. The closer has to keep every sales step in its proper order and not leave out any phase of the overall sales presentation. If he does forget something it is just like a car without wheels — it won't work.

5. The closer has to develop a degree of tolerance for the customer's problems and views if he ever expects to be the best.

6. The closer has to learn that if he disagrees with the customer he shouldn't be disagreeable.

7. The closer has to remember to always take the time to listen to the customer, because sooner or later they will tell everything about themselves.

8. The closer's sales presentation means nothing unless he gets the customer's signature on a contract and a check. FACT.

9. If the closer honors the customer with sincerity and genuine appreciation, the customer will buy the closer's product.

10. If a closer makes the customer's mediocre job look important and responsible, and shows a sincere interest in that job, the customer wil be like putty in the closer's hand.

Sam said this finished my lesson on "closing." He told me a closer above all other things has to love his profession and his customers first, if he wants to be the best. There simply is no other way.

NOTES

Chapter Nine

THE CLOSERS

THE TWENTY GREATEST "CLOSES" ON EARTH

Chapter 9

THE CLOSER

THE TWENTY GREATEST "CLOSES" ON EARTH

The Book Close

DESCRIPTION: This "close" is especially designed for this book. The closer can use this "close" with any customer, anytime he wants to, and it will get positive results. This "close" is intended to embarrass and control the customer, and it does just that.

How the Book Close is Used . . . (example)

When the customer tells the closer, "I'm going to have to talk to my brother in Chicago before I buy this product, because he's in the same kind of business you are, Mr. Closer," the closer should calmly take out this book, "THE CLOSERS," and say to the customer, "Mr. Customer, let me show you something that you've never heard of or seen before. This book that I'm holding tells me in Chapter 3, exactly what kind of attitude people like yourself, in your type of business, have. Then in Chapter 10, page 270, this book tells me exactly the objection you just stated and the book shows me how to answer your objection in three different ways. Again in this book, in Chapter 4, page 68, I can tell how you planned all along, from the first time we met, to think of and develop an objection. Mr. Customer, just think, there has even been a book written that tells all about you personally, what you're thinking and what you're going to say. Now let's be realistic: that excuse about your brother isn't real. We're really talking about finances, aren't we?" When the customer says "Yes," the closer should work the money matter (the real objection) out and then ask the customer to give his product a try.

(NOTE: When the closer uses this "close" he has to make the customer's objection look ridiculous to the customer himself, and then find out what the true objection is so he can "close" again.)

The Power of Suggestion Close

DESCRIPTION: This "close" will work if the closer plants "imagination and suggestion seeds" in the customer's mind early in the sales presentation. By doing this the closer can actually get the customer to "close" himself by using these positive thoughts. The customer will actually think at the end of the sales presentation that these "closer-planted ideas" were his originally.

How the Power of Suggestion Close is Used...(example)

When the closer is with his customer during the early stages of the sales presentation he should deliberately drop little hints and make positive suggestions concerning the customer and the product. For instance, the closer could say, "Mr. Customer, do you know that by putting my product on your home, you will have the most beautiful home on your whole block?" or "Mr. Customer, did you realize that by starting an investment plan now with my company, your children's education will be paid for when it's time for them to go to college?" or "Mr. Customer, by buying my product at this time in the off-season you will save a lot more money." After making these suggestive statements the closer has to give the customer plenty of time, so these thoughts will sink in and take hold in the customer's subconscious. When the closer thinks the timing is right (during the last stages of the sales presentation) for him to ask the customer for the order, the closer should say (1) "Mr. Customer, remember you wanted to have the best looking house on your block, something your family could really be proud of? Then why don't you give my product a try?" or (2) "Mr. Customer, remember you wanted your children to have a good education and at the same time you didn't want to worry about that financial burden when that time comes? Then why don't you give my company a try?" or (3) "Mr. Customer, remember you wanted to get the best buy for your money on my product? This is absolutely the best time to buy. Why don't you give my product a try?"

What has happened in this "close" is this: The closer, by hinting and planting suggestions early in the sales presentations, has actually activated the customer's mind early in the presentation. During the rest of the presentation the customer has been thinking and toying with these "closer-planted suggestions." When the closer finally asks for the order and brings up these suggestions again (making them sound as if they were the customer's suggestions and thoughts in the first place) the customer, because of the time span and all of the sales activity during the total sales presentation, will actually believe these ideas were his originally. The customer will usually forget the closer subtly suggested them first. So the closer can go ahead and "close" this customer, with his full and enthusiastic cooperation.

The Sharp Angle Close

DESCRIPTION: In this "close" the closer throws the customer's objection right back at him and makes him eat his own words.

How the Sharp Angle Close is Used...(example)

The customer says something like this to the closer:

1. "Mr. Closer, I want to see the lake from my property and I can't from this piece of real estate." The closer should immediately respond with, "Mr. Customer if I show you some property for the same price where you could see the lake, would you give it a try?"

2. "Mr. Closer, I don't like the color combinations on that car — I like royal blue." The closer should say, "Mr. Customer, if I can get that same automobile in royal blue, would you take it?"

3. "Mr. Closer, I don't have enough money for the down payment right now." The closer should say, "Mr. Customer would you give it a try if I made arrangements so you could comfortably handle the down payment?"

4. "Mr. Closer, I think your product is overpriced — I'm not going to pay that much money for it." The closer should say, "Mr. Customer, if I can talk to my boss and get the product's price down to where you think it's fair, would you try it?"

The Demonstration Close

DESCRIPTION: This "close" is to be used by the closer only after he has demonstrated his product to the customer. This "close" speaks for itself, and does its own "closing." All the closer has to do is set this "close" up properly, then follow it through and Bingo! The closer automatically has a sale. FACT!

How the Demonstration Close is Used...(example)

The first thing the closer has to do is set the customer up for this "close." For example: "Mr. Customer, if I could show you the prettiest view you could ever hope to find of a lake, and the price was right, would you buy it?" The customer, knowing the odds are with him in the fact that he has seen beautiful views before, will say "Yes" or "Probably." All the closer has to do is show the customer the view property (and it had better be beautiful,) make sure it fits into the customer's budget, then use an assumption attitude and start writing up the order. If the customer stops the closer from writing, the customer will most likely give the closer a real objection. All the closer has to do is overcome that objection and say to the customer, "Mr. Customer, remember you said you'd buy the property if it was exactly like I described?" The closer should again start writing up the order in a positive and assuming way.

Here are three more examples of how this "close" works:

(1) "Mr. Customer, if I proved to you beyond a shadow of a doubt that my product would make you more money than any investment you now have, would you give my company a try?"

(2) "Mr. Customer, would you give my company five dollars a day every day for a year if at the end of that period of time, my company gives you back all your original money *plus* one thousand dollars? Would you do that if I could prove it to you?"

(3) "Mr. Customer, if I could show you that this automobile has the best ride in the world plus being very economical beyond any doubt that you might have, would you buy it?"

(NOTE: The closer had better be able to back up his statements if he wants this "close" to work. PERIOD.)

The Three Devil Close

DESCRIPTION: This "close" is great for the older, reserved customer, and especially good for preachers. This "close" actually tells the customer to go to hell when he says he has to think about buying the product. The good thing about this "close" is that the customer won't realize what the closer has just said to him until it's too late to do anything about it. This "close" will absolutely destroy the "I have to think about it" customer.

How the Three Devil Close is Used. . . (example)

When the customer tells the closer he has to think about it, the closer should look directly at the customer and say "Mr. Customer, have you ever heard the story about the three devils?" When the customer says "No," the closer should continue. "Well, Mr. Satan was down in hell one day, and he was trying to figure out how to get all the people on earth down there with him and away from heaven. When along comes a devil who walks up to Mr. Satan and says, 'I know how to get fifty percent of all the people on earth down here with us. So Mr. Satan says, How are you going to do that?' The first devil answers, 'I'll dress up as a mortal and go to the earth and tell everyone there is no God, no devil, no heaven, no hell, no good nor any evil, and they can do whatever they want — wild women, booze, gambling — anything at all. And I promise I'll get fifty percent of the people on earth down to hell.'

"Mr. Satan said he liked that idea. Suddenly a second devil walks up and tells them both *he* can get seventy-five percent of all the people on earth down to hell. Mr. Satan and the first devil asked the second devil how he would do that. The second devil said, 'I'll go up to earth dressed as a mortal also, but I'll tell all the people there is a heaven, there is a hell, there is a God, and there is a devil, so they'd better go to church every Sunday morning and evening, plus on Wednesday nights. But during the rest of the week they can do anything they want to do — no limit. This way the people will rationalize their wild conduct during the week, because they still go to church. We'll pull the wool over their eyes and get seventy-five percent of the people down here to hell.

"Mr. Satan really liked that idea. He thought that plan was the one to go with, when a third devil walks up and tells them they are all wrong. This third devil says he could get *everyone* on earth down to hell, one hundred percent of the people. Mr. Satan looked shocked and asked the third devil how he would do it. The third devil said he too would dress up as a mortal and go up to earth, but he would tell all the people there was a God, and there was a devil, there was a heaven and there was a hell, there was good and there was evil and if everybody didn't follow the straight and narrow, the teachings of the Bible and accept the Lord, then they would automatically go straight to hell. But before they had to accept these things, the third devil was going to give the people on earth all the time in the world to think about it."

When the closer has finished with this devil story he should look straight at the customer and in a soft and serious voice, say, "Now let's be realistic, why don't you give my product a try?"

NOTE: After the customer hears the devil story he will laugh a little, thinking it's cute, but when the closer asks for the order the customer will get serious again.

The Ben Franklin Close

DESCRIPTION: This "close" uses logic to get the closer's point across to the customer. It is a good "close" to use on a customer who is a thinker or who is reserved and overly cautious when buying a product.

How the Ben Franklin Close is Used. . . (example)

"Mr. Customer, in America everybody has always regarded Ben Franklin as a pretty smart fellow. When Ben Franklin had a problem to solve or a matter to figure out and make a decision on, he would take piece of paper and draw a line down the middle of it. On the left side of the paper he would write the word "Yes" and on the right half of the paper he would write the word "No." In the "Yes" column Ben would make a list of all the good and beneficial factors that would favor his decision to pursue something or purchase something. And in the "No" column he would list all of the reasons for not doing something or for not buying something. When Ben was finished with this "Yes" and "No" process, he could simply look at the list and his decision was already made for him. He would either have more yesses or more noes. It was that simple. Mr. Customer, why don't we try that and see what happens, it sure can't hurt?"

(NOTE: The closer should hand the customer a sheet of paper and a pen and have the customer fill out the "Yes" and "No" column. The closer should tactfully assist the customer on the "Yes" side by giving out suggestions, but on the "No" side keep quiet and not say a thing. The "Yes" side will always, with the closer's help, win. When this process is finished the closer should look at the customer and ask him to give the product a try.)

The Kids vs. Parents Close

DESCRIPTION: In this "close" the closer uses the excitement and innocence of the customer's children against the customer himself. This close is powerful — in fact it could backfire and kill a sale, but if the closer handles it tactfully and with class the customer won't get too upset, plus he will wind up purchasing the product.

How the Kids vs. Parents Close is Used. . . (example)

When the closer first meets the customer and his family (providing the customer has children) if at all possible in the sales situation, the closer should have a small live pet available for the kids to play with while the closer makes his first pre-pitch introduction. (Note: The small pet could be anything from a hamster to a puppy dog to a shetland pony. It doesn't really matter that much, just as long as the customer's kids like the animal and have fun playing with it.) When the closer shows the customer his product, he can go back to the subject of small pets and say to the customer's kids, "Did you kids like that little dog you were playing with when we first met?" The kids will automatically say "Yes." Then the closer should say, "Let me ask you kids this, if that little dog was yours what would you name him?" The kids will say something like, "We'd name him Cookie." The closer should immediately say (in front of the whole family) "Well, I'll tell you what, if your dad buys my product then Cookie is your very own dog, free!" Then the closer should say to the customer and his family, "Why don't you all talk about it for a few minutes," and walk away, not letting the customer stop him.

This is where the fun begins, because the customer's kids will go wild with excitement and beg dear old dad to buy the product. The closer doesn't have to do a thing except stay away from the customer long enough for the customer's kids to have time to work on and break down their dad's resistance. The customer won't appreciate the closer using this trick on him but there is a very good chance the customer will buy. When the closer comes back to the customer all he has to do is give a sincere smile and ask the customer how he wants his name on the contract.

The Summary Close

DESCRIPTION: This "close" should be used by the closer when he has a customer who either says he has to think about buying the product, or seems confused and unable to literally make a buying decision. (NOTE: When a customer says he has to think about buying, he is simply not sold on the product yet. The closer not only has to work a little harder on this type of customer to "close" him, but the closer has to get the statement of "I have to think about it" into a real and conquerable objection. The excuse of "I have to think about it" is not an objection but a worthless set of words. It's the closer's responsibility to change that "it" into a real and tangible objection so he can overcome it.)

How the Summary Close is Used. . . (example)

When the customer tells the closer he has to think about it, the closer should calmly and sincerely say, "Mr. Customer, just to get my thoughts straight, exactly what is it about my product that you wanted to think about (without taking a breath the closer should continue) is it my company's reputation?" If the customer says "No," the closer should immediately continue without pausing and say, "Is it the size of the property?" If again the customer says "No" the closer should keep right on talking and say, "Is it the down payment?"

The closer shouldn't stop asking the customer what he wants to think about until the customer finally says, "Yes, that's what I have to think about, the down payment." Now the closer has a solid objection he can work with and conquer.

(Note: When the closer is asking the customer "is it" questions he'd better not go too slowly in his delivery or pause, because the customer will have time to think and automatically say, "That's it, I have to think about the whole thing." And if the customer says this, then the closer is in serious trouble.)

The Intimidation Close

DESCRIPTION: This "close" is designed to embarrass and shame the customer into buying the product through pressure and emotions. The closer can be very effective with these "closing statements" if he executes them properly. This kind of "close" has to be used on the customer subtly and tactfully for full effect; if the closer misuses this "closing procedure" he could kill a sale.

How The Intimidation Close is Used. . . (example)

The closer can use "closing statements" in many ways, for example:

1. "Mr. Customer, I'll bet you that when you and your wife first got married you would have bought two of my products for her, wouldn't you? Well, don't you love her one-half as much now?"

2. "Mr. Customer, I don't think you need a shirt that expensive. Can I show you something a little cheaper?"

3. "Mr. Customer, I don't want to bother my boss with an offer unless it's serious and I'm sure, since you're so young, you don't have the financial capability to own a product such as this. So make an offer when you're serious."

4. "Mr. Customer, my product only costs a few dollars a day to own. Why, your kids could pick up pop bottles and make that much money."

5. "Mr. Customer, I'll tell you what: If as you say, you can make more money on another investment than you can with my product, then here, you take my check for three thousand dollars and invest it for me. Who do I make it out to?"

NOTE: The closer should just keep throwing out these "closing statements" until the customer really reacts to one and then the closer should focus on that particular objection or problem and go in for the kill.

The Negative Close

DESCRIPTION: This "close" has a lot of power and effect if the closer knows how to use it properly. The closer can turn the "toughest customer" around into a "weak pup" if he uses this "close" in the right manner. If used correctly, this "close" will get the closer more sales than he ever thought possible, and at the same time the "tough customer" will never know what happened to him. FACT.

How The Negative Close is Used. . . (example)

When the closer has a customer who thinks he knows everything or thinks he is too good to talk to the closer or purchase the product, the perfect solution the closer has in his trick bag for this customer is the "negative close." It works in this fashion: When he is with this type of customer, the closer has to act nonchalant, professional, polite, and really uninterested in selling him anything. The closer has to act as if he couldn't care less if this customer purchases the product or not, due to the fact that the closer has let this customer know tactfully that he has sold two or three of his products already that day. (It doesn't matter if the closer hasn't sold anything, just as long as this customer thinks he has).

This kind of attitude on the closer's part will automatically spark the curiosity and interest in this customer every time. FACT. The reason is simple: If the closer acts as though this customer can't afford to buy the product, or is not qualified to buy it, or it won't make a big difference to the closer's company if this customer buys or not, then this customer will tend to buy the product every time just to prove the closer wrong, and show the closer he is important and should be treated with more respect. For example: the closer could say something like this to this kind of customer, "Mr. Customer, my product doesn't appeal to everyone, if you know what I mean." (At this point the customer really doesn't know what the closer is talking about, the closer has started to arouse his interest.) My company is a highly specialized real estate company that only handles certain clients. I'm sure you know we have a reputation for being very selective in our properties and our customers. Now I'm sure that you have good intentions in looking at some of our property, but I hope you understand that you have to qualify first. You know, in this industry you run into some pretty strange people, and I'm not talking about you, who have champagne taste on a beer budget. You know what I mean?" The closer should then wait until sometime later in his sales presentation with this customer and say, "Mr. Customer, do you know if you could qualify for one of our properties if you were interested? I'll tell you what, before we continue why don't we fill out a simple credit application to see how you look on paper. That way I won't be wasting your time and you won't be wasting mine." When the customer starts to justify his qualifications and show the closer his capabilities for buying, the closer should continue to stay somewhat nonchalant and start warming up slowly to this customer and get prepared to make an ordinary but reserved assumption "close."

The Alternate Choice Close

DESCRIPTION: This "closing qusestion" gives the customer two or three choices to choose between. This "close" will not only take the customer's mind off of just one single and scary buying decision, but when the customer answers this "closing question," no matter what choice he makes, he's bought the product. He's made a decision. Then all the closer has to do is start writing up the order.

How the Alternate Choice Close is Used...(example)

The closer should ask the customer questions similar to the following examples.

1. "Mr. Customer, do you want to use your own financing or do you want to go ahead and use ours, since you've already been approved?"

2. "Mr. Customer, which one of these two colors would you prefer on this particular model?"

3. "Mr. Customer, which piece of property do you like the best, the one overlooking the golf course or the one overlooking the lake?"

4. "Mr. Customer, do you write your name using your full middle name or do you just use an initial?"

5. "Mr. Customer, how many do you want: two or all three?"

The Contest Close

DESCRIPTION: This is used when the closer wants the customer to feel he is getting a very special deal or a real break when purchasing the product. This "close" makes the customer think he has lucked out and happens to be in the right place at the right time for buying the closer's product.

How the Contest Close is Used...(example)

Near the end of the sales presentation at the closer's own discretion, the closer should tell the customer something like this: "Mr. Customer, you might not believe what I'm going to tell you, because it's going to sound exactly like a sales pitch. I haven't told you something, because when we first met it didn't make that much difference. But now things have changed a little and I have to tell you. Every year, my company runs a sales contest for its closers. Well, we're at the tail end of that contest right now; the winner gets not only a large cash bonus, but he gets to take his family for a free two-week vacation in Hawaii. I have been leading all the other closers in the company for the whole contest, but just about an hour ago my top rival sold three of these products. Now he's ahead of me, only in dollar volume — that's how the company chooses the winner. All kidding aside, I want you to listen to me very closely. This contest ends in one hour, and that's a fact, and I can beat that other guy if I have one more sale. And believe me, it means a lot to me, not only to win but to be able to give my family a super vacation. In fact it will be the first real vacation we've had in over three years. Here's what I can do if you just keep it to yourself, or I will get in trouble. My product costs X number of dollars — my company won't take anything less, and that's the way it is. To win that vacation I'll do this if you buy my product: you won't have to pay the total price for it. I have a big bonus coming, so I can let you have the product for five hundred dollars less than anyone else can even hope to get it for, and I'll make up that five-hundred-dollar difference out of my bonus money. So not only do you get the product for five hundred dollars below our bottom-line price, but I still get the rest of my bonus money plus the

Hawaii vacation, and my company sold the product for exactly what they wanted to in the first place. So help me and yourself out, and give it a try?"

(NOTE: The first thing the closer has to do is "pad" the product's price by five hundred dollars so that he winds up selling the product for the real price. Secondly the closer has to make the customer believe him. This "close" works on the larceny factor in the customer's heart, and it works wonders.)

The Airplane Close

DESCRIPTION: This "close" is intended to gently and logically show the customer how ridiculous his objection "Well, I don't know for sure, a buying decision like this is hard to make," really sounds. The closer can usually use this "close" with great success on older customers, who tend to get scared when buying a product, always wondering if they made the right decision.

How the Airplane Close is Used...(example)

When the closer has a customer who can't make up his mind, the closer can make a simple and thought-provoking statement like this, "Mr. Customer, you know you told me that you liked my product but it was hard for you to make a decision. Well, that's normal, so don't feel bad. You know when you make a decision you're always going to wonder a little if it was the right one or not. In fact, it's just like getting on an airplane to, let's say, New York or Los Angeles. Did you know that every day, of all the planes that take off, fly, and land, three percent crash. Now I'm talking about all the planes in every country of the world. Three percent do not make it, and that's a fact. So tell me, when you get on that airplane in New York flying to Los Angeles, knowing that three percent of them crash, are you going to cut off three percent of your body and leave it in the terminal? Or are you going to get on that airplane one hundred percent without even knowing the captain and crew and fly to Los Angeles? Of course you're going to make the decision to get one hundred percent of you on board, even though three percent of you may be scared. Mr. Customer, buying this product is the same thing, you might be a little uneasy about buying, but don't worry about it — get on board one hundred percent and you will thank me a year from now. So why don't you give it a try?"

The Order Sheet and Assumption Close

DESCRIPTION: These two "closes" are first cousins. The first "close" (the order sheet) works with paper, the second "close" (the assumption) works with a handshake, but both closes are used in the same basic way to "close" the customer.

How the Order Sheet and Assumption Close is Used...(examples)

The Order Sheet Close — When the closer has overcome the customer's basic objections, the closer should say something like this, "Mr. Customer, now let me show you what it [finances and facts] looks like on paper." Then the closer should take out an order sheet and ask the customer, "Mr. Customer, what exactly is your full name?" If the customer doesn't stop the closer from writing down information then the customer has automatically bought — he's "closed." But if the customer does try to stop the closer from writing, he will nearly always bring out the real and final objection. The closer should just conquer the objection and then continue to write down information on the order sheet, acting as though it were normal procedure. When the entire order sheet is filled out the closer should sign it first and then calmly hand it over to the customer and say, "Mr. Customer, I just need your name right here with mine and then we can have this approved." The closer's casual attitude of assuming the customer was going to buy all the way will only help convince the customer it is all right to sign the order sheet. (Note: The closer should also take notes on the actual order sheet, if possible, during the sales presentation. This way the customer will become accustomed to seeing this paper and when it becomes time for him to sign, the customer won't be surprised and scared by the sight of the order sheet.)

The Assumption Close — When the closer has conquered all of the customer's objections and the closer knows the customer is ready to be asked to buy the product, the closer should say, with a confident voice, "Mr. Customer, why don't you give my product a try?" (With his arm outstretched waiting to shake hands and congratulate the customer.) In most cases the customer will automatically shake the closer's hand (having the same effect as an unvoiced affirmative buying answer). This sudden and impulsive response on the customer's part will make him feel committed; the closer, acting as if there is nothing more to be said, should immediately start writing up the order sheet. (NOTE: The Assumption Close is knowing that you are going to "close" the customer the minute you first meet him.)

The Referral Close

DESCRIPTION: This "close" is designed to be used by the closer on a customer who can't afford the down payment, monthly payments, or the product itself. This "close" works wonders if the customer believes the closer.

How the Referral Close is Used. . . (example)

When the closer sees he has the customer sold but the customer doesn't have enough money to buy the product, the closer should say something like this, "Mr. Customer, my company has found through the years that the best form of advertising is the simple method of 'word of mouth.' In other words, good recommendations from a satisfied customer to a prospective customer. My company is willing to take advantage of this form of advertising in the nature of a referral program, which has been very successful for us. This is how it works: If you bring a prospective customer into our sales office who buys, my company will make your monthly payment for you. So if you just brought in one customer a month and he bought, then your monthly payments would be taken care of. The same process works for the down payment. If you start bringing in new customers we can arrange to take care of the down payment also. This way my company has new customers, and you have my product without any expense to you at all, and I'm sure you know enough people to at least get you started with your investment."

The closer should immediately hand this customer a "referral sheet," or a piece of paper and a pen and say, "Now, who would be the very first person you would recommend?" If the customer starts to write down a name, he is sold on the idea. If the customer doesn't go for the idea at first the closer should repeat the referral program to him, showing its advantages and then ask him to give the product a try.

"The Change Places Close"

DESCRIPTION: This is a good "close" for the closer to use when he has tried about everything he knows, but doesn't really want to use a lot of pressure yet to get the sale. This type of close is easy-going and doesn't offend the customer at all.

How the Change Places Close Is Used...(example)

When the customer won't budge and the closer has built up a good rapport with him and doesn't want to get rough, the closer can say something like this (with sincerity), "Mr. Customer, let me ask you this — just for a minute would you put yourself in my shoes? What I mean is this: What if you had a fantastic product and you knew that it was priced right, and you also knew the product would be beneficial to your customer and his family, but your customer won't buy the product and really won't even give a reason why he won't buy. Now, Mr. Customer, let me ask you what would you do?" (NOTE: In most cases the customer will tell the closer the real hidden objection for not purchasing. Then the closer can start "closing" again. This "close" is a good one for discovering customer secrets.)

After the closer says this, he should shut up and wait to hear what the customer says. If the customer gets kind of embarrassed and says, "I don't know," the closer can assume it's a financial problem he's dealing with and ask the customer, "We're really talking about money, aren't we?" When the customer says "Yes," the closer can continue to solve the problem and "close" again.

"The Multiple Unit Close"

DESCRIPTION: This "close" is designed to embarrass or shame the customer into purchasing the product. The closer has to program the customer throughout the entire sales presentation for this "close" if it is to be used effectively at the end of the "closing process."

How the Multiple Unit Close Is Used...(example)

When the closer is describing and talking about his product to the customer, he should make the customer think the only way someone could buy the product would be in groups, sets, or a package of four. For instance: The closer is selling real estate lots, so he makes the customer believe the only way to purchase any real estate from him is to buy four lots. When it becomes time for the closer to ask the customer for the order he simply says, "The price of this group [unit of four lots] is X amount of money. Why don't you give it a try?"

If the customer still thinks he can't afford the property, the closer should excuse himself, get away from the customer for a few minutes, then return and say, "Mr. Customer, I've talked to my boss and in very special cases, like yours, where I know you would like to own property, our company will — if you don't tell anyone else — let you purchase a quarter of the package [one lot]. Surely, Mr. Customer, you can afford one-quarter of a unit for yourself and your family, so why don't you give it a try?"

When the closer uses this "close" he will more often than not sell two or three pieces of property instead of just one. This "close" makes the customer feel intimidated if he can't at least afford to buy one-quarter of the unit (one lot).

"The Think About It Close"

DESCRIPTION: This "close" is one the closer can make fun of the customer with, if the customer says he has to think about buying the product.

How the Think About It Close Works...(example)

When the customer tells the closer he has to "think about it" after the closer has asked him to give it a try, the closer should look surprisingly happy and with some excitement say, "Mr. Customer, that's perfect, you'll fit right into my company's Think-About-It program. What my company has done is develop a program for people like yourself, who have to think about the product. The program works like this: You, Mr. Customer, go ahead and put down the down payment and then hold on to my product [real estate] for twelve months. Every month, all you have to do is just send in that small monthly investment. Now during this twelve-month period my company wants you to come back as many times as possible to visit and see how everything is developing. Then, at the end of the twelve months, if you don't like the product we will help you sell it. That way you not only make a little money — more than you would have if you had put your money in a bank — but you had a whole year to think about whether you like my product or not. You can have your cake and eat it too."

The closer should then proceed to write up the sale. If the customer stops the closer and says, "Wait, hold on, I have to think about that," then the closer can look right at the customer and in a startled voice say, "Mr. Customer, you mean to sit there and tell me that you have to think about the Think-About-It program?" Then the closer should get a frustrated look on his face and start writing up the sale again.

(NOTE: In most cases the customer will feel like an idiot and go ahead and purchase.)

"The Lost Sale Close"

DESCRIPTION: This "close" should be the very last "close" that the closer uses on his customer. When the closer delivers this close he must look sincere and defeated, as though the customer has won and the closer has lost the sale.

How the Lost Sale Close is Used. . . (example)

The closer should sheepishly say something like this to the customer, "Mr. Customer, I was wondering if you would help me with something before you go. I know you're not going to buy anything, but would you tell me confidentially and personally why you really don't like my product [Do not pause, keep on talking] because this is how I make a living and support my family. If you could, just between the two of us, tell me the reason, then if it happens again with another customer I won't make the same mistake. And I might be able to answer the other customer's questions better than I did for you."

When the customer gives the closer the real reason for not buying, thinking he is off the hook, the closer can immediately act surprised and say, "Mr. Customer, no wonder you didn't buy. It's my fault for not explaining that item to you properly. Here, let me show you how it really works." Then the closer can proceed to go in for the kill.

The Safety Deposit Box Close

DESCRIPTION: This "close" is nothing but raw power and force. It not only works but is so strong the customer will definitely become activated. FACT. (Note: WARNING, when the closer uses this "close" he had better be on his toes and far enough away from the customer, so if the customer becomes violent the closer can take defensive precautions.) This "close" should be used when everything else fails, including the "lost sale close."

How the Safety Deposit Box Close is Used...(example)

When the closer has used everything in the book he knows of to try to "close" the customer, and the customer by this time has said he wouldn't buy the product a hundred times, the closer should take out a work sheet or order sheet, right in front of the customer and his whole family (it helps if the customer has kids) and say something like this, "Mr. Customer, this is an order sheet with all of the facts and figures about the product, plus today's date on it. I want you, right in front of your family to go ahead and sign it for me." The customer will get angry and say, "No, I told you I'm not signing anything today!" The closer should sternly continue, "Mr. Customer, I want you to sign this order sheet right now, right here in front of your family, because I don't even want it, I don't even want a copy of it, all I want you to do is sign it and then fold it up and take it home with you. And when you get home I want you to put that order sheet in your safety deposit box or a safe place along with your other valuable papers, such as your will, your insurance or homeowner's papers, whatever. Because, God forbid, but some day you're going to die and when you do, your wife and kids are going to be going through all of your personal papers and they are going to discover this order sheet dated on this day. Then your wife and kids will look at it and see where you could have bought a prime piece of property years ago for practically nothing, with a little down payment and a small monthly payment. Your wife and kids are going to actually see how close you came to leaving them a lot more financial security. They'll see how close you came, to having enough money so that your wife doesn't have to work and your kids can go to a good university. So Mr. Customer, you go ahead and sign that order sheet and take it with you."

If the customer won't sign the closer should say, "Mr. Customer, sign it. What's wrong, are you afraid that your family is going to learn from your mistakes or see how close they were to being better off?"

If the customer still won't sign the closer should look at the customer's children and say, "Kids, why don't you ask your dad why he won't sign a piece of paper that I don't even want?"

This close will get results. The customer will either sign the order sheet, making the closer a sale, or he will break (fall apart) and give the closer the real objection, which is usually the lack of money, or he will try to hit the closer. Either way this "close" creates excitement.

NOTES

Chapter 10

THE CLOSERS

FIFTEEN CUSTOMER OBJECTIONS
AND
FORTY-FIVE CLOSER RESPONSES

(The Customer's Objection)......"I'll Be Back"

(CLOSER'S RESPONSE)

1. "Great, Mr. Customer. I trust you — know you'll be back tomorrow. Why don't you take my watch with you and bring it back when you return. Here, go ahead and take it; I know you will be back." (Note: This maneuver really puts the customer on the spot and embarrasses him because he's just been trapped and he knows it The closer should then go ahead and find out what the real objection is and "close" it.)

2. "Since you're that interested, let's go ahead and make out an order sheet and take a hold check for the product. That way when you come back we can take care of the paperwork a lot easier."

3. "You don't have to come back to sign the papers or anything. I'm going to be in your neighborhood tomorrow, so I'll just drop by. How's that?"

(The Customer's Objection......
"I Have to Talk to My Dad [Son, Uncle, etc.] First"

(CLOSER'S RESPONSE)

1. "When are you going to see your dad — in a week or so? All right, I'll tell you what I'm going to do. I'll take off work for a week and go see my dad, and while you are asking your dad if you can buy my product, I'll ask my dad if I can sell it."

2. "Let me ask you this, and tell me the truth — does your dad ask for your advice before he buys something?"

3. "Why are you going to talk to someone — you have all the information and facts concerning the product right here in front of you. Whoever you want to talk to sure doesn't, because he's not here. What could you ask him about the product that you don't already know, unless it's a financial question?"

(The Customer's Objection)......
"We Never Buy on the Spur of the Moment"
(CLOSER'S RESPONSE)

1. "We don't want you to buy outright right now, we don't want cash; all we want you to do is try our product for a while. Put a little down payment on it and make some comfortable monthly payments, then during that time come back to visit and watch the progress my company is making. If you're not satisfied you can always resell your product."

2. "If you just came in this sales office and said you wanted to buy the product, *that* would be on the spur of the moment. But you've seen how my product works, all its advantages and benefits, plus you have all the facts needed to make an intelligent buying decision. So why don't you give it a try?"

3. "Well, I know you like my product, so why don't I give you time to think about it. I'll tell you what I'll do so you won't lose any money, I'll go ahead and postdate the contract, all of the working papers for a couple of days. That way you can get the product at today's price, but you'll have a few days to think about it."

(The Customer's Objection)......
"I Just Can't Make a Decision Now"

(CLOSER'S RESPONSE)

1. "Do you mean to tell me that you are fifty-five years old and don't have the capability to make an intelligent business decision?"

2. "You don't have to think about making money, do you? All right, that's exactly what we're talking about."

3. "Mr. Customer, a decision is like playing football — you can't make a touchdown by sitting on the bench. You have to get out on the field and participate. Now you know you have enough facts and information about my product to make a buying decision. All I want you to do is give it a try."

(The Customer's Objection)......
"I'm Just Looking Around, Just Shopping"
(CLOSER'S RESPONSE)

1. "Since you're doing that, why don't you go ahead and invest here, since you know the potential of my company. Then look around and see if you can find anything better. If you do find a better investment, we can liquidate your investment in thirty to forty days and you not only would have made a little more money to invest in your new-found project, but while you were looking you would be enjoying the benefits of my company. But if you don't find a better investment, then you're already an investor with my company at today's special price."

2. "There are lookers and there are doers. Lookers always pass by things, just dreaming and never really having anything, but doers have money, they have a portfolio, something solid to build on. Don't ever fool yourself."

3. "Everyone has to look around. But when you have an opportunity like this, where you can see the potential and advantages of my product and you know that the product is superior to all others, isn't that what you have really been looking around for in the first place? When you find what you want don't overlook it and pass it by; why not give it a try?"

(The Customer's Objection)......
"I Can Make More Money Someplace Else"
(CLOSER'S RESPONSE)

1. "I'll tell you what, let's go on back to a phone in the sales office and you let me talk to those people who make more money on this type of an investment than my company does. Who knows, I might want to get a job with them. What is their phone number anyway?"

2. "Why don't you come on over to my house sometime this week and talk to some of my friends. I'll go ahead and set up the meeting, because I just might want to invest my own money. When can you make it?"

3. "Then what are you doing looking at my product?"

(The Customer's Objection)......"I'm Too Old to Buy"
(CLOSER'S RESPONSE)

1. "No, you're not, you're only as old as you think you are. Why, this product would put a little wahoo in your life. Besides, our company needs people like you. Why don't you give my product a chance, give it a try?"

2. "You're still not too old to think about your wife's care and comfort or your grandchildren, so why don't you buy the product for them — you know they would enjoy it."

3. "I'll bet if you were thirty or thirty-five and you looked into the future and saw yourself talking like that you would have a heart attack. You know life goes on, and you now have the time to enjoy the product and all its benefits. So do something good for yourself and give my product a try."

(The Customer's Objection)......
"We Can't Buy, Because We Have Other Obligations at Home: Sickness, The Farm, Kids in School, etc.
(CLOSER'S RESPONSE)

1. "Those obligations come first, you're right. But now, this is an opportunity that just doesn't present itself every day — that's a fact and you know it. If we could work out the payments with you so that they're compatible with your present obligations and don't interfere, would you give it a try?"

2. What are you going to have tomorrow, more problems? What did you have yesterday, old problems? You're always going to have problems and obligations — everyone does. You just have to start building a future for your family sometime, and now is the perfect time to get started. Not yesterday or tomorrow, but now while you can, while you have the chance."

3. "You know you don't have a monopoly on problems and obligations, we all have them. But some people are better off than others because they started with a plan and followed it through, knowing they would have problems but were willing to work around them and deal with them. That is the only difference between people with money and folks who don't have as much money as they really need. All you have to do is plan and carry that plan through. You'll find out your problems aren't as bad as you thought, so why don't you start planning and give my product a try?"

(The Customer's Objection)......
"I've Already Bought Someplace Else"
(CLOSER'S RESPONSE)

1. "Then go ahead and buy here too, you know the potential. Don't make the mistake of putting all your eggs in one basket. Diversify your monies."

2. "Then write the people you bought from and tell them you're not satisfied with their product and want your money back. [Note: The customer shouldn't call or go back personally because the other company will try to hold him to the contract.] Then you will be free to invest in my product, knowing that you not only saved money, but you purchased a better product."

3. "Then what you should do, knowing my product's potential and liking it, is purchase one of my products for another member of your family, someone who would really appreciate it."

(The Customer's Objection)......
"I Have to Think About It"
(CLOSER'S RESPONSE)

1. "Let me ask you this: If you owned this product and you wanted me to sell it for you, and a customer came up to me and said, 'I have to think about it,' would you want me to let him go, or would you want me to show him what he's missing by not buying the product and try to sell him?"

2. "The only thing you have to really think about is money, isn't it? Well, you know your finances better than I do, so why don't you sit here and have some coffee and see how your finances look. I'll be back in a minute."

3. "I don't blame you. I've got to make a phone call, so why don't you think about it while all the product information is still fresh in your mind, and I'm here to answer any of your questions. Now that makes sense, doesn't it?"

(The Customer's Objection)......
"Your Product Costs Too Much"
(CLOSER'S RESPONSE)

1. "Compared to what the product you now have or some other product that doesn't have as many benefits as this product has, tell me, what are you comparing my product's price to?"

2. "You can go first class or second class, that's your decision; but you get exactly what you pay for. You have to remember that my product is the top of the line and if it doesn't fit into your future plans then I don't think you need it."

3. "If my product is too expensive, as you see it, what do you think it will be worth a year from now? So why don't you try it before it gets even more expensive, and I can assure you it will. Believe me, if you can't afford my product now, you sure won't be able to afford it later."

(NOTE: The closer can very easily turn this objection around and say to the customer, "Well, what do you think my product should be worth?" If the customer answers, the closer should write it up and submit it. A lot of sales have been made that way.)

(The Customer's Objection)......
"Why Is This Product for Me? Why Should I Buy?"
(CLOSER'S RESPONSE)

1. "Because no one in this world is adverse to making money and you can see the potential of my product. If you know it will help you in your financial future you should buy my product. But if you really think my product won't help you, then don't buy it. I don't need the problem, my product is that good."

2. "Why wouldn't this product be for you? You answer me that."

3. "This product is for you because it benefits you. The product provides protection for your hard-earned money in today's economy. And besides, this product wouldn't be near the success it is if it weren't for people like you who understand the product and its potential. Now only do you need the product, but the product needs you."

(The Customer's Objection)......"I Can't Afford It"

(CLOSER'S RESPONSE)

1. "I know what you mean. If someone asked me for that kind of money, I'd say I couldn't afford it either. In fact, I was in the same boat as you are in now, not long ago. Let me show you how I got out of that situation." (NOTE: The closer should then show the customer how the product or some other event made money for him. The customer can relate to that, and the closer has created a common bond with the customer, thus making the "close" that much easier.)

2. "What do you mean, you can't afford it? Can you afford not to? Do you realize how much the price of everyting is going to rise in the future? If you can't afford the buy my product now — something that you want — then you better get a new job that pays more."

3. "Do you mean to tell me you worked your whole life and you can't save X amount of money each month? Did you realize you were in that bad of a financial situation? Here, let me show you how you can get out of it." (NOTE: Then the closer should proceed to solve the customer's money problems by showing and giving examples of other people who were in the same boat, but solved their problems.)

(The Customer's Objection)...... "We Can't Buy, We Just Got Married"

(CLOSER'S RESPONSE)

1. "Well, could you think of a better wedding present for each of you to give the other?"

2. "You can start to build your future together as man and wife right now, in your very first investment. This investment will be a starting point for your future family and a nest egg for times to come."

3. "You have, believe it or not, an opportunity that very few newlyweds enjoy. By buying this product you can share a feeling of accomplishment for years to come. You'd be surprised how many people say they are going to start an investment when they first get married, but don't because they say they don't have the money — you know, the expense of setting up housekeeping and all. Then they say they are going to invest when they have their first baby, but don't

because of the hospital costs and doctor bills. Then they say they will invest when the kids leave home, but don't because now they have to pay for the kids' college. Then they say they will invest when the kids are out of school, but don't because by that time they're trying to save for some type of retirement, and really can't because of the economy. So they retire together years later without any money because they never started an investment for the future. It's a sad story, but it's very true. You people have the chance to direct your lives away from that kind of ending now. So why don't you give my company a try?"

(The Customer's Objection)......
"I Have to Talk to My Lawyer or Money Manager"
(CLOSER'S RESPONSE)

1. "That's a good idea. Let's get him on the phone right now and you explain to him how good everything is about this product and then ask him if he thinks it's a good investment. Now what do you think he is going to say? I'll tell you what he'll say. He'll say, 'How should I know if it's a good deal or bad, I'm not there to see it. You are, how can I tell you about the product?' "

2. "Does your lawyer call you when he's going to buy something in your line of business?"

3. "All your lawyer can really do is say, 'Don't sign anything.' That way he's protected. Even if he knew it was a good investment, he wouldn't dare tell you to go ahead and purchase something he hasn't seen before. If he thinks his decision could lose a client, he'll be overprotective in his statements every time, and what kind of sound advice is that?"

Conclusion

THE CLOSERS

The first of September finally arrived and my summer job at Green Vista Estates was coming to an end. I would be going back to school, but I wasn't as excited about it as I guess I should have been. Green Vista Estates was a total success. I never saw anything grow and develop more in three short months in my entire life. I asked "Big Bill" if I could have my same job back next year and he said he had better things planned for me, so I guessed that meant I had a job.

I think the reason I felt kind of sad about having to go back to school was the fact that I wouldn't be seeing Sam anymore. That morning Sam walked up to me and told me my lessons on "closing" were over. He said if I stayed with Green Vista Estates and practiced what he had taught me, there was no way on earth I couldn't become a Master Closer.

Sam said he wouldn't be coming back next summer because he had completed his job here, whatever that meant. He said I had been a good student and I not only deserved to see what the inscription on the inside of his gold ring said, but he gave me the ring as well. When he handed it to me he had tears in his eyes and told me to always wear it.

I forgot about the inscription and just stood there watching as Sam turned around and walked toward the guard house. About halfway across the parking lot he turned around and looked at me one last time and said, "Now you can 'Sam' 'em."

I felt like crying because my old friend was going to leave me just like that. I put the ring in my pocket and started to run after Sam, wanting to thank him for everything I had learned, and tell him how much I cared about him. I ran right up to Sam's guard house and jerked open the door to say, "Sam, what are you doing, giving me your ring?"

When I looked inside the guard house it was empty. I looked outside, but Sam was gone — he had been there just a second ago. He couldn't have gone somewhere else that fast. So I ran back to the old hotel sales office and right into "Big Bill's" office (which *no one* did) and told him Sam had disappeared — just vanished.

"Big Bill" just looked at me, with his mouth open, as though I was a nut. He asked me who was missing, and I said Sam, the security guard. That's when I think I fainted because "Big Bill" said Green Vista Estates never had a security guard — he had never heard of Sam.

Later that night I drove back to my folks' home, trying to figure out if I was crazy or not, plus feeling sick at my stomach. I felt in my pocket and there was Sam's gold ring. I felt like I was going to faint again, so I pulled off the highway into a rest area and just stared at his old, worn-out ring. Then it dawned on me to see if there was an inscription in the ring, to see if my imagination was working on me. Maybe I had had too much sun that summer.

I opened the glove box to get some light and there, inside the gold ring, was a real inscription. Sam told me (or at least I think Sam told me) if any person wanted to be a Master Closer all he had to do was follow the rule of the ring's inscription. The ring's inscription read simply *Sum Tertius* — "I Am Third."

From listening to Sam I knew what it meant: Put God first in your life, the other fellow second, and yourself always third. If a closer kept that kind of attitude, there is no way he could fail. "I Am Third," that sounded like Sam. Sometimes he was kind of rough, but he always had a heart of gold.

Well, that is what happened to me seventeen years ago when I was going to school and working at Green Vista Estates in the summer. I kept working there, always wearing that ring, and never mentioned Sam again to anyone. Today I'm the president of the Duron Corporation. All thanks to my make-believe friend? But the story doesn't end there.

This past December I was in New York City for the company's anniversary party, where I was introduced as the new president of Duron Corporation. I had finished by speech and was walking around the huge hall, meeting people and really enjoying my new position, when out of nowhere an old man came up to me and said he had noticed my ring and wanted to look at it. I lifted my hand a little, because I never took the ring off, and showed him. He looked up at me and said the inscription on the inside said, *Sum Tertius,* meaning God first, the other fellow second, and always put yourself third. I asked him how in the world he knew that, because through all these years I had never told a living soul what the ring said.

The old man looked sad but he told me he used to be the valet for Edward Duron, Sr., the founder of the Duron Corporation. He said Mr. Duron had that ring made especially for him in Tasco, Mexico. Then on a fishing trip off the coast of Mexico he drowned at sea.

Now that all happened over twenty years ago, three years before I started working for the company. This old man said Mr. Duron never took the ring off and believed in that inscription more than anything else in the world. I was startled. I asked the old man how in the world it could be the same ring, because I got the ring from (I whispered so no one would hear) some old, rough-looking man by the name of Sam Johnson. That's when the valet told me that when Mr. Duron acquired new property across the country, since everyone knew him, he had to use another name. So he used "Sam Johnson."

After I got over the initial shock, I tried in some way to figure out exactly what really did happen to me seventeen years ago. How did Edward Duron's gold ring get to me? Was it my overactive imagination? Or was Sam Johnson a ghost? To this day I never really understood what took place that special summer. Except that I knew I had met a friend who gave me his ring and taught me some very valuable lessons about life and "closing" sales. I cherish the memory of Sam Johnson, no matter who he was or what he was. And I now know that there is a "Sam Johnson" living in every Master Closer's heart.

I hope I'm always "third" and that Sam is proud of me. Thank you, Sam.

The End

Additional
Educational Titles
from
Hampton Books

The Closers

The Original Sales Closer's Bible!

Become a Sales Pro Overnight with the Famous Blue Book!

This is the famous *Blue Book* that has caused thousands of sales-people to double or even triple their earnings. The *Secret Book* that has boosted sales for hundreds of real estate developments, direct sales companies, insurance agencies, automotive dealer-ships, and every type of sales office across America. *The Closers* can do the same for you! Give the 300-page book a try. Better yet, try our "Super Deal," where you get $439.90 in FREE GIFTS!

– *Quantity Discounts Available* –

Item #2301 – *The Closers*: 300-page book - $24.95

Item #2401 – *The Closers*: 8½-hour, 15-cassette audio program - $99.95

To order, call toll-free
800-248-3555
(ask for Operator #624)
Or use the handy order forms in the back of this book!

HOW TO SELL
*Timeshares ★ Vacation Homesites and Homes
Campsites ★ Fractionals ★ Memberships*

This is the new definitive book on selling and closing Timeshares, Vacation Homesites, Vacation Homes, Campsites, Fractionals and Memberships!

From Rio de Janeiro to Brisbane and Seville to Atlantic City, top resort sales trainer Dennis McCann will teach you resort selling with his easy to learn, day-by-day proven method that can put you among the high income top producers!

– *Quantity Discounts Available* –

Item #07-1 – *Art & Science of Resort Sales* book - $19.95

To order, call toll-free
800-248-3555
(ask for Operator #624)
Or use the handy order forms in the back of this book!